Key Issues

RACE

The Origins of an Idea, 1760–1850

Key Issues

RACE

The Origins of an Idea, 1760–1850

Edited and Introduced by
HANNAH FRANZISKA AUGSTEIN
Wellcome Institute, London

Series Editor
ANDREW PYLE
University of Bristol

THOEMMES PRESS

© Thoemmes Press 1996

Published in 1996 by
Thoemmes Press
11 Great George Street
Bristol BS1 5RR, England

US office: Distribution and Marketing
22883 Quicksilver Drive
Dulles, Virginia 20166, USA

ISBN
Paper : 1 85506 454 5
Cloth : 1 85506 455 3

Race
The Origins of an Idea, 1760–1850
Key Issues No. 14

British Library Cataloguing-in-Publication Data
A catalogue record of this title is available
from the British Library

Printed in Great Britain by Antony Rowe Ltd., Chippenham

CONTENTS

ILLUSTRATIONS

Fig. 1: Blumenbach's skull formations. From J. C. Prichard's *Researches into the Physical History of Mankind*, 2 vols, 2nd ed. (London: John and Arthur Arch, 1826).

Figs 2 & 3: The 'Ethiopian variety of mankind' and the 'American variety of mankind', from part 1 of J. F. Blumenbach's *Beyträge zur Naturgeschichte*, 2 parts (Göttingen: J. C. Dieterich, 1790–1811).

Fig. 4: Examples of Georges Cuvier's 'Caucasian' variety of mankind. From vol. 1 of his *Le règne animal*, 3rd ed., 22 vols, ed. by Jean Victor Audouin et al. (Paris: Fortin, Masson, 1836–49).

Fig. 5: Examples of Georges Cuvier's 'Negro' variety of mankind. As Fig. 4 above.

These pictures are reproduced by curtesy of the Wellcome Institute Library, London.

INTRODUCTION

The English term 'race' is derived from the French. Originally it designated the royal families who governed France in the middle ages. By the eighteenth century the term was often employed as one of many synonymous translations of the Latin words 'gens' and 'genus'. Other translations included the terms 'stock' and 'tribe', 'family' and 'nation'. During the age of Enlightenment the word 'race' was unproblematic because the Latin texts, in which its meaning largely resided, merely distinguished between nations as political entities and tribes or families as natural entities. The ambiguity of the nineteenth-century understanding of the term 'people', with its cultural, genealogical and political connotations, was not at issue in the Latin texts which lay at the basis of pre-modern learning. Even though the usages of the term 'race' were decisively to change, some sort of continuity can be perceived. The nineteenth-century notion of races was one answer to questions about the biological nature of man which were put forward systematically in the middle of the eighteenth century. The discourse on man, as one may term it, evolved without interruption from the 1750s to the 1850s. The origins of nineteenth-century racial theory can be grasped only through an understanding of the eighteenth-century view of mankind.[1]

Nineteenth-century racial theory[2] combines several

---

[1] The history of racial theory has been discussed, eg. in Michael Banton, *Racial Theories* (Cambridge and New York: Cambridge University Press, 1987); Nancy Stepan, *The Idea of Race in Science: Great Britain 1800–1960* (London: Macmillan, 1982); George Stocking, *Victorian Anthropology* (New York: Free Press, 1987).

[2] The biologically founded racial theory developed in the nineteenth century lasted well into the twentieth century culminating in the racial

elements: the first is the notion that mankind is divisible into a certain number of 'races' whose characteristics are fixed and defy the modifying influences of external circumstances. Secondly, it contains the idea that the intellectual and moral capacities may be unevenly spread within the various human races. Thirdly, it advocates the notion that mental endowments are bound up with certain physiognomical specificities which, being defined as racial characteristics, are considered to reveal the inward nature of the individual or the population in question. In the nineteenth century, this basic definition of modern racial theory was accompanied by the idea that 'race' was the be-all and end-all of history.

There is no single philosophy, no single movement or author who can be considered as having paved the way for nineteenth-century racial theory. Instead, it grew out of the combination of previously rather distinct traditions – a liberal, lay, anti-monarchical political outlook; the rise of the nation-state; biological and zoological investigations; phrenological and physiognomical fortune-telling; a political interest in finding a scientific justification for slavery; and the philological investigation of languages as a mirror of national character. Nineteenth-century racial theory resulted in a unification of the various approaches to the study of mankind which had evolved during the preceding age.

In early modern times, human tribes had been classified intuitively according to a simple dichotomy. Civilized

ideology of the German National Socialists. In recent years there have been attempts to revivify pseudo-scientific notions of racial theory. Serious scholars have approached the question through a systematic genetical analysis. Their investigations have yielded the result that it is useless to talk of 'human races' unless one is prepared to take the existence of many thousands of races into account: specific genetic configurations can be discerned in various populations, but they are by far more diverse than contemporary racial theoreticians would have it. See L. Luca Cavalli-Sforza, Paolo Menozzi, Alberto Piazza, *The History and Geography of Human Genes* (Princeton University Press, 1994). For a historical analysis of the terms 'race' and 'racism' see Robert Miles, *Racism* (London, New York: Routledge, 1989).

nations, endowed with recorded history, were the domain of political historians; savage tribes, by contrast, were devoid of history, development, and individual distinction. They were, by and large, rather part of nature than of the human world. Peoples who did not adhere to one of the monotheist religions were occasionally excluded from the realm of humanity on the grounds of their paganism. The policy was readily reconcilable with the Bible: had not Ham and his posterity been cursed by God?

In the age of Enlightenment the polarization of Christians and heathens lost its anthropological connotation. It became increasingly common to accept 'savage' tribes among the human family. As God's image changed from active ruler of the world to disengaged 'clock-maker', the human sciences thrived. Starting from medicine, natural history, and political science, the rising discipline of anthropology stood on three legs: dealing with the individual, medicine told people how to be legislators of their personal bodily constitutions. Cultural and political philosophers, by contrast, treating society, turned towards inquiring into the historical laws according to which civilization grew up. The naturalists, finally, became increasingly interested in trying to devise natural systems which assigned mankind a place among their fellow creatures. Savages were still deemed unfit for historicity. But it was precisely their supposed vicinity to the animal creation which made them, as humans, into an object of study. Being part of the realm of descriptive natural history, they were considered analogous to animal tribes.[3]

Until the end of the eighteenth century, natural history was largely a static science. It did not investigate the

---

[3] The cross-relations of the human sciences during the eighteenth century are set out in, among others, Christopher Fox, Roy Porter, Robert Wokler (eds.), *Inventing Human Science. Eighteenth-Century Domains* (Berkeley: University of California Press, 1995); G. S. Rousseau, Roy Porter (eds.), *The Ferment of Knowledge. Studies in the Historiography of Eighteenth-Century Science* (Cambridge University Press, 1980); Londa Schiebinger, *Nature's Body. Gender in the Making of Modern Science* (Boston: Beacon Press, 1993). Also helpful is J. S. Slotkin (ed.), *Readings in Early Anthropology* (London: Methuen, 1965).

history of things but their classificatory relationships. Its criteria were derived less from anatomical and physiological insights than from external observation. This method was congenial to the notion of the 'chain of being' which designated creation as a continuous chain of gradations of resemblance, leading from heavenly creatures down to mankind and further on to the animal realm, plants, and the mineral. Within its framework the Swedish naturalist Carl Linnaeus devised a matrix of the natural creation in which mankind was classified in the same order with apes. Linnaeus was no materialist, but he wanted to be the 'Luther of science';[4] his classification of mankind annoyed many pious contemporaries who were not content that, from the viewpoint of natural history, man should be no better than an ape. Within a few decades Linnaeus's classification was dismissed as arbitrary. In part this was due to his relinquishing man's special station within creation. Moreover, intensified interest in anatomical investigation, in comparative anatomy in particular, proved Linnaeus's *Systema naturae* in many respects wrong. At the same time, the 'chain of being' fell into disrepute. When the Manchester doctor Charles White (1728–1813) put forward his *An Account of the Regular Gradation in Man* (1799), in which he depicted the gradual descent from man to apes, the liberal *Monthly Review* published a scathing commentary: the time of the 'chain of being' was over (see item 5).

The position of mankind within the animal creation was not the only problematic issue. The development of mankind itself also posed questions: given that all human tribes were supposed to be ultimately descended from Noah and his family, it remained to be explained why they looked so different. Why did some tribes civilize themselves while others had seemingly failed to develop? How was it possible that some nations, such as the ancient Greeks and Romans could have retreated from their former

[4]   Lisbet Koerner, 'Carl Linnaeus in his time and place', in N. Jardine, J. A. Secord, E. C. Spary, *Cultures of Natural History* (Cambridge University Press, 1995), pp. 145–62, p. 157.

height of civilization, while others, such as the Indians, the Egyptians, or the Chinese seemed historically to stagnate? What were the preconditions for these developments?

Harking back to Hippocratic writings, the almost universal answer the Enlightenment offered to all these questions was: climate. The proto-sociological theory which Montesquieu advanced in his *De l'esprit des lois* (1748) devised correlations between climatic and geographical circumstances on the one hand, and the state of civilization on the other hand. The Scottish Enlightenment school of philosophy emulated and enlarged Montesquieu's doctrines. The 'four stages theory', which such authors as Adam Smith, Adam Ferguson and William Robertson developed, provided a matrix in which the state of civilization a people had attained was related to their means of subsistence.[5] Such writers believed that mankind was bound to pass through several stages, from the hunter/gatherer state to agriculture, and from thence to commerce. Their doctrines were adopted by many scholars within and outside Britain. In France, the discussions among the Idéologues displayed the same diversity of approach as those in the British context.

The theory of climate prevalent at the close of the eighteenth century saw geographical and climatic circumstances as influences which promoted or retarded the process of civilization. Climate was deemed to be the source of human physical diversity: tribes living in unfavourable conditions developed in response to their station darker and coarser skin. Human physiognomy and civilization were regarded as a function of external living conditions. Since the latter half of the nineteenth century this notion has been known as environmentalism.[6] Before then, however, it was simply the 'theory of climate'.

---

[5] Ronald Meek, *Social Science and the Ignoble Savage* (Cambridge University Press, 1976).

[6] Herbert Spencer has been credited with having coined the term 'environmentalism'. See Armin Hajman Koller, *The Theory of Environment, an Outline of the History of the Idea of Milieu, and its Present Status* (Menasha, Wisc.: University of Chicago, 1918), p. 5.

It was the most widespread explanatory device to account for human variations. But it was not the only one. An alternative was the doctrine of polygenism, that is, the idea that not all human tribes were the offspring of the same act of creation. In 1655 the French Protestant, Isaac de La Peyrère, published a book, *Prae-Adamitae*, in which he argued that there had been humans before Adam was created. It was from this tribe of 'pre-Adamic' humans that Cain chose his wife after he had been expelled by his people for the murder of Abel. Later on, the Scottish Enlightenment philosopher Henry Home, Lord Kames (1696–1782), took up the idea of different human creations (see item 2). Kames combined environmentalist notions with polygenism. He considered the former as the framework within which the development of civilization took place. As for the origin of human varieties, however, Kames did not believe that climatic influences had much to do with it. Hence he advanced the bold idea that the human tribes might have been engendered in different acts of creation. He was very well aware that his assumption contradicted Scripture. Though he paid lip-service to the Biblical story of the tower of Babel he left no doubt that this was not what he actually believed.

Kames's polygenist theory very quickly became the focus for exercises in refutation. Authors intent upon proving Kames wrong had to illustrate, first of all, how mankind could have spread across the earth. The dispersion of mankind over the globe was one of the central topics eighteenth-century students of mankind had to tackle. William Robertson, professor of history in Edinburgh, toyed with the idea that in prehistoric times some tribes might have traversed the oceans in primitive vessels. The French naturalist, Georges Louis Leclerc, Comte de Buffon, suggested that America and Asia had once been connected through a land-bridge. In Germany, the biogeographer Eberhardt August Wilhelm von Zimmermann (1743–1815) set out to solve the riddle of human dispersion within the framework of natural history. Through his insistence on monogenesis Zimmermann aimed to refute materialist doctrines of Voltaire and Hume as well as dangerously fanciful hypotheses such as Monboddo and Rousseau's conjectures on the development of man from apes. Zimmermann's *Geographische Geschichte des Menschen* (*Geographical History of Man*) was praised for its attempt to prove the unity of mankind through the elucidation of their natural history and to refute Kames's polygenism (see item 3).

Another widely-admired author who delved into the natural history of mankind was the Comte de Buffon (1707–88). The French natural historian, whose *Histoire naturelle* was published in forty-four volumes between 1749 and 1804, developed a theory of environmentalism which centred on mankind's physical aspects. Buffon inquired into the evolution of physiognomical characteristics such as skin colour and stature. In his view, the human mind and physicality were a result of environmental influences: a savage tribe transported to Europe and fed on European food would gradually become not only civilized, but white. During the French Revolution and the era of the Napoleonic wars, when transmutationists such as Jean-Baptiste de Lamarck and Erasmus Darwin based their notion of species evolution on Buffon's theories, the Frenchman came into disrepute. For the British audience his theories were too revolutionary, while in France he was deemed too aristocratic. Before the Revolution, however, as well as after Napoleon's defeat, Buffon's systematic application of zoological tenets to mankind was greatly admired. From his viewpoint as a natural historian one of the most salient distinctions between human tribes was that between civilization and the savage state. This was immediately referable to the difference between domesticated and wild animals. Hence, Buffon concluded, all the insights of professional livestock breeders could be exploited to explain mankind. This drawing of parallels between human and animal physiology was called the 'analogical method'.

In the attempt to provide a new classification of the animal creation, Buffon devised a definition for species, based not on the criterion of resemblance but rather on that of lineage: all those animals were part of one species which could procreate with each other and engender fertile offspring. Since all human tribes could pair off with each other, it was no question for Buffon that they were all members of one species. Cross-fertilization was not only possible, it was even desirable. As the example of horses showed, it was necessary to cross breeds in order to maintain the quality of the parent generation. Buffon wrote: 'the produce of two animals, whose defects are exactly balanced, will be the most perfect production of that kind' (item 1, p. 5). A beneficent law of nature ensured that cross-fertilization led to the accumulation of good qualities. Thus, the 'argument from analogy' led to notions of species development which were genuinely different from the ideal of racial purity which infested nineteenth-century theory.

Buffon was immensely influential. His *Histoire naturelle* greatly inspired authors like the above-mentioned Zimmermann (item 3, pp. 24ff.), the Scottish-born London naturalist John Hunter (1728–93), and the Göttingen professor of anatomy Johann Friedrich Blumenbach (1752–1840). Nevertheless, the cornerstones of his monogenism, his environmentalism as well as his definition of species, were increasingly called into question. Blumenbach, for one, doubted whether the criterion of hybridization was valid (see item 7, p. 62). The dog-kind, for instance, appeared to him not necessarily as one single species. Of course, all races of dogs could crossbreed and engender fertile offspring, but if the assumption was correct and there were, indeed, several species of dogs, then Buffon's definition of species was invalid.[7]

Since Blumenbach agreed with Buffon's monogenism he

---

[7] Blumenbach's main anthropological writings are collected in Thomas Bendyshe (ed.), *The Anthropological Treatises of Blumenbach and Hunter*, published for the Anthropological Society of London (London: Green, Longman, Roberts, and Green, 1865). For natural history in Germany see James L. Larson, *Interpreting Nature. The Science of Living Form from Linnaeus to Kant* (Baltimore: Johns Hopkins University Press, 1994).

attempted to provide other criteria for the unity of species. For this purpose he extended the analogical method. He suggested that comparative anatomy and the comparative study of physiology might enable the scientist to draw the dividing line between specific and variational distinctions respectively. What he considered decisive were the functions of the animal economy: if any two different varieties agreed in physiological particulars – such as length of gestation, life span, number of offspring, and proneness to diseases – then it could be inferred that these variations belonged to the same species. With respect to mankind, Blumenbach's view was unequivocal: all human tribes belonged to the same species, physical variation was due to varying climatic circumstances. Correcting Linnaeus's classification, Blumenbach referred mankind to the order of 'bimana' which by definition excluded the ape-kind. There were, Blumenbach believed, five different human varieties: Caucasian, Mongolian, Ethiopian, American, and Malay. These names served as typological classification. In reality the five great families shaded by gradation into each other. Blumenbach's anthropology was Christian and enlightened at the same time. While the review included in this collection was critical of Blumenbach's criteria for distinguishing man from animals (see item 7, p. 66–7), he was later credited with being 'the founder of ethnology' (see item 19, p. 217). His great collection of human skulls was particularly admired. Like John Hunter's collection of animal specimens and the stone relics of ancient cultures which travellers brought home from foreign parts, Blumenbach's skulls were regarded as immensely valuable. They enabled the naturalists to advance from mere philosophical speculation to empirical investigation.

Distinctions between a certain number of human variations had been made by other scholars as well: the London surgeon John Hunter believed that mankind was diversified into seven different varieties; Immanuel Kant had conceived of four basic human types; the Göttingen professor Johann Christian Polycarp Erxleben devised six different human varieties, as did the British naturalist and playwright Oliver Goldsmith. Some of these authors spoke of 'races', the philologist Sir William Jones, for instance, combined his belief in monogenism with the assumption that 'we see *five* races of men peculiarly distinguished' (item 4, p. 42). Inevitably, they have been accused of having paved the way for racialism.[8] Yet it is important to bear in mind, that the ubiquitous eighteenth-century theory of environmentalism impeded the development of a racial theory. On the one hand, the universal belief in a standard of taste and morality naturally led to disdain for the cultural 'other'. On the other hand, however, the Enlightenment was permeated by the notion that cultural and physical improvement was generally possible.

The break-up of the eighteenth-century anthropological framework was in no small part due to the fact that rising empirical evidence seemed to defy the theory of climate. As a result of intensified colonial activities, many dark-skinned people came to live, as servants and labourers, in European countries, while many white families settled permanently in the colonies. Black slaves on American and overseas plantations served as illustrative material to anthropologically interested observers. A pious monogenist such as the Edinburgh-trained American Samuel Stanhope Smith (1750–1819) endorsed the theory of climate so wholeheartedly that he claimed to perceive the transmutation towards white skin colour in black domestic slaves. Other naturalists, however, ridiculed Stanhope Smith's alleged observation. One reviewer poked fun at Stanhope Smith's philanthropic faith in the ability of blacks 'to mend in their colour, features, and hair'. The reviewer was of different opinion: as can be seen from the review (item 6), its author was sarcastic about the blacks. Environmentalism was attacked from many sides, and not every

---

[8] See most recently Martin Bernal, *Black Athena. The Afroasiatic Roots of Classical Civilization*, 2 vols., 2nd ed. (London: Vintage, 1991), vol. 1, pp. 219f. for Blumenbach. Harold E. Pagliaro (ed.), *Racism in the Eighteenth Century, Studies in Eighteenth-Century Culture*, vol. 3 (Cleveland: Case Western Reserve University Press, 1973) contains some useful essays on eighteenth-century racialism.

critic was a polygenist. The Jamaican colonist Edward Long, the doctor James Cowles Prichard, the surgeon William Lawrence, and the famous German naturalist Alexander von Humboldt emphasized that whites stubbornly engendered white offspring, while parents of colour brought forth identically coloured children, under all climatic conditions.

By the 1810s doubts in the theory of climate were broadly publicized. The English schoolmaster John Bigland (1750–1832), whose popular digests of contemporary science found many readers, maintained that race not climate might be accountable for varying human constitutions. 'Reason and revelation', Bigland wrote, 'concur in representing the whole human species as issuing from the same stock; but experience shews, that families are often distinguished not only by certain peculiarities of external organization, but also by particular dispositions of mind, which prevail through all or the greater part of their branches' (item 8, p. 69). Was it inconceivable that all these differences had resulted in genuine, racial distinctions? One of the prime examples at the time were the Jews: the adherents of environmentalism pointed out that their skin colour changed according to their habitat; the proponents of some theories of race, by contrast, claimed that the Jews displayed always, as Bigland put it, 'incontestable evidences of the race to which they belong' (item 8, p. 73; see also p. 156 in item 13, and p. 257 in item 20).

Bigland's *Historical Display of the Effects of Physical and Moral Causes on the Character and Circumstances of Nations* (1816) illustrates how far the spirit of the times was under the spell of recent developments in cerebral anatomy. The Viennese doctor, Franz Joseph Gall, in particular, appealed to Bigland: Gall had maintained that intellectual faculties were – like the physical shape of the future individual – impressed on the creature already in its foetal state. Being fixed, they were displayed in the shape of the head. Starting from this physiological stipulation, Gall and his collaborator Johann Caspar Spurzheim embarked on establishing phrenology as a science, thereby plunging the whole of learned Europe into heated discussions. During the first two decades of the nineteenth century Gall and Spurzheim toured through learned institutions in Germany, England, and France in order to convince their scientific peers that the conformation of the skull was indicative of individual character and abilities.

The doctrines of phrenology were new in the nineteenth century. But they grew in well-prepared ground: quite a few eighteenth-century anatomists had endeavoured to uncover the cerebral peculiarities characterizing various races. The Göttingen anatomist Samuel Thomas Soemmerring (1755–1830) had claimed that the degree of intelligence depended on the proportion between the weight of the brain and the thickness of the nervous strings linking the brain to the rest of the body: the finer the connection, the higher the state of the animal within nature's hierarchy. In his inquiry *Ueber die körperliche Verschiedenheit des Negers vom Europäer* (*On the Physical Difference between the European and the Negro*, 1784) he applied his physiological theories to anthropology. In the latter decades of the eighteenth century, the Dutch anatomist Pieter Camper (1722–89) devised the idea of the facial angle. It grew out of his occupation with anatomical drawings. Camper intended to provide helpful guidelines for correct anatomical illustrations. (In English they were published in 1794 as *The Works of the late Professor Camper, on the Connexion Between the Science of Anatomy and the Arts of Drawing, Painting, Statuary*.) His audiences, however, understood that he had devised a scale of gradation for the creatures of the animal realm: greater perfection and intelligence were mirrored in an increasingly less receding forehead. The ideal-typical profile of Greek statues defined the greatest degree of beauty and intellectual potency. The Dutchman was not aiming at a racial system of the distribution of intelligence. Later, however, many racialist authors read Camper's manual on drawing as having anticipated a system of racial differentiation in which the European type was superior to all other human races.

Another brainchild engendered in the eighteenth century was the technique of physiognomical character studies. The Swiss pastor Johann Caspar Lavater (1741–1801) maintained that the facial appearances of living creatures indicated their internal, moral conformation. Lavater's physiognomy was rejected by many scholars. Yet the core of his theories stuck in the contemporary imagination.

All these attempts to correlate physical form and psychological character were derived from the technique of comparative observation. Georges Cuvier (1769–1832), the great French anatomist and Perpetual Secretary of the Institut de France, had shown that comparative anatomy could be undertaken with a view to elucidate the historical past of the animal creation. Cerebral anatomists, physiognomists and phrenologists aimed, by contrast, at describing the state of human diversity. Their endeavours were basically of a classificatory nature. They were either not interested in the historical development of mankind, or they admitted that the contemporary state of anatomical knowledge was not sufficiently advanced to elucidate the past of the human races.

Some such endeavour was undertaken in a wholly different field: philology developed into a historical science. In the 1780s Sir William Jones (1746–94), a judge at the British High Court in Calcutta, had discovered the genealogical relationship between ancient Sanskrit and the major European languages. The success of his theory induced him to believe that the historical comparative study of language might furnish a key to unlock the mysteries of the earliest ages of the human race. Jones entertained no doubts about the truth of Scripture, he was a convinced monogenist. Historical linguistics, he believed, might illustrate how Noah's posterity had disseminated over the globe. His investigations were eagerly taken up by scholars in other countries. Apart from the works of the Dane Rasmus Kristian Rask, the main impulses in comparative-historical linguistics came from German scholars, namely the brothers Friedrich and August Wilhelm Schlegel, Franz Bopp, Wilhelm von Humboldt, and Jacob Grimm. They all were part of what is referred to as the Romantic movement, their understanding of language implied an organicist philosophy. Languages were considered as 'living' bodies whose laws of generation and decay were to be uncovered. They were thus intimately linked up with the history of man. By virtue of this connection, philology was a historical science and thus on the same level as other historical sciences such as geology and Cuvier's comparative anatomy.

The nineteenth century was to witness the integration of the various approaches to anthropology which hitherto had been treated independently. The question of race resolved itself into the polygenist-monogenist controversy. Some authors maintained that philology alone was the appropriate method for probing into the human past. Others asserted that only comparative anatomy yielded reliable information on the natural history of mankind. There is a certain correlation between the monogenist belief in the common descent of all mankind, philanthropist attitudes, and anti-slavery agitation. But it would be exaggerated to stipulate this as a general rule.[9]

However, there was one country where, indeed, religious monogenism and anti-slavery agitation went hand in hand. In Britain the evangelical William Wilberforce (1759–1833) managed to canvass great support for the abolition of slavery. Already in 1787 Prime Minister William Pitt had attempted to put in a bill against the slave trade. But due to the French revolutionary wars the issue was postponed. In 1807, the Whig Foreign Minister Charles James Fox finally succeeded in abolishing the slave trade. Subsequently, France, Spain, and Portugal were pressed into putting an end to their slave trade as well. But the agitation of Wilberforce's abolitionists and the Anti-Slavery Society went on until finally, in 1833, the possession of slaves was banned. The act 'for the abolition of slavery throughout the British colonies' stipulated that all slaves

[9] This has been pointed out by William Stanton, *The Leopard's Spots. Scientific Attitudes Toward Race in America, 1815–1859* (University of Chicago Press, 1960), p. 173.

had to be freed within a year. (Slaves employed in agriculture were forced to stay in 'apprenticeship' until 1838.) Their owners were compensated. In the wake of the February Revolution in 1848, the new French government abolished slavery as well. In 1822, American slaves wishing to return to Africa were given the opportunity to form their own government in a West-African settlement called Liberia. It was an experiment, keenly observed by abolitionists and the supporters of slavery alike. While the former tended to praise discipline and order in the black settlement, the latter regarded Liberia as a proof for the blacks' inability for self-government (see p. 198 in item 17 and pp. 175ff. in item 14).

One of the contemporaries who combined knowledge in natural history with a staunchly abolitionist attitude was the Bristol doctor James Cowles Prichard (1786–1848). Starting with his MD dissertation, he made the study of mankind his lifelong occupation, being nowadays regarded as 'the leading student of biological races in Britain in the early part of the nineteenth century'.[10] He considered the question of the unity of mankind as the cutting edge in the fight between religion and materialism. Adhering to the evangelical wing of Anglicanism, Prichard strove to uphold the Scriptures. In his *Researches into the Physical History of Man* (1813) and many subsequent publications he attempted to prove that the story of Genesis was correct and that all human tribes had, indeed, descended from one original couple (see item 9). Thanks to his enormous erudition he dominated British ethnology and anthropology until his death in 1848. He served as President of the Ethnological Society of London, founded in 1843, and in the British Association for the Advancement of Science he had the last word on anthropological matters.

Being well aware of the multi-faceted nature of anthropological investigation, Prichard had recourse to arguments

[10] Nancy Stepan, 'Biology and Degeneration: Races and Proper Places', in J. Edward Chamberlin, Sander L. Gilman (eds.), *Degeneration. The Dark Side of Progress* (New York: Columbia University Press, 1985), pp. 97–120, p. 106.

drawn from physiology, anatomy, the study of mythology, archaeology and historical linguistics. He, too, was critical of the theory of climate. But instead of replacing it with the notion of originally different races, he supported a theory of heredity. The diversities of human physiology were, for him, due not to the influence of climate but to sudden variations in the hereditary fabric. Prichard's refutation of the theory of climate resided in his hostility towards the doctrine of transmutationism which relied on the idea that acquired characteristics could become hereditary. Prichard found abhorrent the idea that any alterations in the physiological conformation of the parent should become hereditary. Had this been so, he sneered, the whole of creation would display a picture of utter chaos. Since monogenism was traditionally supported by some sort of climatic theory, Prichard faced the enormous task of proving the unity of mankind without having too much recourse to eighteenth-century environmentalism. He greatly relied on the 'analogical method' which Blumenbach, Buffon and John Hunter had so successfully employed. The comparison between animal domestication and human civilization led him to assume that the civilized state was conducive to the accidental eruption of new variations in the human kind. Emulating Hunter, he believed that all mankind had originally been black and that differentiation was a result of civilization. One of the writers who took up Prichard's stance towards the theory of climate and many of his anthropological tenets, was the British surgeon William Lawrence (1783–1867). Christian faith meant less to him than to Prichard, yet his *Lectures on Physiology, Zoology, and the Natural History of Man* (1819) agreed in many particulars with Prichard's book. Over the years, Prichard amassed a welter of ethnological data from travel literature, anatomical descriptions, and other sources. In order to accommodate the information while preserving the doctrine of monogenism, Prichard modified his argument. He admitted, for instance, that the theory of climate might, after all, play some role in forming a predisposition for the surge of physical variation. By the

1830s, he distinguished between external characteristics such as hair and skin colour, and the internal constitution. Prichard thought that the former were highly susceptible to variation according to environmental influences. As for the inward constitution and the bony structure, by contrast, Prichard took these to be of a relatively stable nature. He went so far as to embrace the idea that there was a certain number of 'permanent human varieties'. Still, all mankind was ultimately related to each other. Prichard never forsook his pious monogenist conviction. As we will see, the very first full-blown racial theories were put forward by men who did not much care for religion. The notion of inherently different races was somewhat alien to the anthropological doctrines of Christian orthodoxy.

The incentive for the formulation of biologically founded racial theories characteristically came from France where indifference to Christianity was more widespread than in the rest of Europe. Georges Cuvier had suggested that there might be genuine differences between the physiological types of savages and Europeans. But in his writings these notions remained on a speculative level – possibly due to his Protestant convictions Cuvier did not follow them up systematically. One of his pupils, however, did. It is noteworthy that Louis-Antoine Desmoulins' *Histoire naturelle des races humaines* (*Natural History of the Human Races*) was written after he had fallen out with Cuvier. Having lost his patron, Desmoulins (1794–1828) advanced theories full of angry enthusiasm. His colleagues and former supporters thought that they were too fanciful to be true. He divided mankind into sixteen originally different races. Not only was the number exceptional: Desmoulins detected racial distinctions in the history of civilized Europe itself. Samuel Taylor Coleridge remarked in the margins of Desmoulins' work that 'no other nation [but the French] could have produced the author of this work'.[11]

Already in the eighteenth century the world of

---

[11] Coleridge's copy of Desmoulins' *Histoire naturelle des races humaines* is in the British Library, London.

antiquarian learning had been shaken by a quarrel over the historical value of ancient Celtic culture. A period of 'Celtomania', which took the ancient Celtic traditions as nobler than those of over-refined modern times, gave way to the brash rejection of Celticism. The notoriously anti-Celtic geographer John Pinkerton (1758–1826), for example, dismissed the Scottish Highlanders and the Irish as 'radical savages' who had nothing in common with the superior Anglo-Saxon family.[12] But neither eighteenth-century Celticists nor their adversaries considered the question from a biological viewpoint. Their discussion had remained within the paradigmatic confines of Montesquieu's *Spirit of the Laws* and the Scottish proto-sociological philosophy. When Desmoulins turned to the racial distinctions among European nations, he applied the terminology of natural history to the history of European nations. Initially, his efforts were not to much avail. His book was criticized as 'a strange production', the outlandish product of an outsider (see item 11). But this opinion did not prevail for long. Besides, Desmoulins was not the only French naturalist who advanced a racial theory. More in line with traditional tenets, the naturalist Julien-Joseph Virey (1775–1846) divided the human race into two originally distinct species: blacks and non-blacks. His huge *Histoire naturelle du genre humain* (*Natural History of Mankind*, 2nd ed., 1824) was very welcome among American proponents of slavery who were looking for scientific justification for the subordination of African blacks. One of them summarized Virey's opinions, giving due weight to the racialist opinions of the Frenchman (see item 14).

During the late 1820s, a group of anti-aristocratic French scholars, including the historians François Guizot, Adolph Thiers, and the brothers Amédée and Augustin Thierry as well as William Frédéric Edwards, a physiologist of Anglo-French origin, tried historiographically to outmanoeuvre

[12] John Pinkerton, *Dissertation on the Origin and Progress of the Scythians or Goths, being an Introduction to the Ancient and Modern History of Europe* (London: John Nichols, 1787), p. 69.

the French nobility. Traditionally, almost the entire French aristocracy and royalty was referred to the Franks who had invaded the country in the fifth century, while the original French populace was said to be of Gallic or Celtic origin. Based on this assumption the third estate tried to challenge aristocratic rule: being merely foreign intruders the nobility had no right to govern those who were the original French population. In the context of this discussion interest in the Celts was rekindled. In 1828, Amédée Thierry published a history of the Frankish invasion on the territory of the ancient Gauls. The republican theory of race proposed in this book was later given biological foundations: in 1829, William Frédéric Edwards (1776–1842) published *Des caractères physiologiques des races humaines* (*On the Physiological Characters of Human Races*).[13] Unlike Desmoulins' speculations, Edwards' theories were considered as well-founded (see pp. 148ff. in item 13). Edwards asserted the permanency of racial types. And he inquired into the laws which governed the intermixture of human races. He doubted whether racial mixture was permanently possible. In most cases, he claimed, the stronger racial type would ultimately reassert itself and finally dominate the entire population.

Edwards' political leanings did not deter him from anthropological investigation. He was decisive in engineering the foundation of the Société ethnologique de Paris (1839). As of its inception the Society considered it as its task to inquire into human racial differences. The type of ethnology which was practised by Prichard and his British followers was not universally well received by the French. Many members of the Société ethnologique deplored the British obsession with Scriptural doctrines. Instead, they followed Edwards' anatomical division of races and the researches of natural historians such as

[13] For William Frédéric Edwards' theory on race see, for example, Claude Blanckaert, 'On the Origins of French Ethnology. William Edwards and the Doctrine of Race', in George W. Stocking (ed.), *Bones, Bodies, Behavior. Essays on Biological Anthropology* (Madison: The University of Wisconsin Press, 1988), pp. 18–55.

Cuvier's disciple, François Désiré Roulin (1796–1874), who had shown that instincts of domesticated animals degenerated into the natural state of their wild brethren once they were left to go wild (see item 17, p. 197). From this theory inferences were readily made about mankind. For an Enlightenment physician like Johann Friedrich Blumenbach, degeneration had merely signified 'deviation' from the 'original' state (see pp. 62ff in item 7). But his basically value-free usage of the term did not find many followers. In the nineteenth century the notion of moral degeneration became one of the historical guiding principles for racial theoreticians. During the 1840s the environmentalist aspects of Roulin's investigations, too, were important. The embryologist and naturalist Marcel de Serres (1780–1862) was one among many scholars who were impressed by Roulin's findings: despite all the attacks on the theory of climate, the environment seemed, indeed, to compel the animal economy to adapt to its physical exigencies (see item 17). Thanks to authors like Roulin, environmentalist theory again gained ground. But since environmentalism was reconcilable with racial theories, it did not materially alter the direction of the discussion.

It was not only in France that political sentiments stimulated thoughts on race. Exuding Anglo-Saxon pride, Thomas Arnold (1795–1842), the famous headmaster of Rugby school, linked, in his *Introductory Lectures on Modern History* (1842), the course of history to the unfolding of racial potential.[14] The same sort of historical theorizing had been put forward in Germany since the late eighteenth century. That country, divided into petty monarchies, had served for centuries as a central European battlefield. Already in 1784 Johann Gottfried Herder had set out the idea that the spirit of a nation resided not in the government but in the people. This notion was eagerly taken up by many German republicans and liberals.

---

[14] For the background of British political racialism see Hugh A. MacDougall, *Racial Myth in English History. Trojans, Teutons, and Anglo-Saxons* (Montreal: Harvest House, Hanover: University Press of New England, 1982).

German nationalism rose as an anti-monarchical movement. The philological investigations of Wilhelm von Humboldt and Jacob Grimm were imbued with the notion that there was a German national spirit which, transcending all arbitrary political divisions, permeated the German language and hence the mind of the German people. Still, there is a difference between this type of self-assertive German nationalism and a biological theory of race. Even the philologist Friedrich Jäkel, who in an act of hearty patriotism claimed the Germanic origins of the ancient Romans, would not have agreed that it was 'race' which governed German history. (It is interesting to notice that John Gibson Lockhart, reviewing Jäkel's book, was not alarmed by its 'Teutonic interpretation' – on the contrary he took it for a source of 'a little amusement and food for speculation': see pp. 146–7 in item 12.)

There were polygenists in Germany, too. The physiologist Carl Asmund Rudolphi (1771–1832), for example, maintained that the peoples of the earth were too diverse to be referred to as only one species. Also the naturalists C. F. Philip von Martius and Johann Baptist von Spix, who were sent by the Bavarian king on an expedition to South America, believed that the local Indians were radically different from the Europeans.[15] On the whole, however, biologically founded racial theory did not especially flourish in Germany before the 1840s. If German nationalism arose out of the Romantic sentiment, which asserted the supremacy of internal (national) essence over external (political) semblance, it was precisely this attitude which prevented German physiologists from placing too much emphasis upon the external physiological differences between the human varieties. In his *Beyträge zur Anthropologie und allgemeinen Naturgeschichte* (*Remarks on Anthropology and General Natural History*, 1842), Rudolphi professed his adherence to polygenism. At the same time, however, he condemned slavery and stressed

---

[15] J. B. von Spix, C. F. P. von Martius, *Travels in Brazil, in the Years 1817–1820*, trans. by H. E. Lloyd (London: Longman, Hurst, Rees, Orme, Brown, and Green, 1824), see esp. pp. 19–38.

that all individuals deserved respect as humans because they all were able to feel joy and sorrow, pleasure and pain. The doctor James Cowles Prichard expressly exempted Germany when deploring the contemporary materialist tendencies conducive to polygenist theorization. As he saw it, France was a hotbed of ill-founded theories on race; and Britain was increasingly invaded by French doctrines. Only in Germany Prichard found fellow-souls who stayed aloof from polygenism and supported the idea that the term 'race' was merely a synonym for 'human variety'.

The first fully-fledged expositions of a biologically founded racial theory were advanced by Robert Knox (1793–1863) in Britain and by Joseph Arthur Comte de Gobineau (1816–82) in France. Knox was a Scottish anatomist. He was a respected member of his faculty until, in 1828, a scandal put his career in jeopardy: it was common practice for anatomists to obtain bodies for dissection from dubious sources; rather often they had to rely on body-snatchers who stole the recently deceased from their graves. The unfortunate Knox, however, had unwittingly fallen prey to two murderers who precipitated the course of nature to provide the anatomist with the desired goods. The crime was uncovered – Knox was widely attacked and even burnt in effigy. Knox's students stood loyally to their teacher. But subsequent to the incident Knox's lectures became more and more unorthodox. Anatomical transcendentalism which linked mankind to the nature of apes meant a lot more to him than Christian philanthropy. As of the beginning of the 1830s his popularity declined. In 1842 he found himself without a class. As a result Knox shifted the focus of his lectures to the history of human races. In 1850 he published a collection of his lectures, *Races of Men*. In the introduction he stated that 'race is everything', in any case it was his attempt to make sense out of the revolutionary movements of 1848.[16] These had shaken Germany and

---

[16] Quoted from p. v of Knox's *Races of Man*. For Knox as racialist see Michael Biddiss, 'Dr. Robert Knox and Victorian Racism', *Proceedings of the Royal Society of Medicine*, vol. 69 (1976), pp. 245–50. For Knox's biological tenets see Philip F. Rehbock, *The Philosophical*

France in their foundations. Britain, too, went through difficult political times. Many contemporaries felt that the whole of Europe was out of joint. In the medical sciences, theories of degeneration began to flourish.

The Enlightenment hope that the progressive course of civilization would one day stretch to all mankind was lost. On the contrary, even the Europeans seemed to fall back into states of disorder. Knox referred the negative tendencies of the times to race. Like Thomas Arnold, he believed that the Anglo-Saxon race was endowed with superior qualities. But unlike Arnold, who put forward his theory as part of the philosophy of history, Knox reintroduced the notion of race into biology. Thus he stipulated that 'races' could not 'amalgamate'. The theories of eighteenth-century naturalists were wrong: hybridization of human 'races' could not succeed, in the end the mixed race was bound to perish; it was a 'pleasing fiction' to believe that human races where shaped by the environment.

As for Gobineau, many of his thoughts were derived from the German liberal Gustav Klemm who in his *Allgemeine Cultur-Geschichte der Menschheit* (*Universal Cultural History of Mankind*, 1843–52) distinguished between 'active' and 'passive' races. Another source of inspiration was the Saint-Simonian author, Victor Courtet de l'Isle who regarded racial intermarriage in analogy to chemical processes. Both Klemm and de l'Isle warned against unhealthy racial mixtures. Michael Biddiss has shown that Gobineau's theoretical radicalism went hand in hand with an overwhelming feeling of nostalgia.[17] Being convinced of the desirability of aristocratic leadership, Gobineau witnessed with disgust the turmoils of French politics. He had little faith in the ordering powers of Christianity. By the 1840s he had turned into a pessimist. The result of his theorization of this pessimism was a racial theory. In his view, even the naturally superior races had degenerated

Naturalists. Themes in Early Nineteenth-Century British Biology (Madison: The University of Wisconsin Press, 1983), chap. 2.

[17] Michael Biddiss, *Father of Racist Ideology. The Social and Political Thought of Count Gobineau* (New York: Weybright and Talley, 1970).

into effeminacy, a process which was largely due to ill-advised intermixture.

The student of nineteenth-century racial theory gains the impression that its first formulations were deeply imbued with cultural misgivings. In its inception nineteenth-century racial theory was the fruit of an angry world view, it reflected the personal discontent of those who formulated it. At the same time, the Christian foundations of theories on man were crumbling. Once natural historians no longer felt obliged to align their tenets to the story of Genesis, the playground for all sorts of racialist speculations was opened. Thereafter, racial theory very quickly grew into the leading explanatory device for human history.

The texts in this collection are taken partly from original monographs. More often, however the views of leading philosophers and natural historians are delineated through contemporary reviews of their works. In eighteenth-century Britain the *Monthly Review* and the *Critical Review* were most widely read. While the *Critical Review* propounded conservative, religiously orthodox opinions, the *Monthly* was politically more liberal and very interested in Continental contributions to natural history. It is, therefore, no accident that this collection includes many reviews from the *Monthly* and none from the *Critical Review*. In the nineteenth century learned journals were mushrooming. In 1808 the conservative *Quarterly Review* was founded, followed, in 1812, by the Whig *Edinburgh Review*. These two mark the beginning of a wave of periodical publications. In 1826 the geologist Robert Jameson became the editor of the *Edinburgh New Philosophical Journal*. His scientific inclinations determined the editorial line of the journal for the coming years. As the contributions of Marcel de Serres and Pierre Flourens show, the periodical solicited translations of articles which had previously appeared in non-English journals. That the name of a contributing author was mentioned was a rare exception. Customarily, reviews were published anonymously. In the few cases in this collection where the reviewer is known, his personal details have been added in the introductory paragraphs that begin each document.

Hannah Franziska Augstein
The Wellcome Institute for the
History of Medicine, 1996

THE NATURAL HISTORY
OF THE HORSE
To which is added, that of the Ass, Bull,
Cow, Ox, Sheep, Goat, and Swine.
Translated from the French of the
celebrated M. de Buffon.

[William Bewley]

Source: Monthly Review, vol. 27, 1762

Buffon's history of the domesticated quadrupeds was part of the Histoire naturelle which he and his collaborator Louis Jean-Marie Daubenton (1716–1800) published from 1749 onwards. After Buffon's death in 1788, the remaining eight volumes were published until 1804 by Bernard de Lacépède. The review was written by William Bewley (1726–83), a frequent contributor to the *Monthly*, who as a surgeon and apothecary had a particular understanding of the physiological side of Buffon's argument.

Natural History has always been considered as a useful and instructive science, as it enlarges our ideas, by making us acquainted with the nature and properties of the many objects that surround us; and accordingly many authors, in different parts of Europe, have exerted their talents in elucidating a subject so beneficial to society. Among these the famous M. de Buffon, and his coadjutor M. Daubenton, have distinguished themselves, and blended the curious with the useful Parts of this science; and as they have formed no system, but followed nature closely in every particular, they have exploded a multitude of errors committed by other authors, in support of a favourite hypothesis, and sufficiently shewn, that it is not by contracting the sphere of nature within a narrow circle, but by extending it to immensity, that we can obtain a true knowledge of her proceedings.

"The views of the illustrious[1] author of nature," says M. de Buffon, "are not to be fathomed, by attributing to him our ideas: instead of curtailing the limits of his power, they must be widened, and extended to immensity. We are to consider nothing impossible; we are to imagine everything, and to suppose that whatever can does exist. Ambiguous species, irregular productions, anomalous beings, will then cease to stagger us, and will be found, in the infinite order of things, as necessary as others. They fill up the intervals of the chain; they form the links, the intermediate points, and also indicate the extremities. These beings are, to the human mind, valuable and singular copies, in which nature, though apparently less consistent with her usual method, shews herself more openly; in which we may perceive marks and characters, denoting her ends to be much more general than our views; and that, as she does nothing in vain, she also does nothing with the designs we impute to her."

On such extensive principles, unbiassed by system, or the authority of any other writer, the natural history of M. de Buffon is executed; and, at the same time, all the particulars relating to each species of animals, that have the least tendency to improve its qualities, or display its character, are carefully enumerated.

As a specimen of this large work, the piece before us, containing the natural histories of some of the most useful animals in nature, is published, and contains complete treatises on the horse, ass, horned cattle, sheep, goats, and swine, in which the manner of breeding, fattening, and improving these valuable creatures is particularly explained, and a great variety of curious questions relative to their nature and properties are discussed, and satisfactorily answered.

The degeneracy of horses has been long known, and several methods have been taken to prevent it. It is apparent, that these differences proceed from the air and food; but the only method of preventing it is by crossing the breed. Our author's reasoning will throw considerable light upon this practice.

"Nature," he observes, "has, in every species, a general prototype, after which each individual is formed: this, in the realization, degenerates or improves from circumstances: so

---

1   We do not remember ever to have seen this inadequate epithet applied to the Supreme Benefactor.

that with regard to certain qualities, there is apparently a capricious variation in the succession of individuals, and, at the same time, a remarkable stability in the whole species. The first horse, for instance, was the external model, and internal mould, by which all horses that have ever existed have been formed: but this model, of which we only know the copies, may, by the communication of form, and by its increase, have undergone some disadvantageous changes, or, on the other hand, received improvement. The original form wholly subsists in each individual. But though there are millions of these individuals, not two of them are, in every particular, exactly alike, nor consequently any one of them the same with the model from whence it received its form. This difference, which at once demonstrates how far nature is from fixing any thing absolutely, and the infinite variations she spreads through her works, is seen in the human race, in every species of animals and vegetables, and, in a word, in every series of beings. But what deserves attention is, that the model of beauty and goodness seems distributed throughout the whole earth, every climate affording only a portion; and this continually degenerating, unless re-united with another portion from some distant country: so that to have good grain, beautiful flowers, &c. the feeds must be changed, and never sown in the soil that produced them. In the same manner, to have fine horses, &c. foreign stallions must be given to native mares, or foreign mares to native stallions: for otherwise, the mother will so powerfully influence the form, as to cause an apparent degeneracy: the form remains, but disfigured by many dissimilar lineaments. Whereas, let the breed be mixed, and constantly renewed by foreign species, and the form will advance towards perfection, and recruited nature display her choicest productions.

"The general reason for these effects does not belong to this place; yet we may be permitted to mention the conjectures which at first offer themselves. Experience shews, that animals, or vegetables, transported from a remote climate, often degenerate, and sometimes greatly improve, in a small time; I mean within a very few generations. That this is the effect of a difference of climate and aliment, is easy to conceive: and, in length of time, the influence of these two causes must render such animals exempt from, or susceptible of certain affections and distempers. Their temperament must gradually alter; the formation, which partly depends on the aliment, and partly on the quality of the juices, must also undergo a change in the succession of a few generations. This change in the first generation is almost imperceptible, as the two animals, the male and female, which we suppose to be the progenitors of the species, had obtained their full shape and constitution before they were brought from their native country: and that however a new climate and food may change their temperament, they cannot act on the solid and organical parts, so as to alter their shape; especially if they had attained their full growth: consequently, in the first generation, there will be no disadvantageous change; no degeneracy in the first production of these animals; the impression of the model will be exact. At the instant of their birth, there will be no radical defect; but the young animal, during its weak and tender state, will feel the influences of the climate. They will make other different impressions on him, than they did on his full-grown sire and dam. Those of the aliment will be much greater, and act on the organical parts during their growth, so as to vitiate a little the original form, and produce germs of imperfections, which will very sensibly appear in a second generation, when the parent, besides its own defects, I mean those it derives from its growth, has also the defects of the second generation, which will be then more strongly marked: and at the third generation, the defects of the second and third stock, caused by the influence of the climate and aliment, being again combined with those of the present influence in the growth, will become so palpable, as to obliterate the marks of the original stock; so that these animals of foreign extraction will have nothing foreign in them, but be exactly similar to the natives. Spanish or Barb-Horses, whose breed are thus managed in France, very often at the second, and always at the third, become so entirely French horses, that, instead of preserving the breed, there is a necessity of crossing and renewing it at every generation, by importing Barb and Spanish horses for the use of native mares. And it is very remarkable, that this manner of renewing the breed, which is only in part, or as it were by halves, has a much better effect than if the renovation was total. A horse and mare of Spain will not, in France, produce such fine horses as a Spanish stallion with a mare of the country. This, however, will be easily comprehended, if we consider, that when a stallion and mare of different countries are put together, the defects of both are compensated. Every climate, by its own influences, and those of the food, imparts a certain conformation, which is faulty through some excess or defect. But in a hot climate there will be an excess of fire, in a cold climate there will be a defect, and *vice versa*. So that, by joining animals of these opposite climates, the excess of the one supplies the defects of the other. And as that reaches nearest to perfection in nature, which has the fewest faults, and the most perfect forms being only such as have the fewest deformities, the produce of two animals, whose defects are exactly balanced, will be the most perfect production of that kind. And this equality is the most accurately adjusted, the more distant the countries are, or rather the more opposite the climates natural to the two animals are to each other. The compound result is the more perfect, as the excesses or defects of the stallion's constitution are more opposite to the excesses and defects of the mare."

These observations of our author sufficiently shew, that the long pedigrees of horses, displayed with so much ostentation, prove the very reverse of what they are intended to prove; for it is evident, that the farther any horse is removed from the first production between a foreign stallion and a native mare, so much greater its defects will be; and consequently, a horse will be better in proportion to the shortness of his pedigree. A great variety of other remarks, equally useful and entertaining, are interspersed in the natural history of the horse, and which are therefore recommended to the perusal of every lover of that generous animal.

In the natural history of the Ass, M. de Buffon has discussed one of the most curious questions in natural history, namely, the degeneration of animals. He asks, whether the horse and the ass are originated from the same stock, or whether they are not and have not ever been different animals? This curious question he has answered, by considering nature in a new point of view. He very justly observes, that those animals which produce together individuals capable of producing others, are of the same species, while those that produce together only such animals as are defective and barren, are of different species. And as the mule, produced between the horse and the ass, is not capable of propagation, these two animals are of different species. In the natural history of the Ox, M. de Buffon has advanced a philosophical hypothesis, which seems to deserve attention, as it tends to elucidate the course of nature with regard to the food of different animals; and as the thought is new, we shall insert it for the satisfaction of the reader.

"The surface of the earth," says this ingenious naturalist, "decked in its verdure, is the inexhaustible and common source from whence man and beast derive their subsistence: whatever lives in nature, lives on what vegetates; and vegetables, in their turn, live on whatever has lived and vegetated. It is impossible to live without destroying; and indeed it is only by the destruction of beings that animals can subsist themselves, and propagate their species. God, in creating the first individual of each species of animal and vegetable, has not only given a form to the dust of the earth, but has rendered it living and animated, by inclosing in each individual a greater or lesser quantity of active principles, of organical moleculæ, living, indistructible, and common to all organised beings. These moleculæ pass from body to body, and equally contribute to present life, and the continuation of life, to the nutrition and growth of each individual; and after the dissolution of the body, after it is reduced to ashes, these organical moleculæ, on which death has no power, survive, circulate in the universe, and pass into other beings, bringing with them nourishment and life. Thus every production, every renovation, every increment by generation, by nutrition, by development, supposes a preceding destruction, a conversion of substance, an accession of those organical moleculæ, which do not multiply, but ever subsisting in an equal number, render nature always equally full of life, the earth equally peopled, and equally shining in the original glory conferred on it by its Creator.

Considering therefore beings in general, the total of the quantity of life is perpetually the same; and however death may appear to destroy every thing, it destroys no part of that primitive life which is common to all organized beings:

death, like all other subordinate and subaltern powers, attacks only individuals, strikes only the surface, destroys only the form; he makes no impression on the substance, and, instead of injuring nature, causes it to shine with greater lustre by his depredations. If nature permits death to cut down individuals, and, in process of time, to destroy them, in order to shew her superiority to death and time, to exercise her ever-active power, manifest her fulness by her fecundity, and to make of the universe, by the reproduction and renewal of beings, a theatre ever crowded, a spectacle ever new: yet she never permits death to annihilate the species.

That beings may succeed each other, it is necessary that there be a destruction among them; in order to the nourishment and subsistence of animals, they destroy vegetables or other animals, and the quantity of life continuing ever the same after as well as before the destruction, it seems to be indifferent to nature, how much such or such a species is destroyed; yet, like a provident mother, in the midst of her inexhaustible abundance, she has limited the expence, and prevented any waste, by implanting the carnivorous instinct in very few animals; and even these voracious species she has reduced to a small number of individuals, multiplying, at the same time, both the species and individuals of those which feed on herbage; and, in vegetables, she seems to have been profuse, both with regard to the number and fertility of the species. Perhaps man has not a little contributed to second her views, with regard to maintaining, and even establishing, this order on earth; for in the sea that indifference, we supposed above, is conspicuous; all species there being more or less voracious, living on themselves or others. They are perpetually preying on, without ever destroying, each other; because the fecundity is equal to the depredation, and the whole consumption increases the reproduction.

Man is known to exercise his power over the creatures in a lord-like manner; those, whose flesh pleases his taste, he has selected, made them domestic slaves, multiplied them beyond what nature would herself have done, formed of them numerous herds and flocks, and, by his care to bring them into being, he seems to be entitled to the power of slaying them for his use; but this power, this right, he extends far beyond his wants: for, exclusive of those species which he has tamed, and disposes of at pleasure, he also makes war on the wild creatures, birds, and fishes. Instead of confining himself to those of the climate in which he lives, he travels far from home, he even visits the seas for new dainties, and all nature seems hardly sufficient to satisfy his intemperance, and the inconstant variety of his appetites. Man consumes, he alone swallows, more flesh than all the beasts together devour; thus is he the greatest destroyer, and even more from wantonness than necessity. Instead of enjoying, with moderation, the good things within his power; instead of liberally distributing them, instead of repairing when he destroys, and renewing when he annihilates, the man of substance places his whole glory in consuming; he prides himself in destroying more in one day, at his table, than would afford a comfortable subsistance to several families. Thus he exercises his tyrannical power equally over animals and men; others pining with hunger and toil, only to satisfy the immoderate appetite, and the still more insatiable vanity of this man; who, while he is destroying others by want, is destroying himself by his excesses.

Yet man, like the beasts, might live on vegetables; for flesh, however analogous it may be to flesh, does not afford better nourishment than grain, pulse, or bread. True nourishment, that which contributes to the nutrition, the growth, and the subsistance, is not that inanimate matter which seems to constitute the texture of the flesh or the herb, but the organical moleculæ contained in the one or the other; as the ox, which feeds on grass, acquires as much flesh as man, or any other carnivorous animal. The only real difference between aliments is this, that an equal quantity of flesh, corn, and grain, contains many more organical moleculæ than grass, the leaves, roots, and other parts of vegetables, as we have ascertained from infusions made with these different substances: so that man, and those beasts whose stomachs and intestines are not of a capacity to receive a very large quantity of aliments, could not hold a sufficiency of grass to furnish the quantity of organical moleculæ necessary to their nutrition. And it is on this account, that man and the other animals, which have but one stomach, can only subsist on flesh or corn, which contain, in a small volume, a very large quantity of the nutritious organical moleculæ; but the ox, and other ruminating animals, which have several stomachs, particularly one very large, and which will consequently contain a large volume of grass, find it sufficient to furnish the necessary quantity of organical moleculæ for their nourishment, growth, and multiplication. Here the quantity conpensates for the quality of the nourishment, which, in effect, is the same; it is the same substance, the same organical moleculæ, by which the ox, man, and all animals are nourished."

It would extend this article far beyond the bounds allotted it, to enumerate the many curious remarks contained in this treatise; we are therefore persuaded that the reader, if he has any taste for natural history, or any regard for, or interest in, the animals described in this work, will thank us for recommending it to his perusal.

PRELIMINARY DISCOURSE, CONCERNING THE ORIGIN OF MEN AND OF LANGUAGES

Henry Home, Lord Kames

Henry Home, Lord Kames (1696–1782), was a member of the Scottish landed gentry. Having studied law he became Lord Commissioner of Justiciary in Scotland. Kames combined legal, philosophical and literary inquiries with practical experiments in agricultural improvement. His *Sketches on the History of Mankind* were published first in 1774 in two volumes. A second edition, enlarged to four volumes, came out in 1778. In the *Sketches* Kames aimed to depict the adaptive, evolutionary nature of human customs and institutions. It was only in the 'Preliminary Discourse' that he pondered the natural history of man, setting out the highly contested idea that the tribes of mankind had been introduced in different acts of creation.

Whether there be different races of men, or whether all men be of one race without any difference but what proceeds from climate or other external cause, is a question that philosophers differ widely about. As the question is of moment in tracing the history of man, I purpose to contribute my mite. And in order to admit all the light possible, a view of brute animals as divided into different races or kinds, will make a proper introduction.

As many animals contribute to our well-being, and as many are noxious; man would be a being not a little imperfect, were he provided with no means but experience for distinguishing the one sort from the other. Did every animal make a species by itself (indulging the expression) differing from all others, a man would finish his course without acquiring as much knowledge of animals as is necesary even for self-preservation: he would be absolutely at a loss with respect to unknown individuals. The Deity has left none of his works imperfect. Animals are formed of different kinds, each kind having a figure and a temper peculiar to itself: great uniformity is discovered among animals of the same kind; great variety among animals of different kinds. And to prevent confusion, kinds are distinguished externally by figure, air, manner, so clearly as not to escape even a child[1]. Nor does divine wisdom stop here: to complete the system, we are endued with an innate conviction, that each kind has properties peculiar to itself; and that these properties belong to every individual of the kind[2]. Our road to the knowledge of animals is thus wonderfully shortened: the experience we have of the disposition and properties of any animal, is applied without hesitation to every one of the kind. By that conviction, a child, familiar with one dog, is fond of others that resemble it; an European, upon the first sight of a cow in Africa, strokes it as gentle and innocent; and an African avoids a tiger in Hindostan as at home.

If the foregoing theory be well founded, neither experience nor argument is required to prove, that a horse is not an ass, or that a monkey is not a man[3]. Some animals indeed are so similar, as to render it uncertain whether they be not radically of the same kind. But in such instances we need not to be solicitous; for I venture to affirm, that both will be found gentle or fierce, wholesome food or unwholesome. Such questions may be curious, but they are of little use.

Whether man be provided by nature with a faculty to distinguish innocent animals from what are noxious, seems not a clear point: such a faculty may be thought unnecessary to man, being supplied by reason and experience. But as reason and experience have little influence on brute animals, they undoubtedly possess that faculty[4]. A beast of prey would be ill fitted for its station, if nature did not teach it what creatures to attack, what to avoid. A rabbit is the prey of the ferret. Present

---

[1] "And out of the ground the Lord God formed every beast of the field, and every fowl of the air, and brought them unto Adam to see what he would call them. And Adam gave names to all cattle, and to the fowl of the air, and to every beast of the field." *Gen.* ii.19.

[2] See Elements of Criticism, vol. 2. p. 490. edit. 5.

[3] See M. Buffon's natural history.

[4] Brute animals have many instincts that are denied to man; because the want of them can be supplied by education. An infant must be taught to walk; and it is long before it acquires the art in perfection. Brutes have no teacher but nature. A foal, the moment it sees the light, walks no less perfectly than its parents. And so does a partridge, lapwing, &c.

Dente lupus, cornu taurus petit; unde nisi intus Monstratum? *Horace.*

a rabbit, even dead, to a young ferret that never had seen a rabbit: it throws itself upon the body, and bites it with fury. A hound has the same faculty with respect to a hare; and most dogs have it. Unless directed by nature, innocent animals would not know their enemy till they were in its clutches. A hare flies with precipitation from the first dog it ever saw; and a chicken, upon the first sight of a kite, cowers under its dam. Social animals, without scruple, connect with their own kind, and as readily avoid others[5]. Birds are not afraid of quadrupeds; not even of a cat, till they are taught by experience that a cat is their enemy. They appear to be as little afraid of a man naturally; and upon that account are far from being shy when left unmolested. In the uninhabited island of Visia Grandé, one of the Philippines, Kempfer says, that birds may be taken with the hand. Hawks, in some of the South-sea islands, are equally tame. At Port Egmont in the Falkland Islands, geese, far from being shy, may be knocked down with a stick. The birds that inhabit certain rocks hanging over the sea in the island of Annabon, take food readily out of a man's hand. In Arabia Felix, foxes and apes show no fear of man; the inhabitants of hot countries having no notion of hunting. In the uninhabited island Bering, adjacent to Kamskatka, foxes are so little shy that they scarce go out of a man's way. Doth not this observation suggest a final cause? A partridge, a plover, a pheasant, would be lost to man for food, were they naturally as much afraid of him as of a hawk or a kite.

The division of animals into different kinds, serves another purpose, no less important than those mentioned; which is, to fit them for different climates. We learn from experience, that no animal nor vegetable is fitted for every climate; and from experience we also learn, that there is no animal nor vegetable but what is fitted for some climate, where it grows to perfection. Even in the torrid zone, plants of a cold climate are found upon mountains where plants of a hot climate will not grow; and the height of a mountain may be determined with tolerable precision from the plants it produces. Wheat is not an indigenous plant in Britain: no farmer is ignorant that foreign

---

[5]   The populace about Smyrna have a cruel amusement. They lay the eggs of a hen in a stork's nest. Upon seeing the chickens, the male in amazement calls his neighbouring storks together; who, to revenge the affront put upon them, destroy the poor innocent female; while he bewails his misfortune in heavy lamentation.

seed is requisite to preserve the plant in vigour. To prevent flax from degenerating in Scotland and Ireland, great quanities of foreign seed are annually imported. A camel is peculiarly fitted for the burning sands of Arabia; and Lapland would be uninhabitable but for rain-deer, an animal so entirely fitted for piercing cold, that it cannot subsist even in a temperate climate. Arabian and Barbary horses degenerate in Britain; and to preserve the breed in some degree of perfection, frequent supplies from their original climate are requisite. Spanish horses degenerate in Mexico; but improve in Chili, having more vigour and swiftness there, than even the Andalusian race, whose offspring they are. Our dunghill-fowl, imported originally from a warm country in Asia, are not hardened, even after many centuries, to bear the cold of this country like birds originally native: the hen lays few or no eggs in winter, unless in a house warmed with fire. The deserts of Zaara and Biledulgerid in Africa, may be properly termed the native country of lions: there they are nine feet long and five feet high. Lions in the south of Africa toward the Cape of Good Hope, are but five feet and a half long and three and a half high. A breed of lions transplanted from the latter to the former, would rise to the full size; and sink to the smaller size, if transplanted from the former to the latter[6].

To preserve the different kinds of species of animals entire, as far as necessary, Providence is careful to prevent a mixed breed. Few animals of different species copulate together. Some may be brought to copulate, but without effect; and some produce a mongrel, a mule for example, which seldom procreates, if at all. In some few instances, where a mixture of species is harmless, procreation goes on without limitation. All

6 That every species of plants has a proper climate where it grows to perfection, is a fact uncontroverted. The same holds in brute animals. Biledulgerid, the kindly climate for lions, would be mortal to the bear, the wolf, the deer, and other inhabitants of a cold region. Providence has not only fitted the productions of nature for different climates, but has guarded these productions against the extremities of the weather in the same climate. Many plants close their leaves during night; and some close them at mid day against the burning rays of the sun. In cold climates, plants during winter are protected against cold by snow. In these climates, the hair of some animals grows long in winter: several animals are covered with much fat, which protects them against cold; and many birds are fatter in winter than in summer, though probably their nourishment is less plentiful. Several animals sleep during winter in sheltered places; and birds of passage are taught by nature to change the climate, when too hot or too cold.

the different species of the dog-kind copulate together; and the mongrels produced generate others without end.

M. Buffon, in his natural history, borrows from Ray[7] a very artificial rule for ascertaining the different species of animals: "Any two animals that can procreate together, and whose issue can also procreate, are of the same species[8]." A horse and an ass can procreate together; but they are not, says he, of the same species, because their issue, a mule, cannot procreate. He applies that rule to man; holding men to be of the same species, because a man and a woman, however different in size, in shape, in complexion, can procreate together without end. And by the same rule he holds all dogs to be of the same species. With respect to other animals, the rule should pass without opposition from me; but as it also respects man, the subject of the present enquiry, I will examine it with attention. Providence, to prevent confusion, hath in many instances withheld from animals of different species a power of procreating together: but as our author has not attempted to prove that such restraint is universal without a single exception, his rule is evidently a *petitio principii*. Why may not two animals different in species produce a mixed breed? M. Buffon must say, that it is contrary to a law of nature. But has he given any evidence of this supposed law of nature? On the contrary, he proves it by various instances not to be a law of nature. He admits the sheep and the goat to be of different species; and yet we have his authority for affirming, that a he-goat and a ewe produce a mixed breed which generate for ever[9]. The camel and the dromedary, though nearly related, are however no less distinct than the horse and the ass. The dromedary is less than the camel, more slender, and remarkably more swift of foot: it has but one bunch on its back, the camel has two: the race is more numerous than that of the camel, and more widely spread. One would not desire distinguishing marks more satisfying; and yet these two species propagate together, no less freely than the different races of men and of dogs. M. Buffon indeed, with respect to the camel and dromedary, endeavours to save his credit by a distinction without a difference. "They are," says he, "one species; but their races are different, and

7   Wisdom of God in the works of creation.

8   Octavo edit. vol. 8. p. 104. and in many other parts.

9   Vol. 10. p. 138.

have been so past all memory[10]." Is not this the same with saying that the camel and the dromedary are different species of the same genus? which also holds true of the different species of men and of dogs. If our author will permit me to carry back to the creation the camel and the dromedary as two distinct races, I desire no other concession. He admits no fewer than ten kinds of goats, visibly distinguishable, which also propagate together; but says, that these are varieties only, though permanent and unchangeable. No difficulty is unsurmountable, if words be allowed to pass without meaning. Nor does he even adhere to the same opinion; though in distinguishing a horse from an ass, he affirms the mule they generate to be barren; yet afterward, entirely forgetting his rule, he admits the direct contrary[11]. At that rate a horse and an ass are of the same species. Did it never once enter into the mind of this author, that the human race would be strangely imperfect, if they were unable to distinguish a man from a monkey, or a hare from a hedge-hog, till it were known whether they can procreate together?

But it seems unncessary after all to urge any argument against the foregoing rule, which M. Buffon himself inadvertently abandons as to all animals, men and dogs excepted. We are indebted to him for a remark, That not a single animal of the torrid zone is common to the old world and to the new. But how does he verify his remark? Does he ever think of trying whether such animals can procreate together? "They are," says he "of different kinds, having no such resemblance as to make us pronounce them to be of the same kind. Linnæus and Brisson," he adds, "have very improperly given the name of the camel to the lama and the pacos of Peru. So apparent is the difference, that other writers class these animals with sheep. Wool however is the only circumstance in which a pacos resembles a sheep: nor doth the lama resemble a camel except in length of neck." He distinguisheth in the same manner, the true Asiatic tiger from several American animals that bear the same name. He mentions its size, its force, its ferocity, the colour of its hair, the stripes black and white that like rings surround alternately its trunk, and are continued to the tip of its tail; "characters," says he, "that clearly distinguish

10 Vol. 10. p. 1.
11 Vol. 12. p. 223.

the true tiger from all animals of prey in the new world; the largest of which scarce equals one of our mastives." And he reasons in the same manner upon the other animals of the torrid zone[12]. Here truth obliges our author to acknowledge, that we are taught by nature to distinguish animals into different kinds by visible marks, without regard to his artificial rule. And if so, there must be different kinds of men; for certain tribes differ visibly from each other, no less than the lama and pacos from the camel or from the sheep, nor less than the true tiger from the American animals of that name[13]. For proving that dogs were created of different kinds, what better evidence can be expected than that the kinds continue distinct to this day? Our author pretends to derive the mastiff, the bull-dog, the hound, the greyhound, the terrier, the water-dog, &c. all of them from the prick-ear'd shepherd's cur. Now, admitting the progeny of the original male and female cur have suffered every possible alteration from climate, food, domestication; the result would be endless varieties, so that no one individual should resemble another. Whence then are derived the different species of dogs above mentioned, or the different races or varieties, as M. Buffon is pleased to name them? Uniformity invariable must be a law in their nature, for it never can be ascribed to chance. There are mongrels, it is true, among dogs, from want of choice, or from a depraved appetite: but as all animals prefer their own kind, mongrels are few compared with animals of a true breed. There are mongrels also among men: the several kinds however continue distinct; and probably will so continue for ever.

There remains an argument against the system of M. Buffon with respect to dogs, still more conclusive. Allowing to climate its utmost influence, it may possibly have an effect upon the size and figure; but surely M. Buffon cannot seriously think, that the different instincts of dogs are owing to climate. A terrier, whose prey burrows under ground, is continually scraping the earth, and thrusting its nose into it. A hound has always its nose on the surface, in order to trace a hare by smell. The same instinct is remarkable in spaniels. It is by nature that these creatures are directed to be continually going about, to

12 See vol. 8. sect. Of animals common to the two continents

13 No person thinks that all trees can be traced back to one kind. Yet the figure, leaves, fruit, &c. of different kinds, are not more distinct, than the difference of figure, colour, &c. in the different races of men.

catch the smell, and trace their prey. A greyhound, which has not the smelling-faculty, is constantly looking about for its prey. A shepherd's dog may be improved by education, but nature prompts it to guard the flock. A house-dog makes its round every night to protect its master against strangers, without ever being trained to it. Such dogs have a notion of property, and are trusty guardians of their master's goods: in his absence, no person dares lay hold of his hat or his great coat. Waggoners employ dogs of that kind to watch during night the goods they carry. Is it conceivable, that such different instincts, constantly the same in the same species, can proceed from climate, from mixture of breed, or from other accidental cause?

The celebrated Linnæus, instead of describing every animal according to its kind, as Adam our first parent did, has wandered far from nature in classing animals. He distributes them into six classes, viz. *Mammalia, Aves, Amphibia, Pisces, Insecta, Vermes.* The *Mammalia* are distributed into seven orders, chiefly from their teeth, viz. *Primates, Bruta, Feræ, Glires, Pecora, Belluæ, Cete.* And the *Primates* are, *Homo, Simia, Lemur, Vespertilio.* What may have been his purpose in classing animals so contrary to nature, I cannot guess, if it be not to enable us, from the nipples and teeth of any particular animal, to know where it is to be found in his book. It resembles the classing books in a library by size, or by binding, without regard to the contents: it may serve as a sort of dictionary; but to no other purpose. How whimsical is it to class together animals that nature hath widely separated, a man for example and a bat? What will a plain man think of a manner of classing, that denies a whale to be a fish? In classing animals, why does he confine himself to the nipples and the teeth, when there are many other distinguishing marks? Animals are no less distinguishable with respect to tails; long tails, short tails, no tails: nor less distinguishable with respect to hands; some having four, some two, some none, &c. &c. Yet, after all, if any solid instruction can be acquired from such classing, I shall listen, not only with attention, but with satisfaction.

Now more particularly of man, after discussing other animals. If the only rule afforded by nature for classing animals can be depended upon, there are different species of men as well as of dogs: a mastiff differs not more from a

spaniel, than a white man from a negro, or a Laplander from
a Dane. And if we have any belief in Providence, it ought to
be so. Plants were created of different kinds to fit them for
different climates, and so were brute animals. Certain it is,
that all men are not fitted equally for every climate. Is there
not then reason to conclude, that as there are different
climates, so there are different species of men fitted for these
different climates? The inhabitants of the frozen regions of
the north, men, birds, beasts, fish, are all provided with a
quantity of fat which guards them against cold. Even the
trees are full of rosin. The island St Thomas, under the line,
is extremely foggy; and the natives are fitted for that sort of
weather, by the rigidity of their fibres. The fog is dispelled in
July and August by dry winds; which give vigour to
Europeans, whose fibres are relaxed by a moist atmosphere
as by a warm bath. The natives, on the contrary, who are not
fitted for a dry air, have more diseases in July and August
than during the other ten months. On the other hand,
instances are without number of men degenerating in a
climate to which they are not fitted by nature; and I know not
of a single instance where in such a climate people have
retained their original vigour. Several European colonies
have subsisted in the torrid zone of America more than two
centuries; and yet even that length of time has not familiar-
ised them to the climate: they cannot bear heat like the
original inhabitants, nor like negroes transplanted from a
country equally hot: they are far from equalling in vigour of
mind or body the nations from which they sprung. The
Spanish inhabitants of Carthagena in South America lose
their vigour and colour in a few months. Their motions are
languid; and their words are pronounced in a low voice, and
with long and frequent intervals. The offspring of Europeans
born in Batavia, soon degenerate. Scarce one of them has
talents sufficient to bear a part in the administration. There
is not an office of trust but must be filled with native
Europeans. Some Portuguese, who have been for ages settled
on the sea-coast of Congo, retain scarce the appearance of
men. South Carolina, especially about Charlestown, is
extremely hot, having no sea-breeze to cool the air: Europeans
there die so fast that they have not time to degenerate. Even in
Jamaica, tho' more temperate by a regular succession of land
and sea breezes, recruits from Britain are necessary to keep up

the numbers[14]. The climate of the northern provinces resembles our own, and population goes on rapidly.

What means are employed by Providence to qualify different races of men for different climates, is a subject to which little attention has been given. It lies too far out of sight to expect a complete discovery; but facts carefully collected might afford some glimmering of light. In that view, I mention the following fact. The inhabitants of the kingdom of Senaar in Africa are true negroes, a jet-black complexion, thick lips, flat nose, curled woolly hair. The country itself is the hotest in the world. From the report of a late traveller, they are admirably protected by nature against the violence of the heat. Their skin is to the touch remarkably cooler than that of an European; and is so in reality, no less than two degrees on Fahrenheit's thermometer. The young women there are highly prized by the Turks for that quality.

Thus it appears, that there are different races of men fitted by nature for different climates. Upon examination another fact will perhaps also appear, that the natural productions of each climate make the most wholesome food for the people who are fitted to live in it. Between the tropics, the natives live chiefly on fruits, seeds, and roots; and it is the opinion of the most knowing naturalists, that such food is of all the most wholesome for the torrid zone; comprehending the hot plants, which grow there to perfection, and tend greatly to fortify the stomach. In a temperate climate, a mixture of animal and vegetable food is held to be the most wholesome; and there both animals and vegetables abound. In a cold climate, animals are in plenty, but few vegetables that can serve for food to man. What physicians pronounce upon that head, I know not; but if we dare venture a conjecture from analogy, animal food will be found the most wholesome for such as are fitted by nature to live in a cold climate.

M. Buffon, from the rule, That animals which can procreate together, and whose progeny can also procreate, are of one species, concludes, that all men are of one race or species; and endeavours to support that favourite opinion, by ascribing to the climate, to food, or to other accidental causes, all the

---

[14] As the Europeans lose vigour by the heat of the climate, the free negroes, especially those in the mountains, are the safeguard of the island; and it was by their means chiefly that a number of rebellious negro slaves were subdued in the year 1760.

varieties that are found among men. But is he seriously of opinion, that any operation of climate, or of other accidental cause, can account for the copper colour and smooth chin universal among the Americans, the prominence of the *pudenda* universal among Hottentot women, or the black nipple no less universal among female Samoides? The thick fogs of the island St Thomas may relax the fibres of the natives, but cannot make them more rigid than they are naturally. Whence then the difference with respect to rigidity of fibres between them and Europeans, but from original nature? Can one hope for belief in ascribing to climate the low stature of the Esquimaux, the smallness of their feet, or the overgrown size of their head; or in ascribing to climate the low stature of the Laplanders[15], and their ugly visage. Lapland is indeed piercingly cold; but so is Finland, and the northern parts of Norway, the inhabitants of which are tall, comely, and well proportioned. The black colour of negroes, thick lips, flat nose, crisped woolly hair, and rank smell, distinguish them from every other race of men. The Abyssinians on the contrary are tall and well made, their complexion a brown olive, features well proportioned, eyes large and of a sparkling black, lips thin, a nose rather high than flat. There is no such difference of climate between Abyssinia and Negroland as to produce these striking differences. At any rate, there must be considerable mixture both of soil and climate in these extensive regions; and yet not the least mixture is perceived in the people.

Thus upon an extensive survey of the inhabited parts of our globe, many nations are found differing so widely from each other, not only in complexion, features, shape, and other external circumstances, but in temper and disposition, particularly in two capital articles, courage, and behaviour to strangers, that even the certainty of different races could not make one expect more striking varieties. Doth M. Buffon think it sufficient to say dryly, that such varieties may possibly be the effect of climate, or of other accidental causes? The presumption is, that the varieties subsisting at present have always subsisted; which ought to have held as true, till positive

---

15   By late accounts it appears that the Laplanders are originally Huns. Pere Hel, an Hungarian, made lately this discovery, when sent to Lapland for making astronomical observations.

evidence be brought of the contrary: instead of which we are put off with mere suppositions and possibilities.

But not to rest entirely upon presumptive evidence, to me it appears clear from the very frame of the human body, that there must be different races of men fitted for different climates. Few animals are more affected than men generally are, not only with change of seasons in the same climate, but with change of weather in the same season. Can such a being be fitted for all climates equally? Impossible. A man must at least be hardened by nature against the slighter changes of seasons or weather: he ought to be altogether insensible of such changes. Yet from Sir John Pringle's observations on the diseases of the army, to go no further, it appears, that even military men, who ought of all to be the hardiest, are greatly affected by them. Horses and horned cattle sleep on the bare ground, wet or dry, without harm; and yet are not made for every climate: can a man be made for every climate, who is so much more delicate, that he cannot sleep on wet ground without hazard of some mortal disease?

But the argument I chiefly rely on is, That were all men of one species, there never could have existed, without a miracle, different kinds, such as exist at present. Giving allowance for every supposable variation of climate or of other natural causes, what can follow, as observed about the dog-kind, but endless varieties among the individuals, as among tulips in a garden, so as that no individual shall resemble another? Instead of which, we find men of different kinds, the individuals of each kind remarkably uniform, and differing no less remarkably from the individuals of every other kind. Uniformity without variation is the offspring of nature, never of chance.

There is another argument that appears also to have weight. Horses with respect to size, shape, and spirit, differ widely in different climates. But let a male and a female of whatever climate be carried to a country where horses are in perfection, their progeny will improve gradually, and will acquire in time the perfection of their kind. Is not this a proof, that all horses are of one kind? If so, men are not all of one kind; for if a White mix with a Black in whatever climate, or a Hottentot with a Samoide, the result will not be either an improvement of the kind, or the contrary; but a mongrel breed differing from both parents.

It is thus ascertained beyond any rational doubt, that there are different races or kinds of men, and that these races or kinds are naturally fitted for different climates: whence we have reason to conclude, that originally each kind was placed in its proper climate, whatever change may have happened in later times by war or commerce.

There is a remarkable fact that confirms the foregoing conjectures. As far back as history goes, or tradition kept alive by history, the earth was inhabited by savages divided into many small tribes, each tribe having a language peculiar to itself. Is it not natural to suppose, that these original tribes were different races of men, placed in proper climates, and left to form their own language?

Upon summing up the whole particulars mentioned above, would one hesitate a moment to adopt the following opinion, were there no counterbalancing evidence, viz.

"That God created many pairs of the human race, differing from each other both externally and internally; that he fitted these pairs for different climates, and placed each pair in its proper climate; that the peculiarities of the original pairs were preserved entire in their descendents; who, having no assistance but their natural talents, were left to gather knowledge from experience, and in particular were left (each tribe) to form a language for itself; that signs were sufficient for the original pairs, without any language but what nature suggests; and that a language was formed gradually, as a tribe increased in numbers and in different occupations, to make speech necessary?"

But this opinion, however plausible, we are not permitted to adopt; being taught a different lesson by revelation, viz. That God created but a single pair of the human species. Tho' we cannot doubt of the authority of Moses, yet his account of the creation of man is not a little puzzling, as it seems to contradict every one of the facts mentioned above. According to that account, different races of men were not formed, nor were men framed originally for different climates. All men must have spoken the same language, viz. that of our first parents. And what of all seems the most contradictory to that account, is the savage state: Adam, as Moses informs us, was endued by his Maker with an eminent degree of knowledge; and he certainly must have been an excellent preceptor to his children and their progeny, among whom he lived many generations. Whence then the degeneracy of all men unto the savage state! To account for that dismal catastrophe, mankind must have suffered some terrible convulsion.

That terrible convulsion is revealed to us in the history of the tower of Babel, contained in the 11th chapter of Genesis, which is,

> "That for many centuries after the deluge, the whole earth was of one language, and of one speech, that they united to build a city on a plain in the land of Shinar, with a tower whose top might reach unto heaven; that the Lord beholding the people to be one, and to have all one language, and that nothing would be restrained from them which they imagined to do, confounded their language that they might not understand one another; and scattered them abroad upon the face of all the earth."

Here light breaks forth in the midst of darkness. By confounding the language of men, and scattering them abroad upon the face of all the earth, they were rendered savages. And to harden them for their new habitations, it was necessary that they should be divided into different kinds, fitted for different climates. Without an immediate change of bodily constitution, the builders of Babel could not possibly have subsisted in the burning region of Guinea, or in the frozen region of Lapland; especially without houses, or any other convenience to protect them against a destructive climate. Against this history it has indeed been urged,

> "That the circumstances mentioned evince it to be purely an allegory; that men never were so frantic as to think of building a tower whose top might reach to heaven; and that it is grossly absurd, taking the matter literally, that the Almighty was afraid of men, and reduced to the necessity of saving himself by a miracle."

But that this is a real history, must necessarily be admitted, as the confusion of Babel is the only known fact that can reconcile sacred and profane history.

A GEOGRAPHICAL HISTORY OF MAN
and of the Quadrupeds which are dispersed over the different Parts of the Earth; with a zoological Map, adapted to the same.
By E. A. W. Zimmerman [sic]
Anonymous

Source: Monthly Review, vol. 80, 1789

Eberhardt August Wilhelm Zimmermann (1743–1815), Professor of Physics at the Caroline College at Brunswick, was one of those authors who criticized the Linnean classification of nature as 'artificial arrangement'. Zimmermann disagreed with Linnaeus's assumption that there was but one centre of creation, i.e. the Garden of Eden, from which all animals and plants had migrated across the earth. His biogeographical history, in which he referred the natural realm to several centres of creation, was published in three volumes between 1778 and 1883. The text below is the first half of the review; the second part followed in volume 81 of the *Monthly Review*.

Powerful are the objections urged by many celebrated proficients in natural history, themselves, against *artificial arrangements*, in the study of that most extensive science. They allege, and with justice, that no system can be perfect until our knowledge of the subject itself be perfect and complete: that those who form artificial arrangements, ever attentive to more minute similarities, frequently place in the same class, bodies, whose grand and leading characteristics are the most opposite to each other; that too great a predilection for mere classification, (which, in fact, is no other than forming a *general index* to natural history,) is apt to draw the attention from what is the most interesting and important in the science, to things which are the most trivial, and may be merely *accidental*; and that it induces men to imagine, that a familiar acquaintance with some favourite system constitutes the *essence* of the science;

although this absurdity is not greater than it would be to
maintain with Hudibras,

> *That all a Rhetorician's rules*
> *Lie in the* NAMING *of his* TOOLS.

Yet to discard systems altogether, is an opposite error, of,
perhaps, a still more pernicious tendency. Without some
arrangement, a collection of facts is but *rudis indigestaque
moles*, difficult to be retained in the memory; and almost
useless from the want of being directed to some determinate
object. It must further be granted that this natural love of
system, which is but the love of *order*, has been of much
occasional benefit to the science. For the very attention which
has been given to those peculiarities on which systems are
founded, have very considerably increased our knowledge of
the *minutiæ* of nature, whether we receive or reject the
favourite order that gave rise to these discoveries.

The grand desideratum is, to observe the due medium; to
chuse such a plan as may assist and direct the student in his
pursuit of knowledge, and not deceive or embarrass him by
slighter similarities or differences. In our opinion, few plans
have been better calculated to answer this desirable end, than
that proposed by Professor ZIMMERMAN, in the work
before us. This celebrated author has laboured many years,
with indefatigable industry, and no small degree of success,
in the extensive vineyard of *natural history*. His plan of study
has enabled him to contemplate *zoology* in general, in a
singular and very interesting point of view. Yet his principal
attention has been directed to that branch of the natural
history of men and quadrupeds, which relates to their *local
residence*. His professed design is to give a GEOGRAPHICAL
history of men and quadrupeds; and to indicate the climates
best adapted to each species; to enquire how far the different
classes of quadrupeds are capable of being spread over the
various countries of the globe; to trace the changes produced
on those animals which inhabit the most opposite regions,
and to mark, with more accuracy than his predecessors have
done, the effects produced on their form or instincts by the
influence of those different degrees of heat, cold, humidity,
dryness, domestication, and kind of food, peculiar to these
diversities of situation. By *climates*, we are to understand,
not simply or solely those distinguished by the geographical

divisions of the globe, to the exclusion of what he terms *physical* climates, or that which depends on the changes produced in any given latitude by such adventitious circumstances as the lower or more elevated situations of a country, its being encompassed by water or large tracts of land, placed in an extensive plain, or surrounded by lofty mountains. Peculiarities of the like kind, it is well known, frequently prevent the *physical* climate from corresponding entirely with the *geographical*, as a country influenced by them is often much warmer or colder than other regions placed under the same degree of latitude.

Professor ZIMMERMAN published a treatise on the same subject, in the *Latin language*, some years ago: which, as we are informed, was favourably received on the continent, though we do not recollect that it has found its way into this island. The many publications since that period, particularly the works of Lord *Kaims*, Professors *Blumenbach*, *Schreber*, *Erxleben*, and others, have furnished such a rich abundance of new materials, and suggested so many new ideas to the author, that the work before us is to be considered rather as a *new* publication, on the plan of the former, than as an enlargement of that treatise. The present performance, though it keeps its principal object in constant view, is enriched with most of the discoveries which have been more recently made, and interspersed with a great variety of interesting observations of a philosophical and moral nature.

The work is divided into *four* principal parts. In the *first* part, the author takes a view of the nobler animals which are universally diffused over every part of the habitable globe, and are rendered capable of sustaining the extremes of heat and cold, both in the *old* and in the *new* world: in the *second*, the class of quadrupeds which inhabit both worlds, but yet are not so universal as the other: in the *third*, the inhabitants of particular regions only. The *fourth* part, which constitutes nearly the whole of the third volume, is chiefly devoted to various curious speculations, and philosophical inferences drawn from the view of animal nature given in the preceding volumes.

As *man* is allowed to be the lord of this lower world, in regard to the nobler faculties of his mind, so with respect to *corporeal* advantages, he enjoys a decided pre-eminence.

'His frame is better able to resist every extreme than that of any other animal. He walks over the surface of the earth without being checked or limited; and takes up his abode where he pleases, without suffering any sensible diminution of his native strength. The pole, the equator, the highest mountains, and the deepest mines, find him an inhabitant. He visits every place, and degenerates in a much less degree, in consequence of local situation, than any other of those animals that can subsist in a great diversity of climate.'

The author therefore begins his geographical history with *man*, and enquires,

'What *degrees* of heat or cold is man capable of sustaining? *How* and *wherefore* does he inhabit such a diversity of climates? Does this capacity proceed from the toughness and pliability of his corporeal system, or is he, as M. DE BUFFON maintains, indebted to his *mental* powers alone for the advantage? Again, what *influence* have climate, nutrition, and various incidental circumstances, on him? Are they sufficient to effect the differences observable in human beings; or has nature formed, from the beginning, a diversity of individuals, each adapted to his own climate? *Which* is the proper land of his nativity, and the spot from which he migrated? Is he naturally *biped*, or *quadruped*; in size, a *Patagonian* or an *Esquimaux*; in complexion, a *Negroe* or a *Circassian*?'

These are the questions which M. ZIMMERMAN examines, at large, in the first chapter of this interesting work; and which he answers to *our* satisfaction, and, we hope, to the satisfaction of all whom they may concern; as he supports the simplicity of creation, and the dignity of human nature, in opposition to all philosophical levelling. He begins with animadverting on the degrees of cold which the human frame is able to sustain with impunity.

'The greatest degree of natural *cold* that has hitherto been ascertained by the thermometer, is that mentioned by the elder *Gmelin*, at *Jeneseisk*, 58 deg. N. lat. in the year 1735. It commenced in *January*, and was so strong, that the mercury of Fahrenheit's thermometer sunk two degrees below the freezing point. Birds *fell dead on the ground*, and every thing capable of freezing, became ice. This fact, which has been called in question by some, is rendered credible by the narrative given by M. *Pallas*, in his travels through *Siberia*, in the year 1772. He tells us that, at *Krassnoyjarsk*, the cold was so extreme, on the 7th of December, that the mercury sunk to 80 degrees below (0), and some days afterward, it froze in the ball. Unfortunately, this gentleman's thermometer was not graduated sufficiently low to enable him to make more accurate observations: but according to *Brown's* experiments, not less than 370 degrees below (0) are requisite completely to congeal the quicksilver[1]. Not less extraordinary must that degree of cold have been which the English sustained at *Churchill's* River, in *Hudson's* Bay, according to the narrative given by *Middleton*. The Lanoseen was frozen *twelve feet*, and brandy could not be prevented from freezing in the warmest rooms. Whoever exposed himself to the open air was in danger of losing the epidermis of his face and hands. Yet this degree of cold did not prove fatal to those born in a warmer climate; and it is supported by the inhabitants with the utmost safety. The Canadian savages, who live very near to Hudson's Bay, and the *Esquimaux* Indians, hunt, almost naked, the whole winter through, notwithstanding the severity of their seasons. The Dutch under *Hemskirk*, in the year 1597, who were obliged to pass a winter in *Nova Zembla*, resisted the severity of the cold, though the white bear, native of these regions, sought a warmer atmosphere; and the white fox (*canis lagopus*) was the only animal that remained. *Crantz*, in his account of *Greenland*, asserts that the inhabitants are very slightly clothed, and that they go with their heads, necks, and legs, naked; that the *Norwegian* peasants work with their bosoms exposed to the cold, till the hair is frozen together, and when in a perspiration by labour, cool themselves by rolling in the snow, without receiving any injury.'

After having produced several other instances of a similar nature, our philosopher proceeds to enquire what degrees of *heat* the human frame is able to sustain without apparent detriment. *Adanson* observed that in Senegal, 17 degrees N. lat. Fahrenheit's thermometer was risen in the *shade* to 108½

1   Many of our readers will recollect a more ample narrative of the above facts given in Bishop *Watson's* elegant Essays, vol. i. Essay 7th.

degrees; and that near the coast it stood at 117½. The Sicilians, during the *Sirok winds*, resist a heat of 112 degrees; and the negroes frequently to the 120th degree, and sometimes far above it.

But the *artificial* heat which has been sustained, is much more astonishing. M. ZIMMERMAN has collected various instances of this; and quotes, among others, the experiments made by Lord *Mulgrave*, Dr. *Solander*, Sir *J. Banks*, and Dr. *Blagden*, from which it appears that they could resist 211, 224, 260 degrees of heat without being roasted alive. But the resisting powers of Dr. *Blagden* himself, who supported, for eight minutes, a heat exceeding that of boiling water by 48 degrees, must yield to those of the French girls mentioned by Messrs. *Du Hamel* and *Tillet*; who inform us, as they were making inquiries concerning a disease which had infected the grain, that they found at *Rochefoucault* in *Angoumois*, some female servants who bore the heat of their ovens, in which fruits and meats were baked, more than ten minutes, with the utmost composure. These academicians, on accurate examination, found the heat of an oven to be exactly 275 $^1/_{17}$ of Fahr. therm. exceeding that of Dr. *Blagden* no less than 15 degrees. The girls were frequently obliged to expose themselves to this heat; and, through the power of custom, bore it without any pernicious effects[2].

It has been shewn that no animal can withstand the extreme cold of the northern climates, equal to man, excepting the *canis lagopus*; and experiments further prove that he is supreme in the opposite quality. According to Dr. *Blagden*, a bitch resisted the 220th degree of heat. *Tillet's* bird, the Loxia, died in the heat of 169 $^{11}/_{17}$. A rabbit bore tolerably well 164, but a cock could not endure a heat of 169 degrees, without danger. Thus it appears that man, and man alone, is formed to resist the two extremes: that he lives, and continues healthy under all the variations of temperature from the 232d of natural cold to the 130th degree of natural heat.

No less wonderful is the difference of *pressure* which the human body is capable of sustaining without detriment, which

---

[2] It is necessary to inform the English reader, that, in many parts of France and Switzerland, their domestic ovens are very large, and it is customary for the servant maids, instead of using an instrument, to go into these glowing ovens, and fetch out the different articles of grain, fruit, &c. after they have been dried or baked sufficiently.

amounts, according to an accurate estimate made by our author, to no less than a diversity of 153,000 pounds: that is, the pressure of the atmosphere on the bodies of those who inhabit countries level with the sea, is greater by the above weight, than the inhabitants of the *Cordilliers* experience. And it is well known that Divers can occasionally sustain upward of 300,000 pounds more than the weight supported by the inhabitant of a strand, without any material detriment.

This universality of his frame exposes man to a great diversity of atmospheres. He breathes, and often continues healthy, in airs surcharged with watery particles, and laden with noxious vapours. Many thousands pass their days in the mines of *Potosi*; and *Condamine* informs us that he found healthful inhabitants in a country between *Loxa* and *Juen*, where they were free from rains only during two months in the year. Man is no less qualified by nature to derive wholesome nourishment from whatever species of *food* he may find in each climate. Both his *appetite* and his *make* prove him to be *carnivorous*, *granivorous*, *frugivorous*, and *ichthyofagous*. The *Greenlander* satiates his appetite with the raw flesh of a whale, and washes it down with the blood of the seal. The inhabitants of *Jakuti* feed luxuriously on mice, wolves, foxes, horses, &c. while the poor *Lybian* is contented with dried grasshoppers. Numberless sects of *India* feed on rice, while an *European* stomach can bear, at one meal, a farrago of milk, soups, mineral waters, oil, vinegar, mustard, beer, various sorts of wine, butchers meat, poultry, fish, vegetables, and fruits; and afterward, to assist digestion, will take a small mouthful of brandy.

Professor ZIMMERMAN now demands, in opposition to the Count de Buffon,

> 'Is it to *talents* and ingenuity, that the *Greenlander*, the *Esquimaux*, the *Canadian*, are beholden for their power to resist the cold? Do these enable the peasant to expose his open breast and naked limbs to the severity of a Northern winter? or the Negroe to sustain a vertical sun, healthy and strong, though the burning sands scorch the soles of his feet? The mind, it is true, can procure many accommodations for the body; can supply it with warm clothing, shelter it from the sun's rays, teach to man the various uses of iron, and instruct him to form weapons, &c.; but it cannot, with all its

influence, render him the inhabitant of every region, were not his body so adapted, by the toughness and pliability of its frame.'

An enquiry here presents itself of no small moment: are the human beings which possess these various and opposite powers, derived from one common origin: or were different races of men formed and adapted by their original make to their specific climates? M. ZIMMERMAN enters fully into this question, which has been so frequently agitated. Like a true son of Adam, he contends earnestly for the old constitution, in opposition to the bold attacks of a *Voltaire* and a *Hume*. He plainly shews, that the distinct, and almost innumerable, exertions of creative power in the formation of different races of men, is a supposition, as unnecessary as it is extravagant; the influence of natural causes being equal to all the differences observable in the human species. He walks with a firm foot and steady pace, through every region of the habitable globe, examines the stature, form, and complexion of its inhabitants, compares these with the peculiarities of their climate and situation, and satisfactorily proves, that the difference of stature between the *Laplander* and the *Patagonian*, or of colour between the *Circassian* and the *Negroe*, are not so great as to require various exertions of omnipotence to create them; nor are they so great as the changes produced on the brute creation, confessedly ɩ y the influence of climate. The *extreme* of cold, he maintains, is an impediment to growth, not only in the human species, but also in the whole animal and vegetable creation: whereas a more moderate degree of cold, connected with a vagrant life, and perpetual exertions of corporeal strength, are favourable to the gigantic stature; of which he produces the ancient Germans, and modern Patagonians, as examples and proofs. He asserts also, and we think he has made his assertion good, that the complexion of the human species is uniformly correspondent to the degree of heat or cold to which they are habitually exposed. In this part of the argument, our philosopher makes a proper use of his distinction between the *physical* and *geographical* climate; and he ascribes the erroneous reasoning of Lord Kaims in particular, to his inattention to this difference. At Senegal, and in the adjacent lands, the thermometer is often at 112 or 117 degrees in the shade, and here we find the inhabitants jet black, with woolly hair. The heat is equally great in *Congo* and *Loango*: and these countries are inhabited by Negroes only; whereas in *Morocco*, to the North of these regions, and at the *Cape of Good Hope*, to the South, the heat is not so intense; nor are the inhabitants of so deep a hue. – Lord K. asks, wherefore are not the *Abyssinians* and the inhabitants of *Zaara* of as dark a complexion as the moors on the coast of Guinea? M. ZIMMERMAN answers, that 'these countries are much cooler. The desert is not only farther from the equator, but the winds, blowing over the Atlas mountains, which, like the Alps, are covered with snow, and the westerly wind coming from the sea, must considerably mitigate the heat. Nor is *Abyssinia* so warm as either *Monomotopa* or *Guinea*. The North East winds from the side of Persia and Arabia, are cooled by their passage over the Red sea: the Northern winds from Egypt lose much of their heat on the chain of mountains that is extended between the countries; the winds from the *South* and the *West*, are *sea* winds. Thus, the only quarter from which they can derive excessive heat, is from the *West*; as the air on this side must pass over tracts of heated lands.' For a similar reason it is that Negroes are not found either in Asia or South America, under the Equator. The situations of these countries, which he minutely investigates, expose them to sea breezes and cooling winds from the continent. He confirms his hypothesis by observing, that the mountaineers of *warm* climates, as in *Barbary* and *Ceylon*, are much fairer than the inhabitants of the vallies; that the Saracens and Moors, who conquered the north-east part of Africa in 1700, from being *brown*, are become like the negroes near the Equator; that the Portuguese, who settled at *Senegal* in 1400, became blacks: and Tudela, the Jew, asserts, that his countrymen in Abyssinia acquired the dark complexion of the original natives. Lord Kaims enquires, why negroes retain their colour when in more temperate climates? The Professor partly denies the fact; and affirms, on the authority of *Demanet*, that the negroes educated in *America* and in *Europe*, are not of so deep a jet as the natives of *Senegal* or *Guinea*. He further remarks, 'that more time is requisite to change the complexion from *jet* to fair, than the reverse: marks which are accidentally made on the skin, continue for years.' Nor is the difference of climate so great as to effectuate a speedy change. To do justice to the experiment, the negroes should be conveyed to the regions of the north, be kept from intermarrying with the natives, but be continually, like them, exposed to the influence of the cold; and should subsist on the same diet, &c. But our limits will not permit us to do justice to this part of his subject, and we must hasten to another question of no less moment.

It being proved, that verily we are brethren, and that the human race, however we may differ in size or complexion, are all of one family; it is natural to enquire, *Who was our progenitor? Adam*, according to the ancient creed? or the *orang outang*, according to the new system? The pretensions of the *orang outang*, or rather of his partizans, for the old gentleman himself either *cannot*, or *will* not utter a word on the subject, are, that he has been the *man of the woods* for many ages before *gardens* were ever thought of. His claims to humanity are founded on his being able to walk upright occasionally, being furnished with a competent share of muscles requisite for the purpose. The form of his heart, lungs, breast, brains, intestines, are similar with those of men; the *cæcum* has also its *appendix vermiformis*: he can sit upright with great ease; shews more design in his plans, than his associates in the forests; and can handle a stick on occasion with tolerable dexterity. His disqualifications are the following: The position of the *foramen magnum occipitis*, which is farther backward than in the human species, and the sockets of his lower jaw, made to receive the *dentes incissores* of the upper, indicate his relationship to the *monkey* breed. He has also *thirteen ribs* on each side; his arms, feet, and toes, are much longer than those of the human species, &c. and although his foot does not so closely resemble a hand, as that of the ape, yet the *pollex pedis*, or the great toe, is placed at a greater distance from the other toes, which gives it the appearance and uses of a *thumb*. These differences indicate, that although the *ourang* can occasionally act the *biped*, yet he is much better qualified to walk on his fore feet, and to climb trees, than the generality of the modern race of men. But his being destitute of *speech* is a subject of much greater triumph to his adversaries, than any of the differences stated above. For there is no nation of men, however savage, that is destitute of speech; though individuals, secluded from society, may in time lose the faculty. No instances are known in which a company of ten or twelve men have been without a language; but upwards of *thirty* of the ourang species have been found in a herd, without shewing the smallest traces of this faculty. It has been suggested by *Rousseau*, that they may have lost the power from their neglect of using it; but it is very singular that they alone should lose this power, and not that race of men to whom they are supposed to be so nearly related. To these arguments, which have been frequently repeated, it is true, but not more so than the whimsical hypothesis which they oppose has been started, Professor Z. adds a satisfactory one, taken from the *ourang outang*'s being destitute of that *universality* which man so eminently possesses. The *ourang* is confined to the *torrid zone* of the *old* world. But since he possessed strength and agility in his native residence, and is formed for running and climbing, wherefore does he not emigrate to other countries which abound equally with proper nourishment, did he not feel the incapacity of subsisting in other climates[3]?

The above question is closely connected with another which has greatly distressed some philosophic minds, and not without reason, as it hath an immediate reference to a right deportment: *Is man naturally a biped or a quadruped?* Until this point can be decided, he that walketh *uprightly* does not walk *surely*, for he may transgress the fundamental law of nature by every step which he takes. While *Rousseau*, Lord *Monboddo*, *Moscati*, and others, have done their utmost to bend the stubborn neck of man down to the earth, our philosopher unites his efforts with those of Messrs. *de Buffon*, *de Pauw*, and *Blumenbach*, to set him up again; and whether it be from the force of nature, or from habit, the majority of our readers, we presume, will entertain but few scruples about their right to walk erect if they chuse it; and therefore it will be needless to enlarge much on this argument. If any one should have doubts, let him be comforted by the thoughts that this erect position is best adapted to the conformation of the human head, and the ponderous quantity of human brains: – that the articulation of the *os occipitis* with the first vertebræ of the neck, is differently constructed from that of quadrupeds, with the obvious design that man should be able to move his head in every direction with the greatest facility: – that the human species (and also monkies) are destitute of that strong ligament or tendinous aponeurosis, vulgarly called *paxwax*, which quadrupeds possess (as a kind of *stay-tape*), to prevent the head from

---

3   When this first volume was written, Professor ZIMMERMAN was ignorant of the anatomical discoveries of the late Prof. Camper: he mentions them in the second vol. as *decisive*.

sinking to the earth; to which, from its natural position, it must be very prone: – and that our eyes and ears are, fortunately, not placed as those of the quadrupeds. The axis of the human eye is nearly perpendicular with a vertical section of the head; whereas, in the brute creation (the larger ape excepted), the position of the eyes forms an acute angle: – nature has also furnished other animals with a *suspensorium oculi*, a muscle, which the *erect* attitude renders needless, though highly necessary in the *prone*; consequently, whoever tries the experiment will find that, in the inclined direction, both his eyes and his ears are in the most unfavourable situation possible for quick hearing or extensive vision: – the shape, breadth, strength of the vertebræ of the back and loins, are so coincident with the erect attitude of the trunk, that the most conscientious mortal must surely think this attitude innocent and harmless. From the above considerations, and many others which might be adduced, it appears that *Ovid* is no less a philosopher than a poet, when he sings,

Pronaque cum spectent animalia cetera terram,
Os homini sublime dedit, cœlumque tueri
Jussit, et erectos ad sidera tollere vultus.

The author now proceeds to those animals which are best able to sustain a diversity of climate, next to the human species, both domestic and wild. It would be impracticable to follow him in these enquiries, or even to give a summary view of them: we shall select, therefore, the *canine species*, as a specimen of his manner of treating this part of the subject.

'The dog follows man through every region and climate. The *Greenlanders* have no other tame animal but this most useful one, which draws their sledges, hunts their bears, serves them for clothing and for food. Neither is there any animal equally capable of subsisting on so great a variety of substances as this; whose stomach is able to sustain and digest the most opposite kinds of food. But this animal is not equally capable of resisting excessive heat. Heat is frequently the cause of madness; and in warm climates, he soon degenerates. The European dogs conveyed to *Africa* soon become dumb, or rather their bark changes into a low hoarse noise. They grow sharp eared, ugly, lose their hair, and also their natural courage. An European dog is highly prized by the negroes "as long as it can *speak*," as they term it.'

The Professor is strongly persuaded that a due attention to the influence of climate, diversity in food, and state of *slavery*, by which the original instincts of animals are suppressed from the beginning, until they are almost lost; and habits foreign to their genuine nature are acquired; will in many cases enable us to account for that great diversity observable in the animal kingdom, without having such frequent recourse to an original distinction of race or of species[4]. Applying this idea to the canine race, which are so multifarious, he supports, with much ingenuity, the hypothesis, that they derive their origin from different sources, whose blended instincts and forms give such an infinite variety, viz. the *wolf*, the *canis aurius*, or *jackal*, the *fox*, and particularly from the *wolf*. He asserts, and gives several examples in proof of his assertion, that each of these animals have been tamed and domesticated. The wolf, which is by far the most wild and savage of the three, is used by the Americans, instead of dogs, for the purpose of hunting. The she-wolf, mentioned by the Count *de Buffon*, was not only faithful to its master, but fawned and caressed in the manner of a dog. Hence he deems it extremely probable, that in the course of a few generations, the offspring of this animal might become a species of house-dog. The wolf not only copulates with the dog, but the offspring possess likewise the power of propagation; which has been generally considered as the distinguishing characteristic of a *genus*. The periods of gestation are nearly the same; and if the dog be more prolific, this may simply proceed from its being domesticated, which is allowed universally to be the case with the swine. It is not uncommon in *Thuringia*, for the females of the canine species to go into the woods, and return pregnant by the wolves. The three most celebrated comparative anatomists in Europe, *Daubenton*, *Hunter*, and *Bourgelat*, after the most minute examination, assert, that both the external and internal construction of each are perfectly similar. The *jackal*, according to the testimonies of *Pallas* and *Guldenstedt*, has instincts very correspondent with those of the canine race. It is easily tamed; it wags its tail, and caresses the human species; it is fond of dogs, and plays with them; and the sound of its voice is similar. It is known in India to copulate with dogs; and *Chardin* asserts, that the

---

4   He admits that these variations may, in process of time, by the perpetual influence of occasional causes, constitute new and distinct species of animals.

female will admit the caresses of the wolf. M. *Pallas* further adds, that the house-dog of the *Calmuks* so nearly resembles the jackal, that they ought to be considered as belonging to the same race. The *fox* seems to be further removed from the species of dogs, by its having an instinct peculiar to itself, that of digging holes in the earth. But yet it copulates with the dog; is capable of being tamed to such a degree as to follow its master to the chace; and, as to external form, it is universally known that some species of dogs bear a strong resemblance to the fox.

Linné, Erxleben, Pennant, and *de Buffon,* in the natural history of the *squirrel,* have considered certain diversities in colour, size, and also in the presence or absence of a tuft, or rather pencil of hair upon the ears[5], as the characteristic mark of different species. *Gmelin* the younger asserts, on the contrary, from his own observations, that the same animal is of a *brownish red* in the summer months, and changes into an *ash colour* during the winter: and that the same animal has not always this pencil of hair. Hence he concludes, that the *petit gris* of M. *de Buffon* is essentially the same with the common squirrel. M. ZIMMERMAN subscribes to this opinion, and maintains that the above distinctions are too trifling to constitute a difference of species, when instincts and habits of living are the same in each; and adds,

'The durable grey colour of the American squirrel is, to me, less remarkable than this power of becoming grey. If, in the œconomy of nature, an animal be so constituted, that it can, from red, be changed into an ash colour, it is easy to conceive that, in some states, the colour shall be permanent.' – *Erxleben,* in like manner, considers the *petit gris* of America as a distinct species from the *grey squirrel* of the old world, because it is somewhat larger than the European: but this is of small moment. *Daubenton* gives eight inches and a half to the *red* squirrel, and to the American *petit gris,* ten inches. But shall we separate a race of animals, whose instincts, manners, and form, are in other respects perfectly similar, merely on account of so slight a discrepance? This plan of procedure would multiply species *ad infinitum.*'

He applies the same mode of reasoning to the *weezel,* or *mustela vulgaris,* and *ermine,* or *mustela erminea.*

---

5   *Pilis ad aures elongatis.*

'The difference of species, according to M. *de Buffon*, and other naturalists, is taken from their size, and the colour of their tails. The weezel is six inches and a half in length, the other [the ermine] *nine*: the tail of the ermine is tipt with *black*, that of the weezel with *yellow*. They have the same instincts, are found in the same places, and are equally diffused; they both change their hair in the same manner, being red in the summer, and white in the winter, and they equally inhabit hot and cold climates.'

In the second part of this interesting work, which treats of those quadrupeds that are diffused over large districts, without being universal, the Professor commences from the north pole, and thence proceeds to the temperate and torrid zones. A subdivision is here necessarily made between the animals which are common to the four quarters of the world, and such as are not found in *America*. He remarks, that this part is not so rich in materials as the preceding, though the diversity in species is greater, because a greater uniformity of climate keeps each genus and species more distinct; and, accordingly, fewer subjects for speculation present themselves.

The third part is chiefly devoted to the quadrupeds which are found in smaller districts. These are the most numerous of all, as those which are universally or generally diffused, are united with those peculiar to these districts. Hence the author takes occasion to give, under this division, a summary view of all the quadrupeds known, with their characteristic differences, according to the order of *Ray*. This is the more valuable, as he has assembled together the recent discoveries of the most celebrated naturalists, so that it may be considered as a more complete compendium of the natural history of quadrupeds, than any which have preceded it.

In the fourth and last part, the Professor gives catalogues of the animals which are found in each grand division of the world, and also in the different islands. We find at the end of the third volume a *geographico-zoological* chart, or a map of the world, in which animals are made to supplant towns and villages; and by which, with the aid of a few marks or characters, denoting colours and degrees of magnitude, the student may, with little trouble, refresh his memory in those leading articles, local residence, hue, and size.

We cannot accompany this indefatigable and well-informed writer any further, at present. Out of a copious abundance of materials, we have selected such specimens as we thought would prove most acceptable to the generality of our readers, while they gave some just ideas of what was most peculiar in his plan. The speculations and enquiries contained in the third volume, are too important to be overlooked; and some account of them shall be given in a future article. We shall take our leave, for the present, with observing, that notwithstanding we entertain a very high opinion of Professor ZIMMERMAN's geographical history, as being replete with useful information, and as placing the history of the higher order of animals in a new and interesting light: yet it is very deficient in the graces of composition. Through the want of a proper arrangement of his ideas, he perpetually anticipates and repeats. His introduction not only plunges too deeply into subjects which immediately concern the object of his treatise, but into others that have a remote reference. It was unnecessary also to produce so many vouchers for facts which no one will be inclined to discredit; and he dwells on *minutiæ*, oftener, and longer, than an English reader is, in the present day, accustomed to endure. In short, though we wish to do justice to his distinguished merits, we must confess that he is not altogether exempt from the censure which the elegant Count *de Buffon* passes on scientific Germans, when he complains, *qu'ils grossissent à dessein leurs ouvrages d'une quantité d'erudition inutile, en sorte que le sujet qu'ils traitent, est noyè dans la quantité de matières inutiles,* &c.

ON THE ORIGIN AND FAMILIES
OF NATIONS
delivered 23 February, 1792,
by The President

Sir William Jones

In 1783 Sir William Jones (1746–94) was dispatched to
Calcutta to serve as judge to the local High Court. Jones, who
since his youth harboured an interest in classical scholarship
and philology, used his stay in India to study ancient Sanskrit.
In 1784 he founded the Calcutta-based Asiatick Society (later
known as the Asiatic Society of Bengal). Each year Jones
delivered an 'Anniversary Discourse' to the Society. On the
basis of his inquiry into the history of languages he maintained
that the human family was divisible into three varieties who in
turn were referrable to one ancestral tribe. In his ninth and last
'Anniversary Discourse' Jones summed up his inferences on
the common origin of mankind.

You have attended, gentlemen, with so much indulgence to my
discourses on the five *Asiatick* nations, and on the various
tribes established along their several borders or interspersed
over their mountains, that I cannot but flatter myself with an
assurance of being heard with equal attention, while I trace to
one centre the three great families, from which those nations
appear to have proceeded, and then hazard a few conjectures
on the different courses, which they may be supposed to have
taken toward the countries, in which we find them settled at
the dawn of all genuine history.

Let us begin with a short review of the propositions, to
which we have gradually been led, and separate such as are
morally certain, from such as are only probable: that the first
race of *Persians* and *Indians*, to whom we may add the *Romans*
and *Greeks*, the *Goths*, and the old *Egyptians* or *Ethiops*,
originally spoke the same language and professed the same
popular faith, is capable, in my humble opinion, of incontestable proof; that the *Jews* and *Arabs*, the *Assyrians*, or second
Persian race, the people who spoke *Syriack*, and a numerous

tribe of *Abyssinians*, used one primitive dialect wholly distinct from the idiom just mentioned, is, I believe, undisputed, and, I am sure, indisputable; but that the settlers in *China* and *Japan* had a common origin with the *Hindus*, is no more than highly probable; and, that all the *Tartars*, as they are inaccurately called, were primarily of a third separate branch, totally differing from the two others in language, manners, and features, may indeed be plausibly conjectured, but cannot, for the reasons alledged in a former essay, be perspicuously shown, and for the present therefore must be merely assumed. Could these facts be verified by the best attainable evidence, it would not, I presume, be doubted, that the whole earth was peopled by a variety of shoots from the *Indian*, *Arabian*, and *Tartarian* branches, or by such intermixtures of them, as, in a course of ages, might naturally have happened.

Now I admit without hesitation the aphorism of LINNÆUS, that "in the beginning GOD created one pair only of every living species, which has a diversity of sex;" but, since that incomparable naturalist argues principally from the wonderful diffusion of vegetables, and from an hypothesis, that the water on this globe has been continually subsiding, I venture to produce a shorter and closer argument in support of his doctrine. That *Nature*, of which simplicity appears a distinguishing attribute, *does nothing in vain*, is a maxim in philosophy; and against those, who deny maxims, we cannot dispute; but *it is vain* and superfluous *to do by many means what may be done by fewer*, and this is another axiom received into courts of judicature from the schools of philosophers: *we must not*, therefore, says our great NEWTON, *admit more causes of natural things, than those, which are true, and sufficiently account for natural phenomena*; but it is true, that one pair *at least* of every living species must at first have been created; and that one human pair was sufficient for the population of our globe in a period of no considerable length (on the very moderate supposition of lawyers and political arithmeticians, that every pair of ancestors left on an average two children, and each of them two more), is evident from the rapid increase of numbers in geometrical progression, so well known to those, who have ever taken the trouble to sum a series of as many terms, as they suppose generations of men in two or three thousand years. It follows, that the Author of Nature (for all nature proclaims its divine author) created but one pair of our species; yet, had it not been (among other reasons) for the devastations, which history has recorded, of water and fire, wars, famine, and pestilence, this earth would not now have had room for its multiplied inhabitants. If the human race then be, as we may confidently assume, of one natural species, they must all have proceeded from one pair; and if perfect justice be, as it is most indubitably, an essential attribute of GOD, that pair must have been gifted with sufficient wisdom and strength to be virtuous, and, as far as their nature admitted, happy, but intrusted with freedom of will to be vicious and consequently degraded: whatever might be their option, they must people in time the region where they first were established, and their numerous descendents must necessarily seek new countries, as inclination might prompt, or accident lead, them; they would of course migrate in separate families and clans, which, forgetting by degrees the language of their common progenitor, would form new dialects to convey new ideas, both simple and complex; natural affection would unite them at first, and a sense of reciprocal utility, the great and only cement of social union in the absence of publick honour and justice, for which in evil times it is a general substitute, would combine them at length in communities more or less regular; laws would be proposed by a part of each community, but enacted by the whole; and governments would be variously arranged for the happiness or misery of the governed, according to their own virtue and wisdom, or depravity and folly; so that, in less than three thousand years, the world would exhibit the same appearances, which we may actually observe on it in the age of the great *Arabian* impostor.

On that part of it, to which our united researches are generally confined, we see *five* races of men peculiarly distinguished, in the time of MUHAMMED, for their multitude and extent of dominion; but we have reduced them to *three*, because we can discover no more, that essentially differ in language, religion, manners, and other known characteristicks: now those three races, how variously soever they may at present be dispersed and intermixed, must (if the preceding conclusions be justly drawn) have migrated originally from a central country, to find which is the problem proposed for solution. Suppose it solved; and give any arbitrary name to that centre: let it, if you please, be *Iràn*. The three primitive languages, therefore, must at first have been concentrated in

Iràn, and there only in fact we see traces of them in the earliest historical age; but, for the sake of greater precision, conceive the whole empire of *Iràn*, with all its mountains and valleys, plains and rivers, to be every way infinitely diminished; the first winding courses, therefore, of all the nations proceeding from it by land, and nearly at the same time, will be little right lines, but without intersections, because those courses could not have thwarted and crossed one another: if then you consider the seats of all the migrating nations as points in a surrounding figure, you will perceive, that the several rays, diverging from *Iràn*, may be drawn to them without any intersection; but this will not happen, if you assume as a centre *Arabia*, or *Egypt*; *India*, *Tartary*, or *China*: it follows, that *Iràn*, or *Persia* (I contend for *the meaning, not the name*), was the central country, which we sought. This mode of reasoning I have adopted, not from any affectation (as you will do me the justice to believe) of a scientifick diction, but for the sake of conciseness and variety, and from a wish to avoid repetitions; the substance of my argument having been detailed in a different form at the close of another discourse; nor does the argument in any form rise to demonstration, which the question by no means admits: it amounts, however, to such a proof, grounded on written evidence and credible testimony, as all mankind hold sufficient for decisions affecting property, freedom, and life.

Thus then we have proved, that the inhabitants of *Asia*, and consequently, as it might be proved, of the whole earth, sprang from three branches of one stem: and that those branches have shot into their present state of luxuriance in a period comparatively short, is apparent from a fact universally acknowledged, that we find no certain monument, or even probable tradition, of nations planted, empires and states raised, laws enacted, cities built, navigation improved, commerce encouraged, arts invented, or letters contrived, above twelve or at most fifteen or sixteen centuries before the birth of CHRIST, and from another fact, which cannot be controverted, that seven hundred or a thousand years would have been fully adequate to the supposed propagation, diffusion and establishment of the human race.

The most ancient history of that race, and the oldest composition perhaps in the world, is a work in *Hebrew*, which we may suppose at first, for the sake of our argument, to have no higher authority than any other work of equal antiquity, that the researches of the curious had accidentally brought to light: it is ascribed to MUSAH; for so he writes his own name, which, after the *Greeks* and *Romans*, we have changed into MOSES; and, though it was manifestly his object to give an historical account of a single family, he has introduced it with a short view of the primitive world, and his introduction has been divided, perhaps improperly, into *eleven* chapters. After describing with awful sublimity the creation of this universe, he asserts, that one pair of every animal species was called from nothing into existence; that the human pair were strong enough to be happy, but free to be miserable; that, from delusion and temerity, they disobeyed their supreme benefactor, whose goodness could not pardon them consistently with his justice; and that they received a punishment adequate to their disobedience, but softened by a mysterious promise to be accomplished in their descendants. We cannot but believe, on the supposition just made of a history uninspired, that these facts were delivered by tradition from the first pair, and related by MOSES in a figurative style; not in that sort of allegory, which rhetoricians describe as a mere assemblage of metaphors, but in the symbolical mode of writing adopted by eastern sages, to embellish and dignify historical truth; and, if this were a time for such illustrations, we might produce the same account of the *creation* and the *fall* expressed by symbols very nearly similar, from the *Puránas* themselves, and even from the *Véda*, which appears to stand next in antiquity to the five books of MOSES.

The sketch of antediluvian history, in which we find many dark passages, is followed by the narrative of a *deluge*, which destroyed the whole race of man, except four pairs; an historical fact admitted as true to every nation, to whose literature we have access, and particularly by the ancient *Hindus*, who have allotted an entire *Purána* to the detail of that event, which they relate, as usual, in symbols or allegories. I concur most heartily with those, who insist, that, in proportion as any fact mentioned in history seems repugnant to the course of nature, or, in one word, miraculous, the stronger evidence is required to induce a rational belief of it; but we hear without incredulity, that cities have been overwhelmed by eruptions from burning mountains, territories laid waste by hurricanes, and whole islands depopulated by earthquakes: if then we look at the firmament sprinkled with innumerable stars; if we conclude by a fair analogy, that every star is a sun, attracting, like ours, a system of inhabited planets; and if our ardent fancy, soaring hand in hand with sound reason, waft us beyond the visible sphere into regions of immensity, disclosing other celestial expanses and other systems of suns and worlds on all sides without number or end, we cannot but consider the submersion of our little spheroid as an infinitely less event in respect of the immeasurable universe, than the destruction of a city or an isle in respect of this habitable globe. Let a general flood, however, be supposed improbable in proportion to the magnitude of so ruinous an event, yet the concurrent evidences of it are completely adequate to the supposed improbability; but, as we cannot here expatiate on those proofs, we proceed to the fourth important fact recorded in the *Mosaick* history; I mean the first propagation and early dispersion of mankind *in separate families* to separate places of residence.

Three sons of the just and virtuous man, whose lineage was preserved from the general inundation, travelled, we are told, as they began to multiply, in *three* large divisions variously subdivided: the children of YÁFET seem, from the traces of *Sklavonian* names, and the mention of their being *enlarged*, to have spread themselves far and wide, and to have produced the race, which, for want of a correct appellation, we call *Tartarian*; the colonies, formed by the sons of HAM and SHEM, appear to have been nearly simultaneous; and, among those of the latter branch, we find so many names incontestably preserved at this hour in *Arabia*, that we cannot hesitate in pronouncing them the same people, whom hitherto we have denominated *Arabs*; while the former branch, the most powerful and adventurous of whom were the progeny of CUSH, MISR, and RAMA (names remaining unchanged in *Sanscrit*, and highly revered by the *Hindus*), were, in all probability, the race, which I call *Indian*, and to which we may now give any other name, that may seem more proper and comprehensive.

The general introduction to the *Jewish* history closes with a very concise and obscure account of a presumptuous and mad attempt, by a particular colony, to build a splendid city and raise a fabrick of immense height, independently of the divine aid, and, it should seem, in defiance of the divine power; a project, which was baffled by means appearing at first view inadequate to the purpose, but ending in violent dissention among the projectors, and in the ultimate separation of them: this event also seems to be recorded by the ancient *Hindus* in two of their *Puránas*; and it will be proved, I trust, on some future occasion, that *the lion bursting from a pillar to destroy a blaspheming giant*, and *the dwarf, who beguiled and held in derision* the magnificent BELI, are one and the same story related in a symbolical style.

Now these primeval events are described as having happened between the *Oxus* and *Euphrates*, the mountains of *Caucasus* and the borders of *India*, that is, within the limits of *Iràn*; for, though most of the *Mosaick* names have been considerably altered, yet numbers of them remain unchanged: we still find *Harrán* in *Mesopotamia*, and travellers appear unanimous in fixing the site of ancient *Babel*.

Thus, on the preceding supposition, that the first eleven chapters of the book, which it is thought proper to call *Genesis*, are merely a preface to the oldest civil history now extant, we see the truth of them confirmed by antecedent reasoning, and by evidence in part highly probable, and in part certain; but the *connection* of the *Mosaick* history with that of the Gospel by a chain of sublime predictions unquestionably ancient, and apparently fulfilled, must induce us to think the *Hebrew* narrative more than human in its origin, and consequently true in every substantial part of it, though possibly expressed in figurative language; as many learned and pious men have believed, and as the most pious may believe without injury, and perhaps with advantage, to the cause of revealed religion. If MOSES then was endued with supernatural knowledge, it is no longer probable only, but absolutely certain, that the whole race of man proceeded from *Iràn*, as from a centre, whence they migrated at first in three great colonies; and that those three branches grew from a common stock, which had been miraculously preserved in a general convulsion and inundation of this globe.

Having arrived by a different path at the same conclusion with Mr. BRYANT as to one of those families, the most ingenious and enterprising of the three, but arrogant, cruel, and idolatrous, which we both conclude to be various shoots from the *Hamian* or *Amonian* branch, I shall add but little to my former observations on his profound and agreeable work, which I have thrice perused with increased attention and pleasure, though not with perfect acquiescence in the other less important parts of his plausible system. The sum of his argument seems reducible to three heads. First; "if the deluge really happened at the time recorded by MOSES, those nations, whose monuments are preserved or whose writings are accessible, must have retained memorials of an event so stupendous and comparatively so recent; but in fact they have retained such memorials:" this reasoning seems just, and the fact is true beyond controversy. Secondly; "those memorials were expressed by the race of HAM, before the use of letters, in rude sculpture or painting, and mostly in symbolical figures of the *ark*, the eight persons concealed in it, and the birds, which first were dismissed from it: this fact is probable, but, I think, not sufficiently ascertained". Thirdly; "all ancient Mythology (except what was purely *Sabian*) had its primary source in those various symbols misunderstood; so that ancient Mythology stands now in the place of symbolical sculpture or painting, and must be explained on the same principles, on which we should begin to decypher the originals, if they now existed:" this part of the system is, in my opinion, carried too far; nor can I persuade myself (to give one instance out of many) that the beautiful allegory of CUPID and PSYCHE had the remotest allusion to the deluge, or that HYMEN signified the *veil*, which covered the patriarch and his family. These propositions, however, are supported with great ingenuity and solid erudition, but, unprofitably for the argument, and unfortunately, perhaps, for the fame of the work itself, recourse is had to etymological conjecture, than which no mode of reasoning is in general weaker or more delusive. He, who professes to derive the words of any one language from those of another, must expose himself to the danger of perpetual errours, unless he be perfectly acquainted with both; yet my respectable friend, though eminently skilled in the idioms of *Greece* and *Rome*, has no sort of acquaintance with any *Asiatick* dialect, except *Hebrew*; and he has consequently made mistakes, which every learner of *Arabick* and *Persian* must instantly detect. Among *fifty* radical words (*ma*, *taph*, and *ram* being included), *eighteen* are purely of *Arabian* origin, *twelve* merely *Indian*, and *seventeen* both *Sanscrit* and *Arabick*, but in senses totally different, while *two* are *Greek* only, and one *Egyptian*, or barbarous: if it be urged, that those *radicals* (which ought surely to have concluded, instead of preceding, an *analytical* inquiry) are precious traces of the primitive language, from which all others were derived, or to which at least they were subsequent, I can only declare my belief, that the language of NOAH is lost irretrievably, and assure you, that after a diligent search, I cannot find a single word used in common by the *Arabian*, *Indian*, and *Tartar* families, before the intermixture of dialects occasioned by *Mohammedan* conquests. There are, indeed, very obvious traces of the *Hamian* language, and some hundreds of words might be produced, which were formerly used promiscuously by most nations of that race; but I beg leave, as a philosopher, to enter my protest against conjectural etymology in historical researches, and principally against the licentiousness of etymologists in transposing and inserting letters, in substituting at pleasure any consonant for another of the same order, and in totally disregarding the vowels: for such permutations few radical words would be more convenient than CUS or CUSH, since, dentals being changed for dentals, and palatials for palatials, it instantly becomes *coot*, *goose*, and, by transposition, *duck*, all water-birds, and *evidently* symbolical; it next is the *goat* worshipped in *Egypt*, and, by a metathesis, the *dog* adored as an emblem of SIRIUS, or, more obviously, a *cat*, not the domestick animal, but a sort of ship, and, the *Catos*, or great sea-fish, of the *Dorians*. It will hardly be imagined, that I mean by this irony to insult an author, whom I respect and esteem; but no consideration should induce me to assist by my silence in the diffusion of errour; and I contend, that almost any word or nation might be derived from any other, if such licences, as I am opposing, were permitted in etymological histories: when we find, indeed, the same words, letter for letter, and in a sense precisely the same, in different languages, we can scarce hesitate in allowing them a common origin; and, not to depart from the example before us, when we see CUSH or CUS (for the *Sanscrit* name also is variously pronounced) among the sons of BRAHMÁ, that is, among the progenitors of the *Hindus*, and at the head of an ancient pedigree preserved in the *Rámáyan*; when we meet with his name again in the family of RÁMA; when we know, that the name is venerated in the highest degree, and given to a sacred grass, described as a *Poa* by KOENIG, which is used with a thousand ceremonies in the oblations to fire, ordained by MENU to form the sacrificial zone of the *Bráhmans*, and solemnly declared in the *Véda* to have sprung up soon after the *deluge*, whence the *Pauránicks* consider it as *the bristly hair of the boar which supported the globe*; when we add, that one of the seven *dwípas*, or great peninsulas of this earth, has the same appellation, we can hardly doubt that the CUSH of MOSES and VÁLMIC was the same personage and an ancestor of the *Indian* race.

From the testimonies adduced in the six last annual discourses, and from the additional proofs laid before you, or rather opened, on the present occasion, it seems to follow, that the only human family after the flood established themselves in the northern parts of *Iràn*; that, as they multiplied, they were divided into three distinct branches, each retaining little at first, and losing the whole by degrees, of their common primary language, but agreeing severally on new expressions for new ideas; that the branch of YÁFET was *enlarged* in many scattered shoots over the north of *Europe* and *Asia*, diffusing themselves as far as the western and eastern seas, and, at length in the infancy of navigation, beyond them both: that they cultivated no liberal arts, and had no use of letters, but formed a variety of dialects, as their tribes were variously ramified; that, secondly, the children of HAM, who founded in *Iràn* itself the monarchy of the first *Chaldeans*, invented letters, observed and named the luminaries of the firmament, calculated the known *Indian* period of *four hundred and thirty-two thousand years*, or an *hundred and twenty* repetitions of the *saros*, and contrived the old system of Mythology, partly allegorical, and partly grounded on idolatrous veneration for their sages and lawgivers; that they were dispersed at various intervals and in various colonies over land and ocean; that the tribes of MISR, CUSH, and RAMA settled in *Africk* and *India*; while some of them, having improved the art of sailing, passed from *Egypt*, *Phenice*, and *Phrygia*, into *Italy* and *Greece*, which they found thinly peopled by former emigrants, of whom they supplanted some tribes, and united themselves with others; whilst a swarm from the same hive moved by a northerly course into *Scandinavia*, and another, by the head of the *Oxus*, and through the passes of *Imaus*, into *Cashghar* and *Eighúr*, *Khatá* and *Khoten*, as far as the territories of *Chín* and *Tancút*, where letters have been used and arts immemorially cultivated; nor is it unreasonable to believe, that some of them found their way from the eastern isles into *Mexico* and *Peru*, where traces were discovered of rude literature and Mythology analogous to those of *Egypt* and *India*; that, thirdly, the old *Chaldean* empire being overthrown by the *Assyrians* under CAYÚMERS, other migrations took place, especially into *India*, while the rest of SHEM's progeny, some of whom had before settled on the Red Sea, peopled the whole *Arabian* peninsula, pressing close on the nations of *Syria* and *Phenice*; that, lastly, from all the three families were detached many bold adventurers of an ardent spirit and a roving disposition, who disdained subordination and wandered in separate clans, till they settled in distant isles or in deserts and mountainous regions; that, on the whole, some colonies might have migrated before the death of their venerable progenitor, but that states and empires could scarce have assumed a regular form, till fifteen or sixteen hundred years before the *Christian* epoch, and that, for the first thousand years of that period, we have no history unmixed with fable, except that of the turbulent and variable, but eminently distinguished, nation descended from ABRAHAM.

My design, gentlemen, of tracing the origin and progress of the five principal nations, who have peopled *Asia*, and of whom there were considerable remains in their several countries at the time of MUHAMMED's birth, is now accomplished; succinctly, from the nature of these essays; imperfectly, from the darkness of the subject and scantiness of my materials, but clearly and comprehensively enough to form a basis for subsequent researches: you have seen, as distinctly as I am able to show, *who* those nations originally were, *whence* and *when* they moved toward their final stations; and, in my future annual discourses, I propose to enlarge on the *particular advantages* to our country and to mankind, which may result from our sedulous and united inquiries into the history, science, and arts, of these *Asiatick* regions, especially of the *British* dominions in *India*, which we may consider as the centre (not of the human race, but) of our common exertions to promote its true interests; and we shall concur, I trust, in opinion, that the race of man, to advance whose manly happiness is our duty and will of course be our endeavour, cannot long be happy without virtue, nor actively virtuous without freedom, nor securely free without rational knowledge.

AN ACCOUNT OF THE REGULAR GRADATION IN MAN
and in different Animals and Vegetables; and from the former to the latter.
By Charles White. 1799

Anonymous

Source: Monthly Review, vol. 33 ns, 1800

After having studied in London and Edinburgh, Charles White (1728–1813) became a surgeon in Manchester. In the 1780s, he started giving public lectures on anatomy. His essay on *Regular Gradation in Man, and in Different Animals*, went back to a lecture which White had delivered, in 1795, at the Literary and Philosophical Society of Manchester. As a demonstration of the continuity in nature's productions, White had placed several skulls before the audience. They were arranged in such a manner as to illustrate an ascending hierarchy of quadrupeds, apes, black humans, and whites. Thus, White aimed to illustrate the continuous scale of the 'chain of being'. The author of the review below, however, was not willing to follow White's argument.

We opened this volume with the expectation of finding some light thrown on a very curious subject of inquiry, but we have been greatly disappointed in the execution of the work. It consists chiefly of well-known passages, selected from books which are in the hands of every lover of natural history; and we are sorry to say that the author has been very unsuccessful in his attempts to add to the general stock of knowledge. Much of the preliminary matter relates, indeed, to a subject which no one will now contest with Mr. White. The distinction of natural objects into the three great classes of animals, vegetables, and minerals, is allowed to be arbitrary; and to be only a convenient arrangement for the purposes of perspicuity and celerity, in conversation or writing: – but, when the author proposes to ascertain a *gradation* in those objects, we think that he misunderstands his own term. Gradation implies not only an approximation by similarity of appearances, or properties, but an approximation by equal degrees; yet Mr. White owns that 'the gradation from man to animals is not by one way, the person and actions descend to the orang outang, but the voice to birds.' (p. 39.) This is a descent *per saltum*, not by equal degrees; and here is an end, at once, to the object professed by the author in his title-page: since he there expressly mentions *regular* gradation; a phrase which we consider indeed as a pleonasm, but which places his meaning beyond all doubt. The first step, then, of this *regular gradation* below man is, according to Mr. White, a most irregular dispersion of the human qualities; for the voice certainly does not descend to *all* birds, nor to the largest and most perfect birds; and whoever would trace a gradation from man to the parrot must consult some other authority than the book before us.

Notwithstanding this unlucky stumble at the threshold, we still hoped to meet with some new information respecting the varieties of the human species, at least; and we read the chapters on this subject with particular attention. Mr. White supposes that he has discovered some circumstances which discriminate the African from the European, and which approximate him to quadrupeds. We shall omit the consideration of the long details which he has borrowed from Professor Camper and others, and shall confine ourselves to his own remarks; because the opinions which he has quoted have already undergone the decision of the public.

That the African 'seems to approach nearer to the brute creation, than any other of the human species,' is Mr. White's assumption; it remains to be seen by what proofs, drawn from personal observation, he has endeavoured to establish it. The foundation of his opinion was laid in the measurement of a single skeleton of a negro, in his possession: but this is a commencement of ill omen. The radius and ulna of this skeleton, he found 'to be an inch longer than in the European skeleton of the same stature;' from which mode of expression it would seem that Mr. W. had merely compared a single skeleton of one nation, with a single skeleton of another; and from so slight a view, no solid conclusion would be formed by any person of a philosophical mind. Yet this seems to have been the basis of the author's theory. He tells us, indeed, that he afterward measured the arms of about fifty negroes, and, comparing them with those of several Europeans, found the fore-arms of the Africans longer: but he adds that he is 'informed of a negro skeleton in St. Bartholomew's Hospital, in which the radius and ulna are no longer than the medium of Europeans: *but as Africans, as well as Europeans, are liable to some variation in this particular, one or two exceptions have no force against the general inference.*' The latter part of this paragraph contains a complete refutation of the author's own theory. Professor Blumenbach, who has examined a great variety of human skeletons, asserts that every perfection attributed to the form of the European is to be found in that of the African. Mr. White may have met with deformed negroes, or with those who have been injured by hardships and poverty: but it appears to be as unjust to decide on the structure of a numerous nation from a few unfortunate specimens, as it would be to ascribe the form and qualities of the *Cretins* to all the inhabitants of the country in which they appear. Even on the coast of Guinea, considerable differences in the form and spirit of different nations are discoverable. Has Mr. White ever measured a Cormantin negro?

From these very scanty materials, the author proceeds to several general conclusions respecting the diversity of 'cartilages, muscles, tendons, skin, hair,' &c. between the negro and the European: but, though he undertakes to *shew* this variation, he admits that, with regard to the first three subjects, 'we are not in possession of a sufficient number of comparative anatomical facts to allow us to state much.' The same observation may be applied to the remaining points of supposed difference.

Respecting one instance of gradation, the state of the *clitoris* and *nymphæ* in African women, which the author has asserted, without any positive knowledge, we refer him and the reader to a chapter in *Sonnim's Travels*, which clears up the mistake long supported by former travellers, and adopted from them by Mr. White.

In treating of the *speech* and *language*, (which the author has thought proper to distinguish; we do not know why;) Mr. W. has unfairly applied the observations of travellers on the language of the Hottentots, to negroes in general. It would be equally improper to assert that we possess no good books on natural history, because a few bad writers have sometimes exposed themselves by attempting to compose works of that nature, without a competent knowledge of the subject. In p. 69, we are presented with an account of 'the manner in which the human voice and speech *is*[1] effected,' because, we are told, 'it is not to be met with every where:' neither, indeed are the principles of spherical trigonometry, nor the art of dialling, 'to be met with *every where.*' We can direct our readers to a much more copious and satisfactory account of the formation of the letters in speaking, than they will obtain from Mr. White; we mean, the grammarian's lecture, in Moliere's *Bourgeois Gentilhomme*; or that of Mr. *Gruel*, in Foote's Commissary.

After having gone through this unsatisfactory detail, we find the author concluding, p. 83, that there is a *pretty regular gradation* from the European to the tribe of Simiæ. This is almost a *retreat* from the promised demonstration of a regular descent: but we must not confine the author too closely to his terms; for at p. 85, the descending gradation becomes retrograde, and we are again at a loss for his meaning; he thus expresses himself:

> '6. That, in comparing the classes of mankind with each other, and with the brute creation, as in the second article,' [just quoted from p. 83.] 'there is a gradation also discoverable in the senses of seeing, hearing, and smelling, in memory, and in the powers of mastication, *but in a contrary order to that above stated, the European being least perfect, the African more so, and the brutes most perfect of all, in these particulars.*'

While we were puzzling ourselves to discover what could be the nature of a gradation which is *regular* on the face of the book, which is unequally divergent in p. 39, which becomes only *pretty regular* in p. 83, and which is *reversed* in p. 85, and must be traced backwards, like a witch's prayer; we turned again to the Preface for information, and there we found the following passage:

> 'The student must not, however, expect to find an uniform gradation in all the faculties and powers of different subjects; it frequently happens that an inferiority in one particular, is accompanied by a superiority in some other particular; so

---

[1]   This is only one of several grammatical errors which we have observed.

that the ascent or descent is *not always by equal, but often by irregular steps.*'

Where, then, is the alleged regularity of gradation? It is evident that there must be some mistake in this matter; and that the author should either have provided a new title-page for his book, or a new book for his title-page.

As Mr. White has so completely failed in establishing his avowed object, the remaining sections of his book become little interesting. They contain, indeed, nothing that is either new or important. – Some fragments, translated from a paper by Dr. Soemmering, are added; in which one of the paragraphs amounts to a reply, by anticipation, to Mr. White's book.

If we have spoken of this work with apparent severity, we rely not only on the justice of our remarks, but we must add that an attempt to destroy the barrier between any set of human beings, however degraded, and the inferior animals, can serve no good purpose, either in politics or in morals; and the author's protest against the application of his doctrine would have availed little, if he had been able to substantiate them.

AN ESSAY ON THE CAUSES OF THE VARIETY OF COMPLEXION AND FIGURE IN THE HUMAN SPECIES

To which are added, Strictures on Lord Kames's "Discourse on the original Diversity of Mankind." By the Rev. Samuel Stanhope Smith, D. D. London. 1788

Anonymous

Source: Monthly Review, vol. 80, 1789

Samuel Stanhope Smith (1750–1819) was a Presbyterian minister and professor of moral philosophy at the College of New Jersey. His religious views led him to embrace monogenism. In dealing with the causes of human varieties, he focused mainly on the different sorts of skin colour. Having studied for a few years at Edinburgh University, he was well versed in Scottish Enlightenment philosophy. In his *Essay* he argued expressly against Kames's polygenism. Instead, he embraced the theory that human features were shaped by the cultural and climatic environment.

Dr. Smith here pursues, with much ingenuity and labour, a very curious enquiry. From observing nature, and her operations, and the effects produced in them by diversity of climate, by savage and social life, by diet, exercise, and manners of living, the author shews, that all the different nations of mankind may have sprung from one original pair; and he thence infers, that there is no occasion to have recourse to the hypothesis of several original stocks. The subject has been amply discussed by Linné in his *oration on the increase of the habitable world*, printed in the second volume of the *Amœnitates Academicœ*, a work which Dr. Smith has not perhaps seen, and which is not confined to man alone, but treats of animals in general.

Dr. Smith's arguments would lose much of their force if detached or abridged. Recommending therefore the whole work to the perusal of the naturalist and the divine, we shall conclude with one brief remark, *en passant*, on what our author, in contending for the power of climate, and the changes it produces on animals, &c. says of the negroes. He affirms, that the native blacks in America *mend* in their *colour*, *features*, and *hair*, in every generation. This would be controverted, no doubt, by a negro critic, who would certainly object to the word *mend*; which, however, perhaps, he would candidly consider as an error of the press, and shortly say, "for *mend*, read *degenerate*:" – and, "for *hair*, read *wool*."

ON THE NATIVE VARIETIES OF THE HUMAN SPECIES

The Third Edition. To which is prefixed an
Epistle to Sir Joseph Banks, Bart. K.B. P.R.S. By
J. F. Blumenbach, F.R.S. Göttingen. 1795.

Anonymous

Source: *Monthly Review, vol. 20 ns, 1796*

Johann Friedrich Blumenbach (1752–1840) was one of the
most influential scholars of his time. He served as Professor of
Anatomy at the University of Göttingen. Being part of the
Hanoverian domains, Göttingen was endowed with a great
library and a Royal Museum (founded in 1773) one of whose
directors was Blumenbach. He entertained close connections
with the Royal Society of London and its President, Sir Joseph
Banks. His various publications on anatomy, physiology, and
anthropology were widely reviewed in Britain.

We have observed with pleasure that the German philosophers
have lately exerted no inconsiderable portion of their characteristic industry, on the study of the natural history of their
own species. Of their productions several have been either
compilations, like M. *Zimmermann*'s geographical history; or
reasonings, more or less ingenious, on previously ascertained
facts: such as those of Mr. *Grose*, in his *Physikalische
Abhandlungen* (Leipzig, 1793); M. *Herder*, in various places of
his voluminous writings; M. *Kant*; and others: – but there are
some among these inquirers, whose curious and original
observations seem to give them a superior claim to attention.
To that very expert anatomist, M. *Soemmerring*, we are
indebted for an excellent essay on *the Difference between the
Conformation of the European and the Negroe*; and, as there
appears to be a number of persons in this country at the present
moment willing to employ themselves in the version of German
books, we hope that M. *Soemmerring*'s very accurate and
interesting essay will be soon undertaken by a translator who is

properly qualified. For such a work of fact, we could be well contented to be without a work of fancy.

Of all the living authors of Europe, Dr. BLUMENBACH has perhaps bestowed most time in reading and reflecting, as also in making internal and external observations, on the varieties of the human species. The present work is a digested extract of all that he himself and others have thought and done respecting this engaging subject; and though professing merely to be the *third edition* of a former publication, it is a very different and in fact a new work. We deem it, therefore, entitled to attentive consideration.

In his prefatory letter, the author pays Sir Joseph Banks some High-Dutch compliments in High-Dutch Latin. After due mention of Sir Joseph's liberality in allowing Dr. B. free access to his copious and valuable collection, he bestows some reflections on Linné's classification of the mammalia by the teeth. This method he considers as rendered, by modern discoveries, altogether unfit for the purpose of just arrangement, however well adapted it might have been to the state of knowledge some years ago. We are now, says Dr. B., acquainted with two species of rhinoceros, in habit perfectly similar, and yet differing so widely in their teeth, that it would be necessary, according to this method, to refer one to the *belluæ*, the other to the *glires* of Linné; and so the *sus Æthiopicus* (which has no fore-teeth) would be removed from the *belluæ*, and placed among the *bruta*. Dr. B. proposes a more natural system, deduced from the general habit; and of this, for the sake of reference in the succeeding pages, he gives a short specimen, in which the mammalia are distributed into ten orders. These orders are not founded on a principle pervading and connecting the whole, but on some discriminating circumstance proper to the subjects of each order. Thus order I. is *bimanus*, and comprehends one genus, MAN. So order IV. *chiroptera*, the BAT. VII. *Solidungula*, the HORSE.

In another preliminary paper, Dr. B. presents a view of his own collection (*supellex anthropologica*). It contains 82 sculls, foetuses of different ages, hair of various nations, several wet preparations, principally relative to the negroe, and 20 choice *drawings* of Chinese, Tartar, Hottentot, and other portraits. He mentions a Calmuck Tartar, Feoder Iwanowitsch, now a student at Rome, to whom he is indebted for his own portrait, done with admirable taste and exactness.

Having thus noticed the preliminaries, we shall offer first a compressed abstract of the work itself, and afterward remark on some of the most important passages.

The subject of discussion in Sect. I. is the distinction between man and other animals. Linné ingenuously confessed that he could find no criterion, by which man might be distinguished from the ape; and hence he was obliged finally to refer man and the *simia longimana* to the same genus. Dr. BLUMENBACH hopes, however, to accomplish that which Linné found impracticable, by striking into a different road. To establish a solid distinction, he proposes to take into account, 1. the external figure of the human body; 2. its external structure; 3. the functions; 4. the faculties of the mind; 5. the diseases peculiar to man; and 6. those circumstances which have been hitherto falsely assigned as characteristic of our species.

Dr. B. finds four external circumstances of distinction: 1. the erect posture; 2. the broad, shallow pelvis; 3. the two hands; 4. the disposition of the teeth in even rows. Man, he observes, is not only formed for the erect posture, but it is his exclusive attribute; as appears from his whole conformation, and the concurring habits of all nations. The example of a few *solitary* wild individuals, that crept on all fours, proves nothing to the contrary. 'We may as well fix on any monstrous birth as a model for the human form, as on these wretched outcasts for examples of the genuine gait of man. Nay, if we inquire accurately concerning the best ascertained instances, as Peter the wild boy, the girl of Champaigne, and the man of the Pyrenees, we shall find that they went erect. As to others, that have commonly been accounted *quadrupeds*, *e.g.* the *juvenis ovinus Hibernus, Linn.* many circumstances render their history extremely problematical.' *Moscati* and *Schrage*, who have maintained that man is destined to be a quadruped, are confuted by the length of the inferior extremities in comparison with the trunk and the arms; by the strength of those extremities, which is apparent in the formation of the bones; and by the whole disposition of the thorax: 'for quadrupeds, if they be long-legged, have a thorax compressed at the sides and keeled before; they are destitute of a clavicle or collar-bone, whence they are better able to draw the fore-feet together, and more easily and firmly to sustain the body. Quadrupeds have either a longer breast-bone or more ribs to sustain the intestines when the trunk is horizontal.' The shallowness of the human pelvis affords a character by which man is distinguished from the anthropomorph *simiæ* and other *mammalia*: this part deserves the name of *bason* only in our species. The author discovers farther evidence of his opinion in the connected parts; in the full, fleshy, subglobular nates; and in the relation of the axis of the *vagina* to that of the *pelvis*; – whence he says, may be determined a question agitated since the days of Lucretius – *quænam in coitu positura homini maxime conveniat?* In a note, he mentions a great curiosity in the king's collection; the delineation, by Leonardo da Vinci, *viri cum fæminâ concumbentis, unde ea quam innuimus virilis genitalis tensi ad vaginam relatio luculenter patescat.*[2]

The human hand only deserves the title of *organon organorum*. The ape is properly four-handed. The hind-feet have a thumb, instead of a great toe; and these deserve the name of hands much better than their fore-feet, being better contrived for grasping. There is a species of *cercopithecus* which is destitute of thumbs before: but no four-handed animal wants a thumb to the hind hands. Hence it appears that the Ouran Outang is not destined to go either on two or four limbs: for, since the hands are made for holding, Nature must intend these animals for living on trees. 'These they climb; on these they seek their food; and one pair of hands serves for support, the other for gathering fruit. Hence in the *cercopitheci*, which have imperfect hands, a provision is made for security in their station in trees by a prehensile tail.'

The teeth and their arrangement distinguish man from the brute. The shortness of the jaw, the projection of the chin, and the structure of the condyles, all concur to shew that we are intended to be omnivorous. Linné has asserted that there exist (*alicubi terrarum*) apes less hairy than the human species. Our author, however, owns that he is ignorant *where* they exist; and he adds that we are in general more smooth than the monkey race, though we have some parts more hairy.

Among the *internal* peculiarities of man, are reckoned the largeness of the brain in respect to the nerves, and sandy grains in the pineal gland, the position of the heart, and the union of the pericardium with the diaphragm. The tenderness and pliability of the cellular substance is also mentioned as a principal distinction; and the author is persuaded that to this

[2] Allowing the *venus obversa* to be proper to man, what proof of it does this drawing afford? Was it done from fancy, or from nature? *Rev.*

we owe our capability of becoming habituated to any climate. To this head belong also our slow growth, tardy maturity, and protracted life. The difference of stature in the morning and the evening is likewise pointed out; with other peculiarities, not altogether fit for discussion in this place.

The use of reason, says Dr. B., is universally ascribed to man, as his supreme prerogative. Unfortunately, philosophers have not agreed in their notion of reason. Our author believes that it would be best to make reason consist in that which has made man master of the animal creation. Moreover, man is furnished with the power of invention, whence Dr. Franklin acutely styled him a *tool-making* animal. Hence, too, he has fabricated language for his convenience. Whether laughing and weeping be among his peculiarities, Dr. B. does not appear prepared to decide.

Diseases deserve to be briefly noticed, as having their origin in a peculiarity of œconomy. Dr. B. enumerates almost all the exanthemata, and several other disorders, as proper to man. Dr. *Jansen* of Amsterdam assured him, from his own observation, that apes had a local ulcer, but not a variolous fever, from the contagion of the small-pox. As peculiarities falsely ascribed to our species, Dr. B. recounts the proximity of the eyes and eye-lashes, prominence of the nose, immobility of the ear, an organ of touch, the uvula, eructation, and incapability of being fatted.

Sect. II. Causes of the degeneration of animals in general.

It is necessary here to examine two questions: what is a species in zoology? and how a species degenerates into varieties? Dr. B. finds little use in the power of producing prolific offspring, either as a criterion to be generally applied, or as limited by *Frisch* to wild animals. In the first place, we shall scarcely bring together certain animals, inhabitants of distant countries, concerning which we want to know whether they are of the same species; and secondly, the principal doubts respect domestic animals, as in the case of the dog, all the varieties of which proceed, according to some, from the shepherd's dog; according to others, from the jackal; while some again contend that the jackal itself, with the whole family of dogs, originates from the wolf. Dr. B. does not find that the constancy of a certain mark is of more avail in this difficulty. In the white

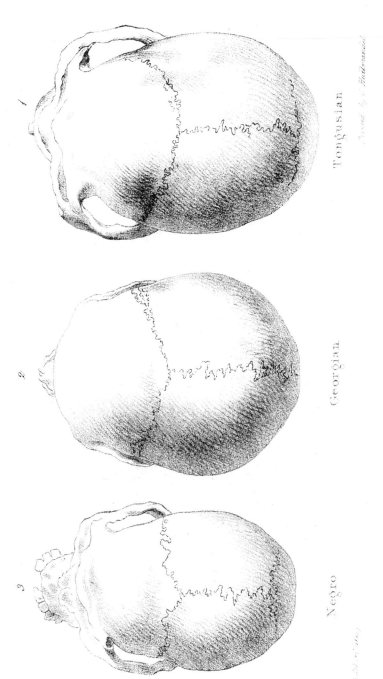

Pl. 1

Tongusian

Georgian

Negro

Blumenbach thought that skulls were best classified if 'seen from above and from behind'. Here: a 'Negro', a 'Georgian', and a 'Tongusian' example. (From J. C. Prichard's *Researches into the Physical History of Mankind*, 2nd ed., 1826.)

In the end of the eighteenth century human tribes were depicted as part of their environmental and cultural surroundings. This is Blumenbach's image of the 'Ethiopian variety of mankind'.

4ᵗᵉ Menſchen Varietät

Blumenbach considered the 'American variety of mankind' as an intermediary between the 'Mongolian' and the 'Caucasian' type.
(From Blumenbach's *Beyträge zur Naturgeschichte*, 1790.)

(Both illustrations taken from Blumenbach's *Beyträge zur Naturgeschichte*, 1790.)

By the 1830s illustrations of human types had become professionalized. Past and present peoples, from higher and lower orders of society were depicted. See here: a Brahman (fig. 1), a 'young Indian' (fig. 2), two heads of 'ancient' and 'modern' Persians (figs 3 and 4).
(From Georges Cuvier's *Le règne animal*, vol. 1, 1836.)

RACES HUMAINES

(Planche 21)

S. Renard imp.

Georges Cuvier believed that the 'Negro' variety of mankind had survived the flood on the top of Mount Atlas. A Hottentot (fig. 1), a Bushwoman (figs 2 and 3), a Kafir (fig. 4).
(From Knox's *Races of Men*, 2nd ed., 1862.)

rabbit the red eye is as constant as any specific character; and yet the white rabbit is merely a variety. The notion of a species can only, then, be derived from analogy and probability. Thus, the grinders differ greatly in the African and Asiatic elephants. As it does not appear that the difference proceeds from degeneration, these elephants must be regarded as separate species, and not as varieties. On the other hand, Dr. B. considers the ferret as a variety of the *mustela putorius*; 'not (he says) because I know the fact of their breeding together: but because I judge from analogy that all animals, destitute of the *dark pigment* of the eye, are a mere altered breed.'

To demonstrate how an original species may degenerate, the author relates some phænomena of this kind in animals, with a view afterward to investigate the causes. Thus in different climates we see animals differing in colour, hair, size, shape, and proportion of parts, and in the form of the scull. In the shape of the head, the hog differs as widely from the wild boar, and the Neapolitan from the Hungarian horse, as the European *man* from the negroe. In the buffalo, there are deep *foveæ lachrymales*; in the ox, these depressions are nearly obliterated. The author's theory is founded on the influence of external agents on the living body. The formation of the young animal may be affected, he says, by these agents in three different ways. A monster, a mule, or a variety, may be produced. The last deviation alone is considered here. 1. The climate operates as a power, producing variation of form. The atmosphere varying in temperature, moisture, &c. in every climate, the blood and other fluids are modified differently by the absorbed air. It is, however, difficult to determine what is owing to mere climate, and what to other causes. The whiteness of the arctic fox, crow, black-bird, &c. seems owing to temperature or cold; because we have various examples of coloured animals turning white in winter. The dark colour, so general in tropical countries, is, on the contrary, ascribed to heat. As an example of the effect of *diet*, the African sheep is adduced: the fleece of which, in its native soil, is more like camel's hair than wool, but, after a year's pasturage in England, it becomes soft and valuable. In marshy countries, as in Friesland, the horse grows large; whereas in dry soils he continues puny. The *mode of living*, which comprehends culture and habits, is another cause of change. None, however, operates so quickly as the mixture of varieties. The propagation of weakness or indisposition, in any way acquired, is the last cause assigned. Whether mutilations can produce varieties, Dr. B. does not decide, but he inclines to the affirmative.

Sect. III. Of the kinds and causes of degeneration in man.

The most obvious kind of variety is that of colour; it is also permanent and hereditary. The complexion is connected with the colour of the hair, and of the pupil, and with the general temperament. Dr. B. constitutes five principal varieties of colour; 1. the white with red cheeks; 2. the yellow or olive, as seen in the mongrel tribes; 3. the copper colour, in the American Indians; 4. the tawny, in the Malays; 5. from tawny-black to jet-black. The tawny-black is not confined to negroe (Æthiopic) nations. It is found 'mixed with the predominant hue' in very different and very remote varieties; as in the people of Brazil, California, India, and of the South Sea Islands. The author's theory of the black colour of the Africans scarcely differs, or differs but in terms, from one that has been proposed in this country. He thinks that the *carbone*, in passing out from the skin with the hydrogene, is precipitated by the oxygene of the atmosphere; and that it remains in the rete mucosum. The liver, he thinks, as well as the skin, serves to excrete carbone; and there is an analogy between various tints from the jaundice and national complexions. From the affinity between the bile and fat, he accounts for the waxy tinge of the latter in dark-coloured tribes; and he imagines, for the same reason, that the Greenlanders, who live much on animal oil, have a dark skin. – Of seasons and climates, as affecting the complexion, – of the Creoles, – Mulattoes, – agreement between the skin and hair, and Iris.

Dr. B. reckons five diversities of national physiognomy: 1. the oval, or what we esteem the most beautiful; and two flatted and two elongated variations of countenance. The two former are exemplified in the Tartar and American visage; the two latter in the Guinea and Malay. Dr. B. deems the climate the principal efficient cause of each variety; for in China all ranks have one and the same countenance; and migration occasions a change, as is apparent in the Jaculatæ and the Creole; and children born of the same parents in Europe and the West Indies will exhibit a marked difference in their physiognomy. Egypt and India on this side of the Ganges, however, afford the clearest examples. The traits of the fierce nations of the North, once the conquerors of Egypt, are only to be recognized in the most ancient monuments; and since Timur, the Monguls in India have sensibly approximated to the Indian face. In one descendant of emigrants, we see the face much altered; the Laplanders and Hungarians are said to come from the same stock. How the climate produces its effect it is difficult to say. *Leibnitz* fancied that the natives bore a resemblance to the indigenous animals, as the Laplander to the bear, the negroe to the ape. The mode of life and certain customs have influence on the features. Among the negroes, the nose, flat of itself, is artificially flattened after birth.

The study of the form of the scull is of great importance to the natural history of man. A blind person would distinguish, at the first grasp, the scull of a Calmuck from that of a negroe. The diversities are almost infinite; yet a certain uniformity is observable in those of the same nation. Hence different anatomists have sought a rule by which they might compare the gradations. Dr. B. objects to Professor *Camper*'s[3] facial line. It does not apply to tribes, distinguished by the direction of the jaw; many heads, widely different in other respects, coincide in the facial line; and M. *Camper* himself fluctuated in its application. The author proposes to supply this defect by what he calls a vertical line, to the illustration of which the first of his two plates is dedicated. The scull being placed on its base, he attends to the projection of the *ossa jugalia*, and of the upper jaw-bone. The Negroe thus appears *beaked*, the Tartar drawn outwards and flatted. Dr. B. assumes and figures five varieties of sculls, owing in part to the same causes that produce the natural physiognomies, and partly to peculiar modes of pressure.

In the remainder of this section, some facts are stated respecting the various shapes of the ear, hands, feet, &c; and the fables concerning the Patagonian giants, the dwarfish Quimos, and men with tails, are treated as they deserve.

In Sect. V. and last, Dr. B. defines the five varieties which he assumes of the human species, *one and indivisible*: 1. the Caucasian variety; the model, according to our estimate, of beauty. The two extremes are, 2. the Mongul, and 3. the Æthiopic. Intermediate, stand 4. the American, and 5. the

[3] See Rev. N. S. vol. vi. p. 206.

Malay. In the vignettes to a little work published six years ago (*Beytraege zur Naturgeschichte*[4]) Dr. B had given some idea of these varieties; and a book like the present, in order to be generally useful and agreeable, should be richly furnished with accurate engravings. The Caucasian he considers as the primitive variety, because the others recede from this in regular gradation to the Negroe or Æthiopic on one side, and to the Mongolic on the other; also because, from his chemical hypothesis, as mentioned above, he conceives the degeneracy much more easy from white to black than the contrary – *quando nempe pigmenti carbonacei secretio et precipitatio semel inveterata radices egit*. Of the Negroe variety, Dr. B. asserts that there is no character so constant and peculiar, but that it may be observed in the others, and fails in many Negroes: 'the footlike powder (he adds) is not, as some pretend, confined to the *rete mucosum* of this race. I have remarked it, though less equally distributed, in many Lascars. In a female Indian servant of my own, a native of Bombay, I observe this very foot imperceptibly vanishing in the face and arms, while the tawny carbonaceous precipitate still continues to be effused under the epidermis.'

Having thus minutely analysed Dr. B.'s tract, we think ourselves entitled to say that, of all the publications which have yet appeared in the natural history of man, it most abounds in exact and curious *facts*. Of the Doctor's *philosophy*, we have not received a very advantageous impression: for we find him often trifling, and often illogical. What, for instance, can be more puerile than to rank an atom of sandy matter in the brain among the attributes of man, when the absence of it in other animals is by no means proved? – Nor can we admit, without evidence, that it is the pliability of the cellular substance which qualifies man to inhabit all climates. Parturition is probably not absolutely without pain and danger in any of the mammalia; and we find Dr. B. much too liberal in conceding to the adversaries of the erect posture in man, that the inclination of the axis of the *vagina* to that of the *pelvis* is the cause of difficult parturition. In undepraved and unenfeebled human tribes, the young are brought forth with as much ease as in any other viviparous animal. – Nor will these speculatists be either convinced or silenced by what our author advances on the

4   See Rev. N.S. vol. xi. p. 559.

fitness of our present conformation for the erect posture. They can easily answer that the erect posture itself has progressively changed the structure. What Dr. B. says of the *faculty of reason* proves only how poorly he can sometimes employ it; and in order to his next edition, we advise him to study the modern philosophy of words; as he may then produce something more satisfactory on the notion of *species*. His doctrine leaves it to the arbitrary will and pleasure of the naturalist, to determine what may or may not be placed to the account of degeneration. His objections to *Ray*'s and *Buffon*'s criterion are feeble and irrelevant. This criterion, applied to our species, appears to be the most convincing proof of its unity; for the progeny of every mixture of the varieties of man is prolific. To found a diversity of species between the elephants of Africa and Asia, on a difference in their teeth, seems the more unwarrantable, since Dr. B. has himself shewn that great diversity prevails in the human teeth: the fore-teeth, in some mummies and other subjects, being blunt, (*non scalpriformes, margine tenui instructi, sed crassi et conis truncatis similes*, p. 224.) and the canine teeth not being distinguishable, but by situation, from the contiguous grinders.

We could extend our strictures: but, from the remarks already offered, we presume that it will appear that Professor BLUMENBACH's efforts have succeeded only as far as they may have furnished matter of reflection to the sagacious, or references to a writer who is capable of treating the subject in a manner suitable to its interest and its dignity.

AN HISTORICAL DISPLAY OF THE EFFECTS OF PHYSICAL AND MORAL CAUSES
on the Character and Circumstances of Nations including a comparison of the Ancients and Moderns in regard to their intellectual and social state. London. 1816

John Bigland

John Bigland (1750–1832) was born into a family of little means in Yorkshire. He worked as a schoolmaster and published several popular books, including *Reflections on the Resurrection of Christ* (1803), *Letters on Natural History* (1806), *A Compendious History of the Jews* (1820). His discussion of the effects of climate and racial lineage was not original and was not quoted by contemporary scholars. Bigland's knowledge of the influence of climate was derived from Scottish Enlightenment philosophers and the French rationalists. But he saw that the theory of climate, which these authors asserted, was flawed. As the excerpt below shows, his turn towards a concept of race was fuelled by the phrenological doctrines of Franz Joseph Gall.

The greatest part of the writers who have made the history of man the subject of their inquiries, have overlooked or paid too little attention to a circumstance which, if thoroughly investigated and fully understood, might contribute to account for various phenomena in his physical and moral existence, that seem to be covered with a veil of impenetrable obscurity. When we contemplate the various characters and dispositions not of individuals only, but also of numerous collections of men, living under the same climate, and nourished by the same kind of food, we are sometimes unable to discover any such difference in their government, laws or religion, or other moral circumstances, as can account in a satisfactory manner for so marked a distinction. In such cases, are we not tempted to believe, that something more than is generally supposed, may be attributed to race? Reason and revelation concur in representing the whole human species as issuing from the same stock; but experience shews, that families are often distinguished not only by certain peculiarities of external organization, but also by particular dispositions of mind, which prevail through all or the greater part of their branches. On the contrary it sometimes happens, that one or two individuals belonging to a family, differ greatly from the rest of its members in exterior appearance as well as in disposition and intellect. While, therefore, the human species was composed of only a few families, some of the individuals might be very different from the others, both in their bodily and mental faculties. It is neither impossible, nor extremely improbable, that the three sons of Noah might greatly differ in strength, courage, genius, and the other gifts of nature; or such a difference might take place amongst the children of these patriarchs, or other parents and founders of tribes or colonies, and be perpetuated in numberless directions and ramifications.

This view of the varieties of race among the human species, is analogous to what is discoverable throughout the whole system of animated nature. A late writer ascribes the distinctive properties and perfection of animals solely to the breed, independent of climate and all other extraneous circumstances, and adduces in proof of his hypothesis the successful practice of jockeys and sportsmen. "The consequence," says he, "of this kind of attention to breed, continued for ages is, that although the climate of Great Britain has never been deemed peculiarly favourable to the horse species, yet it is admitted, that in no part of Europe are horses bred that can equal those of this country, either in swiftness of foot or in strength and perseverance of course. In Arabia, indeed, where this animal may be esteemed the chief support of the family, and where the very existence of the owner depends, on many occasions, on the powers of his horse, this circumstance has obtained a still greater degree of attention than in Britain. The pedigree of a horse is there preserved with as great care as the genealogy of a royal family in Europe, and the interposition of the magistrate is called in upon every occasion of this sort to prevent frauds, and to authenticate the deed. In that country, it is not so much swiftness of foot that they regard, as the faculty of bearing fatigue and abstinence without being exhausted; and this quality, they find runs in the blood, being transmissible to the descendants of a race, which is known to possess it in an eminent degree, with as much certainty as any known quality whatever. And so successful have they been in augmenting it by their uninterrupted care for an indiscernible[1] length of time, always to select the most eminent of this kind to breed from, that they have obtained a race which possesses this quality to a degree that could never have been deemed possible by other nations, had not the evidence of the fact been altogether undeniable."[2]

From the horse, Dr. Anderson transfers his observations to the dog. "How long it is since the Spanish pointer was introduced into this island I am unable to say; but we all know that this breed of pointers is reared every day; and there is reason to believe that some of them are to be found in this country, at the present hour, which possess the distinctive qualities of that kind of dog, in perhaps as great perfection as ever they were known to do at any period of time. The same may be said of the beagle, the hound, the terrier, the spaniel, the bull-dog, pug-dog, and every other variety."[3]

The same philosophical observer of animated nature, supposes that the varieties amongst animals are distinctions which man may change at his pleasure, by mixing the breed, and preserve as long as he pleases, by keeping it unmixed: and that whenever a change in this respect takes place, it is solely by mixture of blood, and happens alike under every climate. "There is, however," says he, "a still less variation that is observed to take place among animals, and which might be ranked by naturalists as a subdivision of varieties; because it never tends to blend one variety with another, but merely to divide it into lesser groups, which might be called families or breeds, each of these possessing certain discriminative peculiarities, which, though not absolutely permanent, are yet so durable as to be sufficient for the most part, clearly to distinguish these breeds from others."[4] The original of this variety," continues Dr. Anderson, "is purely accidental, *i.e.* our knowledge of the nature of animal life is not sufficiently perfect to enable us to trace any circumstance that should give rise to such variations."[5] But experience sufficiently shews, that the

[1]   Dr. Anderson here uses an expression not very common: he evidently means from time immemorial.

[2]   Dr. Anderson's Recreations, v. 1. p. 72–73.

[3]   Dr. Ander. Recreat. v. 1. p. 56.

[4]   Dr. Anderson's Recreations, v. 1. p. 62.

[5]   Ibid.

different breeds of animals possess characteristic distinctions, which cannot be changed or obliterated by the influence of climate or any other extraneous circumstance. It is well known that Merino sheep do not degenerate in England; and we are assured, on unquestionable authority, that they do not degenerate in France.[6] The most eminent breeders of cattle agree, that attention to race is the only effectual means that can be used for the improvement of stock, and the success of their practice proves the truth of their theory.[7]

No one will attempt to deny that there exists an unquestionable analogy between the human frame and other animal bodies; and it is also observable, that the same individual and family differences are seen among men as among brutes. Dr. Anderson pursues this analogy, and after remarking that the diversities among animals are infinitely numerous, and relate to the internal qualities, as well as to the form of the body and external appearance, transfers his observations and theories to the human species. "To this origin," says he, "we must trace the well known phenomenon of family likeness, and although this in the human species is wonderfully weakened among European nations by the law of consanguinity preventing marriages between persons who are near a kin, yet in spite of this, a family likeness and family cast of character have been often known to prevail for several successive centuries. Its influence is still more observable in regard to national appearance and character; but no where is that so distinctly perceptible as among the clans in the Highlands of Scotland, which having each originally sprung from one family that separated itself from all others, like the varieties of other creatures in a wild state, and preserved themselves distinct from the neighbouring clans till of late years, by those never ending feuds and acts of hostility in which they were incessantly engaged, each of them were thus induced always to intermarry among their own clans, so that it sometimes happens that a race of people will be found there, inhabiting one valley, whose features, complexion, stature, and general appearance, are extremely different from the inhabitants of another valley, separated from the first only by a ridge of

6 Bourgoanne's Trav. in Spain, chap. 3.

7 Witness the improvements made in the breeds, not only of horses but also of horned cattle, sheep, &c.

mountains that are easily accessible, insomuch that a person, who is acquainted with this peculiarity, will know by the appearance of the first person he meets what clan he belongs to."[8]

The authority of Dr. Anderson, who was a native of Scotland, and well acquainted with the Highlanders, may be considered as unquestionable in regard to the clans. And he adduces the case of the gipsies and the jews as an additional proof of the influence of race on the exterior appearance of the human species. But the gipsies can scarcely be considered at this day as a distinct race; for although on their first appearance in Europe, they seemed to be a particular colony or tribe wholly different from any that inhabited this quarter of the globe, yet it is certain, that in process of time they have been joined by numbers of vagabonds in all the countries in which they have been permitted to reside;[9] and their singular manner of living, may have greatly contributed to give them that peculiar cast of countenance by which they may in general be recognized.

But the jews furnish the most striking instance of a marked distinction of race that is to be met with in the whole range of physiological observation, so far as it relates to the human species. The perpetuated effect of this distinction, seems to overpower the influence of all other physical, and indeed, of most moral causes. The jews are a numerous people, and extensively diffused over most of the countries of Europe, Asia, and Africa. They subsist, generally speaking, on the same kind of food as the other inhabitants of those countries; for the prohibitions contained in their law are not such as can have any effect on their stature, their features, or their complexion. They follow a variety of professions and employments: many of them are wealthy merchants, having a fixed residence in populous and commercial cities: others, engaged in a great variety of inferior branches of traffic, lead a wandering life;

---

[8]   Dr. Anderson's Recreations, v. I, p. 70–71. The reader, although he cannot approve of Dr. Anderson's embarassed style, and the length of his involved sentences, will acknowledge the accuracy of his observations and the soundness of his arguments.

[9]   Concerning the origin of the gipsies, various opinions have been entertained, and much has been written on the subject; but the most probable account is, that they were Egyptian fugitives who abandoned their country when it was conquered by the Turkish Emperor Selim I. as they are said to have made their first appearance in Europe soon after that event.

and in some countries, as Lithuania, Courland, &c. great numbers of them are agriculturists. Although they rigidly adhere to their peculiar institutions these relate wholly to religious matters: in all other respects they are subject to foreign governments and foreign laws, which are very different in the different countries where they are settled. But in every climate, in every profession and station of life, under every government and every system of legislation, amidst every variety of physical and moral circumstances, the jews preserve, in their external appearance, incontestible evidence of the race to which they belong.

This characteristic distinction by which the jews are so easily recognized, can be ascribed only to their almost invariable custom of intermarrying among themselves, which preserves the race pure and unmixed. The justness of this conclusion appears from an indisputable circumstance; for it has constantly been observed, that whenever any of those people have become converts, and formed family alliances with the nations among whom they are settled, the distinctive marks of their race are soon obliterated. A proof of the perpetuation of those characteristic distinctions, unless when effaced by mixture of breed, may be adduced from what a late traveller says of the Afghans, whose incursions and victories have rendered their names terrible in the annals of Hindostan, and whose princes sat a long time on the throne of Delhi. These people claim their descent from a jewish stock, and had long been seated in Cashmire and the adjacent parts of Little Bocharia. Their numerous adventurers, who at different periods have opened a way with their swords into India and Persia, are mixed with the native inhabitants of those countries; but in their original seats they still discover the distinctive marks of their race; and Mr. Forster was so struck with the general appearance of the Cashmerians, as to be almost inclined to imagine that he had been suddenly transported amongst a nation of jews.[10]

In almost every part of India, the different casts into which the people are divided, exhibit in their external organization and appearance certain peculiar characteristics. The professions and pursuits of the different casts are in a great measure confounded in consequence of the wars, the civil commotions, and scenes of anarchy which have so long

---

[10] Forster's Travels, v. 2. p. 21.

prevailed. The Bramins have taken up the sword and are seen in the ranks of an army: the Kettry, or warrior tribe, engage occasionally in traffic: and the Sooders have acquired principalities. But intermarriages between separate casts are still rare: each tribe has a distinct feature, and the lineaments of the countenance as well as the form of body seems to indicate a particular family.[11]

Almost every part of the world, and every portion of mankind, afford convincing proofs that a family or tribe, remaining without any intermixture with others, will assume and perpetuate a peculiar appearance. The historian of the Decline and Fall of the Roman Empire, describes the shrill voice, the uncouth gestures, and the strange deformity of the Huns. "These savages of Scythia," says he, "were compared, and the picture had some resemblance, to the animals that walk very aukwardly on two legs, and to the mis-shapen figures the Termini, which were often placed on the bridges of antiquity. They were distinguished from the rest of the human species by their broad shoulders, flat noses, and small black eyes deeply buried in the head; and as they were almost destitute of beards, they never possessed either the manly graces of youth, or the venerable aspect of age."[12] Gibbon here refers to the authority of Ammianus Marcellinus,[13] and of Jornandes, who in describing them seems to delineate a caricature of a Calmuc face. Their ugliness was such, that a tradition of the Goths ascribed their origin to the amours of witches and demons who had met in the deserts.[14] Montesquiou who, as well as many other writers, considers the Turks and the Huns as the same nation, says that the Turks were the ugliest people upon earth, and that their women were as frightful as the men.[15]

Such was the exterior appearance of the Hunnish and Tartar nations, when issuing from their original seats on the northern and north western frontiers of China, and traversing the vast regions of central Asia, they at length approached the civilized

11   Chatfield's Hist. Rev. of Hindostan, p. 165.

12   Gibbon's Dec. and Fall of the Rom. Emp. v. 4. 8vo, chap. 26. p. 375.

13   Ammianus Marcellinus, lib. 31. chap. 1.

14   Gibbon ubi supra. Montesquiou Grandeur et Decadence des Romains, ch. 28. p. 225.

15   Montesquiou ubi supra.

countries of Europe.[16] Their conquests introduced a mixture of breed by which their shape, their features, and complexion were gradually improved. China, during a considerable space of time, groaned under their oppression, and contributed to the improvement of their race. The Huns, regarding their own women only as instruments of domestic labour, their desires or rather their appetites were directed to the enjoyment of more elegant beauty. A select band of the fairest maidens of China was annually devoted to their rude embraces, and the alliance of the Hunnish kings was secured by their marriage with the daughters of the imperial family.[17]

The historian of the Decline and Fall of the Roman Empire, ascribes the improvement of the Hunnish race to other circumstances, as well as to mixture of blood. When the power of that people was broken, towards the close of the first century, by their wars with the Chinese and the Siempi, and by the defection of their vassal tribes, two formidable divisions refusing to submit to their conquerors, directed their course one towards the Oxus, and the other towards the Volga. The first of these colonies established their dominion in the extensive plains of Sogdiana, on the eastern side of the Caspian sea. "Their manners," says Mr. Gibbon, "were softened and even their features were insensibly improved by the mildness of the climate, and their long residence in a flourishing province."[18] But the same historian, speaking of the Alani, who were seated between the Don and the Volga, says, "The mixture of Sarmatic and German blood had contributed to improve the features of the Alani, to whiten their swarthy complexions, and to tinge their hair with a yellowish hue, which is seldom found in the Tartar race."[19] In the case of the Huns, Mr. Gibbon here ascribes the improvement of their exterior to the influence of climate and civilization: in regard to the Alani, he refers it to mixture of blood: all these causes might concur in producing the same effect; but the last is undoubtedly the most powerful. A mild climate, and the comforts of civilized life, have an undoubted tendency to

---

16 For the progress of the Huns through the vast regions of Tartary, see De Guigne's Hist. des Huns, tom. 2.

17 De Guigne's Hist. des Huns, tom. 2. p. 62.

18 Gibbon's Dec. Rom. Emp. v. 4. ch. 26. p. 368.

19 Ibid Dec. Rom. Emp. v. 4. ch. 26. 373.

improve both the complexion and features as excessive heat or cold, severe hardships, and long continued labour, darken the skin, and give a harshness and rigidity to the lineaments of the face. But it is proved by experience, that attention to breed is the most effectual means of removing blemishes, or perpetuating desireable qualities in every kind of animal: and, reasoning from analogy, there is no great danger of error in concluding that the same cause must produce, at least, in a considerable degree, similar effects on the human species. In this manner indeed, the Turks and Persians, both of whom appear to have been originally of a very disagreeable exterior, have so greatly improved their race by their continual mixture, during a long succession of ages, with Circasian, Grecian, and other slaves, that they are now the two handsomest nations of Asia, and little inferior in beauty to Europeans.[20]

The reasonings of philosophy, the history of mankind, and the discoveries of the medical art, all concur to shew that various peculiarities in the human frame and constitution are transmissible by hereditary descent. Physicians know this to be the case with several of the most dreadful diseases to which the species is liable;[21] and the same observation may often be made on the different qualities and powers both of the body and the mind. Some of these peculiarities, which seem to be attached to particular tribes, may perhaps be originally owing to climate, food, and mode of life; but when once formed, they are transmitted from one generation to another, and often subsist for a long time after the combination of circumstances by which they were produced has ceased to exist. But the greater number of these distinctions appear to arise from accident;[22] for we may sometimes perceive among a family of children a difference of strength, beauty, and intellect, for which it is impossible to assign any cause. These differences, when not obliterated by mixture of breed, may among men as well as

20   Herodot. lib. 3. chap. 97. Buffon's Hist. Nat. tom. 3. p. 420. Herodotus says that even in the time of Xerxes, the Persians were not inferior to the Greeks in courage and strength.

21   Among those may be reckoned the scrofula, gout, insanity, and several other disorders. The idocy of the Cretins, in the Valais, who are mentioned in chap. 2, is also perpetuated in hereditary descent with unfailing certainty.

22   By accident is here meant some circumstance for which philosophy cannot account: as no effect can exist without a cause, nothing can happen by mere chance, which is a word used to cover human ignorance.

among brutes be perpetuated, and at length become characteristic marks of families and tribes. Nothing but the hereditary
transmission of these peculiarities, which may at first be
deemed accidental, could occasion the difference of external
appearance observable amongst the Scottish clans, who subsist
on the same kind of food, live under the same climate, and have
from time immemorial been surrounded by the same moral as
well as physical circumstances.[23]

This hypothesis may be illustrated by a suppositious
example. If several pairs of the human species were placed in
countries under the same climate, and furnishing the same kind
of food, but each pair entirely cut off from all intercourse with
the rest of mankind, the families that would be raised, in such
circumstances, would be easily distinguishable from each other
in external appearance, and perhaps also in intellect. If the
original parents of one of these families should excel in
strength, those of another in beauty, if, in fine, each of the
separate pairs here supposed were distinguished by any
remarkable qualities or defects, either corporeal or mental, it is
more than probable that these distinctions would be
perpetuated amongst their descendants, and become characteristics of their different tribes. In the primeval world during the
patriarchal ages, it was the general custom to intermarry with
persons of the same family, and accidental peculiarities being
thus perpetuated, the distinctions of race probably arose from
that circumstance.

Whether intellectual as well as corporeal differences be thus
transmitted and perpetuated, it may appear to some a question
of difficult solution. If we could give credit to the fanciful
theory of Dr. Gall, we should readily answer it in the
affirmative.[24] The principle of his hypothesis is, that the
capacities and inclinations of the different kinds of animals and
also of men, are strong or weak in proportion to the largeness
or smallness of the brain in comparison with the other parts of
the body. The Cretins of the Valais, have a far less quantity of

---

[23] See Dr. Anderson's observations on the characteristic distinctions of the
Scottish clans. Recreations, v. 1. p. 70 and 71, already quoted.

[24] Dr. Gall, of Vienna, employed twenty-years, and expended a large fortune
in making his collections of skulls, heads of plaster, brains of wax, &c.
But about the close of the year 1801, his lectures were prohibited by the
Austrian government, as tending towards materialism. His opinions have a
great many abettors among the German physicians and philosophers.

brain than other men. Dr. Gall compared the skull of an old woman who had been an idiot from her infancy, with that of a man distinguished by his talents; and he found the latter to be twice as large as the former. According to the doctor's hypothesis, the germ of every intellectual faculty as well as of every corporeal organ is in the fœtus, and consequently as transmissible in a family or tribe, as the traits of the countenance and other peculiarities of the exterior appearance.[25] If this could be proved, the conclusion would necessarily be, that the distinctions of race would have a far more decided influence on the human species, than any of the other physical or moral circumstances, which, in all their endless variety of combinations, operate on man through the whole course of his existence; for Dr. Gall expressly asserts, that external circumstances may either impede or favour the developement of the organs of mental agency, but cannot in any wise change their nature.[26]

But without adopting the doctrines of this ingenious and fanciful philospher, we must still admit the indications of observation and experience.[27] It is well known that diseases and defects of the mind from whatever causes they may proceed, are often transmitted to descendants, as well as those of the body. This is frequently the case with idiotism, and every species of insanity, of which the Cretins of the Valais are a melancholy instance. It is evident that the intellectual imbecillity of these unfortunate people originates in some unknown property of the climate; but experience proves it to be transmitted by hereditary descent to their posterity. They were formerly permitted to marry, and have consequently

25   "Le germe de l'organe futur de la penetration ou de l'imagination est aussi bien dans le foetus qui vient de se former dans le sein de la mere que le germe de l'oreille, du nez, &c. et que le germe de l'arbre est dans le noyau." "The germ of the future organ of penetration or imagination is as really in the foetus, which is formed in the womb of the mother, as the germ of the ear, the nose, &c. and as the germ of the tree is in the kernel of its fruit." Exposition de la Doctrine du Docteur Gall, chap. 3. p. 35.

26   "Les circonstances, exterieures pourront en contrarier ou favoriser le developpement, mais nullement en changer la nature." Exposition de la Doctrine du Docteur Gall, ubi supra.

27   During the space of nearly thirty years employed in the instruction of youth, the author has frequently observed that in some families, genius and penetration seemed to be in a great measure hereditary, while in others a degree of dullness and stupidity appeared to be prevalent. Both these cases, however, generally admitted of individual exceptions.

become a distinct race, existing in the same melancholy state through several generations.[28]

In comparing the Europeans, the northern and southern Asiatics, the southern Africans, and the aboriginal Americans, there appears to be a visible distinction of races.[29] Although the varieties of complexion may be ascribed to climate and modes of life, yet the differences that are seen in their features and bodily structure, can scarcely be ascribed to these causes. It is difficult indeed to account for that singular shape of the eye, and some other peculiarities which characterise a Chinese and Tartar physiognomy without considering them as the marks of a particular race, and perpetuated in hereditary descent.[30] These observations might be extended to the negroes of Guinea, to the aborigines of America, and to several other nations, in whom the difference of exterior appearance can scarcely be ascribed to differences either in climate or food, or to any other causes physical or moral, except distinction of race.[31]

But among the nations of Europe, at least if we except the Laplanders and some of the Russian tribes, all distinctions of this kind are annihilated by a general intermixture, occasioned in early times by almost incessant revolutions, and afterwards increased by commercial communication. The ancient Greeks

[28] Coxe's Trav. in Switzerland, v. 1. p. 385, &c.

[29] The Hottentots and the Caffres, although so near neighbours, have all the appearances of distinct races. And it is impossible, in viewing the Bojesmans, not to consider them as a race entirely distinct from all others. They seem to have sprung from parents originally defective in size and shape; they are scarcely four feet high, and their lank and deformed limbs give them a singular appearance. Lichtenstein's Trav. p. 117.

[30] See Barrow's China, p. 48. &c. The curious reader may here be referred to an "Essay on the causes of the variety of complexion and figure in the human species," delivered in the annual oration before the philosophical society of Philadelphia, 28th Feb. 1787. By the Rev. Samuel Stanhope Smith, D. D. Little regard indeed is paid to race: all is attributed to climate and moral habits. The disquisitions are curious although sometimes carried to too high a pitch of refinement, and containing much assumption scarcely susceptible of proof.

[31] Mr. Winterbottom has a curious dissertation on the causes of the black complexion of the negroes. See Account of the Africans, ch. 12. p. 181. &c. This attempt, however, to account for so remarkable a phenomenon, is not more successful than that of the Abbè Raynal. But from Winterbottom's account, it appears that the negroes are divided into distinct races, and that the flat nose, thick lips, &c. are not common to all of them. P. 197.

and Romans were a mixture of Egyptians and Phœnicians, with Celts or Cimmerians. The conquests of the Romans, and still more the subversion of their empire, were events that greatly promoted the mixture of the European nations. The Franks and the Saxons, the ancestors of the modern French and English, came from the north western parts of Germany, and might be regarded as kindred tribes. These became blended with the Gauls, Burgundians, Goths, Romans, Britons, and Normans. The Spaniards are a mixture of Carthaginians, Romans, Goths, and Arabians, blended with the aboriginal tribes; and the Italians are descended from Romans, Goths, and Lombards. These intermixtures, indeed, have been so frequent and numerous, that among the European nations, all distinctions of race, which might once have existed, are long since confounded and lost in the general amalgamation.

RESEARCHES INTO THE PHYSICAL HISTORY OF MAN
By James Cowles Prichard, M.D. F.L.S.
London. 1813.

Anonymous

Source: Monthly Review, vol. 75 ns, 1814

James Cowles Prichard (1786–1848) grew up as a Quaker. But shortly after he had taken his MD degree at Edinburgh University he converted to Anglicanism. Already in his doctoral dissertation, he had chosen to investigate the origins of human variation. Its title – *De generis humani varietate* (*On the Origins of Human Varieties*, 1808) – reveals his indebtedness to Blumenbach (see item 17) whom Prichard admired throughout his life. In 1810 Prichard returned to his hometown Bristol where he set up a private medical practice. Subsequently he became physican to the Bristol Infirmary. In 1813 he published an enlarged version of his dissertation, *Researches into the Physical History of Man*. Here he dissented in one major respect from Blumenbach's anthropology: he rejected the theory of climate. Instead, he believed that the process of civilization gave rise to new human varieties. In his view, the human mind and human physicality improved together. The natural history of man led from primitive blackness to the growth of white skin colour.

It is the object of this volume to ascertain whether the human race be derived from one original pair, or whether several distinct species exist among mankind. Dr. Prichard embraces the former opinion, and, in support of it, enters very largely into the nature and causes of the physical diversities which characterize the different races of men.

The investigation pursued in these pages resolves itself into the question, Are the physical diversities observed in man sufficient to constitute *specific differences*, or are they to be considered merely as *varieties*? Under this point of view, the author commences his inquiry, and endeavours to apply to it those rules which have been adopted with respect to other animals. Certain circumstances, however, in this particular instance, prevent the strict application of the rules; so that, for the solution of the difficulty, it is necessary to employ a less compendious, although a more satisfactory method. Dr. Prichard thus describes the general plan of reasoning which is followed in the course of his researches:

> 'In the present state of our knowledge, it will be better to proceed on a cautious and inductive mode, and in the first instance to ascertain as nearly as possible what are the kinds of variation in which Nature chiefly delights. When we have found that any particular deviation from the primitive character has taken place in a number of examples, the tendency to such variety may be laid down as a law more or less general; and accordingly when parallel diversities are observed in instances, which do not afford us a view of the origin and progress of the change, we may nevertheless venture to refer the latter with a sufficient degree of probability to the class of natural varieties, or to consider them as examples of diversified appearance in the same individual species. Thus, if we find mice, rats, or crows, resembling in other respects the animals commonly known to us under those names, but having their hair or plumage perfectly white, and their eyes of a light-red colour, we need not hesitate in referring these peculiarities to variation from the primitive hue of their respective races, because we find a change exactly similar exhibited in many parts of the animal kingdom, concerning which we are well informed.'

The two most obvious sources of diversity, between different species of the same animal, are the colour and the form; and, as the author observes that, in the human race, variations of colour produce distinctions which are more permanent than those of figure, he enters first on the consideration of the former circumstance. He enumerates and describes seven varieties that depend on colour, beginning with the Albino, then coming to the ruddy, sanguine complexion, and passing through the different shades until he arrives at the Black of the negro. He traces the analogy between these several shades of colour, and those which occur in the inferior animals; and he concludes that, as in the latter case they are only *varieties*, and do not constitute *specific differences*, so no specific difference exists in the various colours of the human species. In order that this analogy may be complete, it is necessary to shew that the tendency to the transmission of colour, from the parent to the offspring, prevails in the same degree in the inferior animals and in the human species; and that in both cases the colour of the parent, when connate, however it be produced, is liable to become hereditary and permanent. The same remarks apply to the diversity of form; which has, in like manner, a strong tendency to become hereditary, although it is, on the whole, both less observable and less permanent than that of colour. Yet of the general fact we can have no doubt; and, as we every day observe in other animals that a diversity of form, which becomes permanent in a particular race, does not depend on any distinction of species, we extend the analogy to man.

After some observations on the variation of form in the human species, Dr. Prichard devotes his attention more particularly to that of the skull; and he gives an account of the different methods which have been proposed by physiologists, for classing the varieties that occur in this part, and reducing them to some systematic principles. The plan adopted by Camper, who estimated the form of the skull by the size of what he calls the facial angle, – the method of Cuvier, who compares the size of the vertical and longitudinal sections of the head, – and Blumenbach's remarks on the size and shape of the bones which compose the upper part of the face, – are detailed. The result of these observations is well known, that an obvious gradation prevails in the shape of the skull, from the European to the negro, bearing a ratio to the degree of intellect. These peculiarities of form are, like those of colour, liable to be transmitted by hereditary descent: but Dr. P. endeavours to shew that, in this as in the former instance, the diversities are not absolutely permanent, but sometimes appear promiscuously; so that, among Europeans, we occasionally observe a tendency to the form of the African head, and among the Africans a tendency to that of the European. The same degree of hereditary transmission, with a similar liability to exceptions, occurs in the form of the inferior animals; and, as these are admitted to constitute varieties only, so by analogy we conclude that the different races of men are not to be regarded as distinct species. The other distinctions between the several races of men are less striking and permanent than the colour of the skin, or the shape of the skull: such as the stature, the length of the limbs, the texture of the hair, &c. Dr. P. considers them in detail, and compares them with the analogous circumstances belonging to the brute-animals; concluding the investigation with these remarks:

'We have thus taken a sufficiently ample view of the principal examples of diversity in physical characters, which have been observed in the several races of mankind. Whatever other instances may be found are of inferior importance to those we have mentioned, and less in the degree of their deviation, and the conclusions which we form concerning the greater will hold *a fortiori* of others which are less. All the varieties to which we have adverted in the foregoing pages appear to be strictly analogous to the changes, which other tribes through almost the whole animal creation, have a general tendency to assume.

We are therefore compelled in obedience to the most firmly established laws of philosophical reasoning, to refer these similar phænomena to similar causes, and to consider all the physical diversities of mankind as depending on the principle of natural deviation, and as furnishing no specific distinction.

One accessory argument tending to the like conclusion, which has incidentally appeared in the course of our analogical reasoning, has been separately noticed. Those instances of variety which have been thought to lead most forcibly to the doctrine of distinct species in mankind, and to be the most insuperable difficulties on the contrary opinion, are the diversities of figure. But the varieties of form, are less permanent in mankind than those of colour, and there is none of them so general in any race of men, that it is not in many examples wanting.'

When we have gone through the first part of the inquiry, and rendered it probable that the *genus* of man consists but of one *species*, we may still suppose that the human race was not all the progeny of one original pair, but was produced primarily and separately in different regions. To solve this difficulty, Dr. Prichard has again recourse to the argument of analogy; and, taking the different kinds of mammiferous animals, as those that bear the nearest resemblance to the human species in their power of loco-motion, he proceeds to examine whether every existing species may not be traced with probability to a certain point, which appears, in the first instance, its only abode. He collects a number of facts in natural history, which seem to confirm this opinion; makes many ingenious strictures on those points that are seemingly adverse to the hypothesis; and, on the whole, may be considered as having rendered it at least very plausible. Buffon observes that the animals in the American continent are generally different from those of the old world; and that, where any species is common to both, it consists of those who are able to bear the extreme cold of the arctic regions, and might therefore have passed over from the eastern parts of Asia. Since the time of Buffon, this fact has been denied, but, as Dr. Prichard remarks, without foundation; he therefore again displays his knowledge of natural history, by separately examining the different classes of animals, and observing how far the facts at present ascertained respecting their situation support or controvert the doctrine of the single creation of each kind. The conclusions of Dr. P. are decidedly in favour of his hypothesis. It does not appear that any animal was originally common to the warm parts of the old and the new world; nor that any European species are aboriginal in America, which are inhabitants of the northern parts of each continent. It is farther stated that, with the exception of the dog, which seems to have accompanied the first settlers in almost all parts of the world, the whole stock of Australasian quadrupeds is peculiar, and strikingly different from those that exist in other countries. Although some difficulties remain respecting the manner in which remote islands receive their animal population, yet, for the most part, the facts render it probable that they were transplanted by accidental circumstances, and all originated from one common pair.

The same mode of reasoning, which has been used with respect to inferior animals, is now applied to man; and the author proceeds to inquire, how the more remote and insulated parts of the earth can be supposed to have been peopled from the original stock, in the earliest ages, before the art of navigation could afford them any mode of migration. The question is very curious and interesting, and can only be answered by conjectures: but, on the whole, we do not appear to have sufficient ground for deviating from the same mode of reasoning which we have applied to the inferior animals. The islands of the Pacific Ocean, which are situated at the greatest distance from the main land, and the most widely dispersed from each other, are all inhabited by tribes that seem to have sprung from the same common stock; and several remarkable circumstances would lead us to conclude, that the native Americans originally passed over to the new continent from the eastern parts of Asia.

Having thus endeavoured to shew that the human race must be considered as composing only one species, and derived from one common pair, our next subject of inquiry is to ascertain in what manner the varieties which we now observe were originally produced. The difference of complexion is first investigated; and the author discusses at length the opinion, whether the dark hue of the inhabitants of the torrid zone depends on the effect of the sun's rays. This idea he controverts with much ingenuity and research: adducing facts to prove that, when persons of a white complexion have migrated into warm climates, and their posterity have remained there for a number of successive generations, their colour never experiences any permanent change; and that any degree of brownness which is the consequence of exposure to the sun, or of hard labour, is not transmitted to the posterity. Other proofs of the same position are derived from the circumstances of particular tribes existing in very hot climates, who have never acquired the dark hue of their neighbours; and, on the contrary, of some colder districts that are inhabited by a race of dark complexioned men. If it should then appear that the effect of the sun's rays is not to produce a permanent darkness of the skin, and one that is transmitted to the offspring, and that there are no other external causes which seem in any degree likely to effect this change, we are led to search for internal causes, depending on some peculiar state of the constitution generally, or of the surface of the body in particular. On this point, it appears extremely difficult to arrive at a decisive conclusion: any thing that promotes the vigour of the body seems to have a tendency to darken the skin and the hair; while the effects of civilization and refinement have an opposite tendency. Civilization appears, indeed, to be the most permanent cause of a change in the complexion; and many facts are brought about to prove the influence of this agent in altering the tinge of the skin. The natives of the South-sea islands, who all appear to have sprung from the same common stock, but are now dispersed through a wide extent of surface, who are prevented from communicating with each other, and exist in very different states of refinement, seem to the author to afford all the data for determining this question. The fact is that the most savage tribes among them are quite black, with woolly hair; while the more civilized communities are nearly of the same complexion with Europeans, and have long hair, with the same anatomical structure. It is to be observed that these whiter nations live nearer the equator than many of the more black and savage islanders.

Dr. Prichard recapitulates the train of reasoning employed in this part of his work so judiciously that we shall gratify our readers by giving it in his own words:

'It will be proper to recapitulate in this place our inferences concerning the effects of climate and of civilization on the human species.

We endeavoured in the first instance to shew that there is no foundation for the common opinion which supposes the black races of men to have acquired their colour by exposure to the heat of a tropical climate during many ages. On the contrary the fact appears to be fully established, that white races of people migrating to a hot climate, do preserve their native complexion unchanged, and have so preserved it in all the examples of such migration which we know to have happened. And this fact is only an instance of the prevalence of the general law, which has ordained that the offspring shall always be constructed according to the natural and primitive constitution of the parents, and therefore shall inherit only their connate peculiarities and not any of their acquired qualities. It follows that we must direct our inquiry to the connate varieties, and to the causes which influence the parent to produce an offspring deviating in some particulars of its organization from the established character of the stock. What these causes are seems to be a question which must be determined by an extensive comparision of the phænomena of vegetable and animal propagation. It appears that in the vegetable world cultivation is the chief exciting cause of variation. In animals climate certainly lays the foundation of some varieties, but domestication or cultivation is the great principle which every where calls them forth in abundance. In the human species we endeavoured to ascertain what comparative effect these two principles may produce, and first to determine whether climate alone can furnish any considerable variation in tribes of men uncultivated or uncivilized. We compared the appearances of two great races of uncivilized people, each of which is scattered through a great portion of the world, and which taken collectively, constitute nearly all the savage tenants of the globe. It resulted from this comparison, that little effect is produced by the agency of climate alone on savage tribes. Varieties indeed appear more ready to spring up in moderate than in intensely hot climates, but they are not sufficient to produce any considerable change on the race. Civilization however has more extensive powers, and we have examples of the greatest variation in the human complexion produced by it, or at least which can scarcely be referred to any other cause, viz. the appearance of the sanguine constitution in a race generally black. Lastly, it appears that in races which are experiencing the effect of civilization, a temperate climate increases the tendency to the light varieties, and therefore may be the means of promoting and rendering the effect of that important principle more general and more conspicuous.'

The necessary consequence of the principles which have now been laid down is, that the primary inhabitants of the earth were black; and that the progress of nature has been the gradual transmutation from the negro to the European. Several analogical arguments, drawn from the inferior animals, are adduced in proof of this position, which at least tend to render it probable; and various considerations are also brought forwards to shew that the negro form and complexion are better adapted to his savage condition, while that of the European is more suited to the civilized state in which he is placed. Still, however, all these arguments must be considered as merely giving probability to an hypothesis, which must be established by a reference to facts and historical documents. The author, therefore, devotes the latter part of his volume to an investigation of the physical history of man; in which he collects all the historical data that bear on this question, and endeavours to shew how the different races of men are connected with each other, and thus to refer them to one common origin. We shall not attempt to follow him through this long detail; only remarking concerning it, that the general impression produced in our minds is favourable. It is interesting, comprehensive, and candid; and although, on such topics, much must be left to conjecture, and important conclusions are often built on slender foundations, yet Dr. P. seems to have employed the best arguments that the nature of the subject afforded him. His general conclusion from the historical is the same with that which he draws from the physical argument; viz. that all the different tribes of mankind may be traced to one common origin. Even those who should not agree with us in thinking that Dr. Prichard has made out a plausible case must, we apprehend, allow that he defends it with learning and ingenuity, and that he has produced a work of much amusement and information.

ON THE CAUSES OF THE VARIETIES
OF THE HUMAN SPECIES
William Lawrence

The London surgeon William Lawrence (1783–1867) is
generally known for his involvement in the dispute over the
existence of a 'vital principle' which agitated medical Britain
in the late 1810s. Lawrence professed his disbelief in the
existence of a vital force, instead referring life to the
mechanical functions of matter. He was therefore accused of
materialism. In 1807 he had published a translation of J. F.
Blumenbach's *A Short System of Comparative Anatomy*. In
this extract from his *Lectures on Physiology, Zoology, and the
Natural History of Man* (first published in 1819) the reasons
are delineated why "native differences . . . do not depend on
extraneous causes". Like Prichard, Lawrence believed in the
unity of mankind.

Having examined the principal points in which the several
tribes of the human species differ from each other; namely,
the colour and texture of the skin, hair, and iris, the features,
the skull and brain, the form and proportions of the body,
the stature, the animal economy, the moral and intellectual
powers, I proceed to enquire whether the diversities enumerated under these heads are to be considered as characteristic
distinctions coeval with the origin of the species, or as the
result of subsequent variation; and in the event of the latter
supposition being adopted, whether they are the effect of
external physical and moral causes, or of native or congenital
variety. The very numerous gradations which we meet with,
in each of the points above mentioned, are almost an
insuperable objection to the notion of *specific difference*; for
all of them may be equally referred to original distinction of
species; yet if we admit this, the number of species would be
overwhelming. On the other hand, the analogies drawn from
the animal kingdom, and adduced under each head, nearly
demonstrate that the characteristics of the various human
tribes must be referred, like the corresponding diversities in
other animals, to *variation*. Again, I have incidentally brought

forwards several arguments to prove that external agencies, whether physical or moral, will not account for the bodily and mental differences which characterize the several tribes of mankind; and that they must be accounted for by the breed or race[1]. This subject, however, requires further illustration.

The causes which operate on the bodies of living animals, either modify the individual, or alter the offspring. The former are of great importance in the history of animals, and produce considerable alterations in individuals; but the latter are the most powerful, as they affect the species, and cause the diversities of race. Great influence has at all times been ascribed to climate, which, indeed, has been commonly, but very loosely and indefinitely represented as the cause of most important modifications in the human subject and in other animals. Differences of colour, stature, hair, features, and those of moral and intellectual character, have been alike referred to the action of this mysterious cause; without any attempt to shew which of the circumstances in the numerous assemblage comprehended under the word 'climate' produces the effect in question, or any indication of the mode in which the point is accomplished. That the constitution of the atmosphere varies in respect to light and heat, moisture and electricity; and that these variations, with those of elevation, soil, winds, vegetable productions, will operate decidedly on individuals, I do not mean to deny. While, however, we have no precise information on the kind or degree of influence attributable to such causes, we have abundance of proof that they are entirely inadequate to account for the differences between the various races of men. I shall state one or two changes, which seem fairly referable to climate.

The whitening (blanching or etiolation) of vegetables, when the sun's rays are excluded, demonstrates the influence of those rays on vegetable colours. Nor is the effect merely superficial: it extends to the texture of the plant, to the taste and other properties of its juices. Men much exposed to the sun and air, as peasants and sailors, acquire a deeper tint of colour than those who are more covered; and the tanning of the skin by the summer sun, in parts of the body exposed to it, as the face and hands, is a phenomenon completely analogous. The ruddy and tawny hues of those who live in the country, particularly of

[1] See sect. ii. chap. ii. p. 277, and following; chap. iv. p. 357, and following; chap. vi. p. 406.

labourers in the open air, and the pale sallow countenances of the inhabitants of towns, of close and dark workshops and manufactories, owe their origin to the enjoyment or privation of sun and air. Hence, men of the same race are lighter or darker coloured according to the climate which they inhabit, at least in those parts which are uncovered. The native hue of the Moors is not darker than that of the Spaniards, of many French, and some English; but their acquired tint is so much deeper, that we distinguish them instantly. How swarthy do the Europeans become who seek their fortunes under the tropic and equator, and have their skins parched by the burning suns of "Afric and of either Ind!"

Mr. EDWARDS represents that the Creoles of the English West-Indian islands are taller than Europeans; several being six feet four inches high; and that their orbits are deeper[2].

It has been generally observed by travellers, that the European population of the United States of North America is tall, and characterized by a pale and sallow countenance. The latter effect is commonly produced in natives of Europe when they become resident in warm climates. That both sexes arrive earlier at puberty, and that the mental powers of children are sooner developed in warm than in cold countries, are facts familiarly known.

The prevalence of light colours in the animals of polar and cold regions may, perhaps, be ascribed to the influence of climate; the isatis or arctic fox, the polar bear, and the snow-bunting, are striking instances. The same character is also remarkable in some species, which are more dark-coloured in warmer situations. This opinion is strengthened by the analogy of those animals which change their colour in the same country, at the winter season, to white or gray, as the ermine (mustela erminea), and weasel (m. nivalis), the varying hare, squirrel, rein-deer, white game (tetrao lagopus), and snow-bunting (emberiza nivalis[3]). PALLAS observes "that even in domestic animals, as horses and cows, the winter coat is of a lighter colour than the smoother covering which succeeds it in the spring. The difference is much more considerable in wild animals. I have shewn instances of it in two kinds of antelope (saiga and gutturosa), in the musk animal (moschus

---

[2] *History of the West Indies*, v. ii. p. 11.

[3] LINNÆUS. *Flora Lapponica*; ed. of SMITH, pp. 35, 352.

moschifer), and in the equus hemionus. The Siberian roe, which is red in summer, becomes of a grayish white in winter; wolves and the deer kind, particularly the elk and the rein-deer, become light in the winter; the sable (m. zibellina), and the martin (m. martes), are browner in summer than in winter[4].

Although these phenomena seem obviously connected with the state of atmospherical temperature, and hence the change of colour, which the squirrel and the mustela nivalis undergo in Siberia and Russia, does not take place in Germany[5]; we do not understand the exact nature of the process by which it is effected; and cold certainly appears not to be the direct cause. For the varying hare, though kept in warm rooms during the winter, gets its white winter covering only a little later than usual[6]; and in all the animals, in which this kind of change takes place, the winter coat, which is more copious, close, and downy, as well as lighter coloured, is found already far advanced in the autumn, before the cold sets in[7].

The coverings of animals, as well as their colour, seem to be modified in many cases by climate; but, as the body is naked in the human subject, and as the hair of the head cannot be regarded in the same light as the fur, wool, or hair which covers the bodies of animals generally, the analogies offered by the latter are not very directly applicable to the present subject.

In cold regions the fur and feathers are thicker, and more copious, so as to form a much more effectual defence against the climate than the coarser and rarer textures which are seen in warm countries. The thick fleece of the dogs lately brought from Baffin's Bay exemplifies this observation very completely. The wool of the sheep degenerates into a coarse hair in Africa; where we meet also with dogs quite naked, with a smooth and soft skin.

Whether the goat, furnishing the wool from which the shawls of Cashmere are manufactured, is of the same species with that domesticated in Europe, and whether the prodigious difference between the hair growth of the two animals is due to

---

[4] *Novæ Species Quadrupedum*, p. 7.

[5] Ibid. p. 6, note *h*. The ermine changes its colour in the winter in Germany: but PALLAS states, on the faith of sufficient testimony, that it does not undergo this change in the more southern districts of Asia and Persia.

[6] *Novæ Species Quadrupedum*, p. 7.

[7] Ibid. p. 9.

diversity of climate, are points at present uncertain. Neither do
we know whether the long and silky coat of the goat, cat,
sheep, and rabbits of Angora can be accounted for by the
operation of this cause: it is at least worthy of notice, that this
quality of the hair should exist in so many animals of the same
country. It continues when they are removed into other
situations, and is transmitted to the offspring; so that we may,
probably, regard these as permanent breeds.

It is well known that the qualities of the horse are inferior in
France to those of neighbouring countries. According to
BUFFON, Spanish or Barbary horses, when the breed is not
crossed, become French horses sometimes in the second
generation, and always in the third[8]. Since the climate of
England, which certainly does not approach more nearly to
that of the original abode of this animal than that of France,
does not impede the developement of its finest forms and most
excellent qualities, we may, perhaps, with greater probability,
refer the degeneracy of the French horses to neglect of the
breed. We know that the greatest attention to this point is
necessary, in order to prevent deterioration in form and spirit.

Differences in food might be naturally expected to produce
considerable corresponding modifications in the animal body.
Singing birds, chiefly of the lark and finch kinds, are known to
become gradually black, if they are fed on hemp-seed only[9].
Horses fed on the fat marshy grounds of Friesland grow to a
large size; while, on stony soils of dry heaths, they remain
dwarfish. Oxen become very large and fat in rich soils, but are
distinguished by shortness of legs; while, in drier situations,
their whole bulk is less, and the limbs are stronger and more
fleshy. The quantity of food has great influence on the bulk and
state of health of the human subject; but the quality seems to
have less power; and neither produces any of those differences
which characterize races.

In all the changes which are produced in the bodies of
animals by the action of external causes, the effect terminates
in the individual; the offspring is not in the slightest degree
modified by them[10], but is born with the original properties and

---

8   V. iv. p. 106.

9   *Der Naturforscher*, pt. 1. p. 1. pt. 9. p. 22.

10 When the fœtus in utero has small-pox or syphilis, there is actual
    communication of disease by the fluids of the mother. This is a case
    altogether different from those under consideration. Neither does heredi-

constitution of the parents, and a susceptibility only of the same changes when exposed to the same causes.

The change in colour of the human skin, from exposure to sun and air, is obviously temporary; for it is diminished and even removed, when the causes no longer act. The discolouration, which we term tanning, or being sun-burnt, as well as the spots called freckles, are most incidental to fair skins, and disappear when the parts are covered, or no longer exposed to the sun. The children of the husbandman, or of the sailor whose countenance bears the marks of other climes, are just as fair as those of the most delicate and pale inhabitant of a city: nay, the Moors, who have lived for ages under a burning sun, still have white children; and the offspring of Europeans in the Indies have the original tint of their progenitors.

BLUMENBACH has been led into a mistake on this point by an English author[11], who asserts that Creoles are born with a different complexion and cast of countenance from the children of the same parents brought forth in Europe. In opposition to this statement, from one who had not seen the facts, I place the authority of LONG, a most respectable eye-witness, who, in his *History of Jamaica*, affirms that "the children born in England have not, in general lovelier or more transparent skins than the offspring of white parents in Jamaica." The "austrum spirans vultus et color," which the above mentioned acute and learned naturalist ascribes to the Creole, is merely the acquired effect of the climate, and not a character existing at birth.

"Nothing," says Dr. Prichard[12], "seems to hold true more generally, than that all acquired conditions of body, whether produced by art or accident, end with the life of the individual in whom they are produced. Many nations mould their bodies into unnatural forms; the Indians flatten their foreheads; the Chinese women reduce their feet to one third of their natural dimensions; savages elongate their ears; many races cut away the prepuce. We frequently mutilate our domestic animals by removing the tail or ears, and our own species are often obliged

tary predisposition to particular diseases prove that acquired conditions are transmitted to the offspring. There are natural varieties of organization, disposing different individuals to different diseases on application of the same external causes. These natural varieties, like those of form, and colour, and other obvious properties, are continued to the children.

11   HAWKESWORTH, in *Collection of Voyages*, v. iii. p. 374.

12   *Disp. inaug.*

by disease to submit to the loss of limbs. That no deformity, or mutilation of this kind is hereditary, is so plainly proved by every thing around us, that we must feel some surprise at the contrary opinion having gained any advocates. After the operation of circumcision has prevailed for three or four thousand years, the Jews are still born with prepuces, and still obliged to submit to a painful rite. Docked horses and cropped dogs bring forth young with entire ears and tails. But for this salutary law, what a frightful spectacle would every race of animals exhibit! The mischances of all preceding times would overwhelm us with their united weight, and the catalogue would be continually increasing, until the universe, instead of displaying a spectacle of beauty and pleasure, would be filled with maimed, imperfect, and monstrous shapes."

It is obvious that the external influences just considered, even though we should allow to them a much greater influence on individuals than experience warrants us in admitting, would be still entirely inadequate to account for those signal diversities, which constitute differences of race in animals. These can be explained only by two principles already mentioned[13]; namely, the occasional production of an offspring with different characters from those of the parents, as a native or congenital variety; and the propagation of such varieties by generation. It is impossible, in the present state of physiological knowledge, to shew how this is effected; to explain why a gray rabbit or cat sometimes brings forth at one birth, and from one father, yellow, black, white, and spotted young; why a white sheep sometimes has a black lamb; or why the same parents at different times have leucæthiopic children, and others with the ordinary formation and characters.

The state of domestication, or the artificial mode of life, which they lead under the influence of man, is the most powerful cause of varieties in the animal kingdom. Wild animals, using always the same kind of food, being exposed to the action of the climate without artificial protection, choose, each of them, according to its nature, their zone and country. Instead of migrating and extending, like man, they continue in those places which are the most friendly to their constitutions. Hence, their nature undergoes no change; their figure, colour, size, proportions, and properties, are unaltered;

13   See pp. 357 and following, 382 and following.

and, consequently, there is no difficulty in determining their species. Nothing can form a stronger contrast to this uniformity of specific character than the numerous and marked varieties in those kinds which have been reduced by man. To trace back our domestic animals to their wild originals is in all cases difficult, in some impossible; long slavery has so degraded their nature, that the primitive animal may be said to be lost, and a degenerated being, running into endless varieties, is substituted in its place. The wild original of the sheep, is even yet uncertain. BUFFON conceived that he discovered it in the mouflon or argali (ovis ammon): and PALLAS, who had an opportunity of studying the latter animal, adds the weight of his highly respectable authority to the opinion of the French naturalist. Yet BLUMENBACH regards the argali as a distinct species. Should we allow the latter to be the parent of our sheep, and consequently admit that the differences are explicable by degeneration, no difficulty can any longer exist about the unity of the human species. An incomplete horn of the argali, in the Academical Museum at Göttingen, weighs nine pounds[14].

"Let us compare," says BUFFON, "our pitiful sheep with the mouflon, from which they derived their origin. The mouflon is a large animal. He is fleet as a stag, armed with horns and thick hoofs, covered with coarse hair, and dreads neither the inclemency of the sky nor the voracity of the wolf. He not only escapes from his enemies by the swiftness of his course, and scaling, with truly wonderful leaps, the most frightful precipices; but he resists them by the strength of his body and the solidity of the arms with which his head and feet are fortified. How different from our sheep, who subsist with difficulty in flocks, who are unable to defend themselves by their numbers, who cannot endure the cold of our winters without shelter, and who would all perish if man withdrew his protection! So completely are the frame and capabilities of this animal degraded by his association with us, that it is no longer able to subsist in a wild state, if turned loose, as the goat, pig, and cattle are. In the warm climates of Asia and Africa, the mouflon, who is the common parent of all the races of this species, appears to be less degenerated than in any other region. Though reduced to a domestic state, he has preserved

[14] BLUMENBACH, *Handbuch der Naturgeschichte*, p. 111, note.

his stature and his hair; but the size of his horns is diminished. Of all domestic sheep, those of Senegal and India are the largest, and their nature has suffered least degradation. The sheep of Barbary, Egypt, Arabia, Persia, Tartary, &c. have undergone greater changes. In relation to man, they are improved in some articles, and vitiated in others; but with regard to nature, improvement, and degeneration, are the same thing; for they both imply an alteration of original constitution. Their coarse hair is changed into fine wool. Their tail, loaded with a mass of fat, and sometimes reaching the weight of forty pounds, has acquired a magnitude so incommodious, that the animals trail it with pain. While swollen with superfluous matter, and adorned with a beautiful fleece, their strength, agility, magnitude, and arms are diminished. These long-tailed sheep are half the size only of the mouflon. They can neither fly from danger, nor resist the enemy. To preserve and multiply the species, they require the constant care and support of man. The degeneration of the original species is still greater in our climates. Of all the qualities of the mouflon, our ewes and rams have retained nothing but a small portion of vivacity, which yields to the crook of the shepherd. Timidity, weakness, resignation, and stupidity, are the only melancholy remains of their degraded nature[15]."

The pig-kind afford an instructive example, because their descent is more clearly made out than that of many other animals. The dog, indeed, degenerates before our eyes; but it will hardly ever, perhaps, be satisfactorily ascertained whether there is one or more species. The extent of degeneration can be observed in the domestic swine; because no naturalist has hitherto been sceptical enough to doubt whether they descended from the wild boar; and they were certainly first introduced by the Spaniards into the new world. The pigs conveyed in 1509, from Spain to the West Indian island Cubagua, then celebrated for the pearl fishery, degenerated into a monstrous race with toes half a span long[16]. Those of Cuba became more than twice as large as their European progenitors[17]. How remarkably again have the domestic swine degenerated from the wild ones in the Old World: in the loss of

15   BUFFON, by WOOD; v. iv. p.7.

16   HERRERA, *Hechos de los Castellanos en las Islas*, &c. v. i. p. 239.

17   CLAVIGERO, *Storia antica del Messico*, v. iv. p. 145.

the soft downy hair from between the bristles; in the vast accumulation of fat under the skin, in the form of the cranium; in the figure and growth of the whole body. The varieties of the domestic animal too are very numerous: in Piedmont they are almost invariably black; in Bavaria reddish-brown; in Normandy white, &c. The breed in England, with straight back and large pendulous belly, is just the reverse of that in the north of France, with high convex spine and hanging head: and both are different from the German breed; to say nothing of the solidungular race found in herds in Hungary and Sweden, and already known by ARISTOTLE, and many other varieties.

The ass, in its wild state, is remarkably swift and lively, and still continues so in his native Eastern abode.

The original stock of our poultry cannot be determined, nor can the varieties into which they have run be enumerated. No wild bird in our climates resembles the domestic cock; the pheasant, grous, and cock of the woods, are the only analogous kinds: and it is uncertain whether these would intermix and have prolific progeny. They have constituted distinct and separate species from the earliest times, and they want the combs, spurs, and pendulous membranes of the gallinaceous tribes[18].

There are twenty-nine varieties of canary-birds known by name, all produced from the gray bird[19].

Most of the mammalia, which have been tamed by man, betray their subjugated state by having the ears and tail pendulous; a condition of the former parts, which, I believe, belongs to no wild animal. In many, the very functions of the body, as the secretions, generation, &c. are greatly changed. See the examples mentioned in chap. VI. p. 382.

The application of these facts to the question concerning the human species is very obvious. If new characters are produced in the domesticated animals, because they have been taken from their primitive condition, and exposed to the operation of many, to them, unnatural causes; if the pig is remarkable among these for the number and degree of its varieties, because it has been the most exposed to causes of degeneration; we shall be at no loss to account for the diversities in man, who is, in the true, though not ordinary sense of the word, more of a

---

[18]   BUFFON, v. xii. p. 112.

[19]   Ibid. v. xiv. p. 61.

domesticated animal than any other. We know the wild state of most of them, but we are ignorant of the natural wild condition to which man was destined. Probably there is no such state, because nature, having limited him in no respect, having fitted him for every kind of life, every climate, and every variety of food, has given him the whole earth for his abode, and both the organized kingdoms for his nourishment. Yet, in the wide range through which the scale of human cultivation extends, we may observe a contrast between the two extremities, analogous to that which is seen in the wild and tamed races of animals. The savage may be compared to the former, which range the earth uncontrolled by man; civilized people to the domesticated breeds of the same species, whose diversities of form and colour are endless. Whether we consider the several nations, or the individuals of each, bodily differences are much more numerous in the highly civilized Caucasian variety, than in either of the other divisions of mankind.

Such, then, are the causes by which the varieties of man may be accounted for. Although I have acknowledged my entire ignorance of the manner in which these operate, I have proved that they exist, and have shewn by copious analogies, that they are sufficient to explain the phenomena. The tendency, under certain circumstances, to alterations of the original colour, form, and other properties of the body, and the laws of transmission to the offspring, are the sources of varieties in man and animals, and thereby modify the species; climate, food, way of life; in a word, all the physical and moral causes that surround us, act indeed powerfully on the individual, but do not change the offspring, except in the indirect manner just alluded to. We should, therefore, openly violate the rules of philosophizing, which direct us to assign the same causes for natural effects of the same kind, and not to admit more causes than are sufficient for explaining the phenomena, if we recurred, for the purpose of explaining the varieties of man, to the perfectly gratuitous assumption of originally different species, or called to our aid the operation of climate, and other external influences.

Yet, if it be allowed that all men are of the same species, it does not follow that they all descended from the same family. We have no data for determining this point: it could indeed only be settled by a knowledge of facts, which have been long ago involved in the impenetrable darkness of antiquity.

By the most intelligent and learned writers on the varieties of mankind, their production has been explained in a different manner from that which has been just attempted; they have solved the problem entirely by the operation of adventitious causes, such as climate, particularly the light and heat of the sun, food, and mode of life. These, it is said, acting on men originally alike, produce various bodily diversities, and affect the colour of the skin especially; such alterations, transmitted to the offspring, and gradually increased through a long course of ages, are supposed to account sufficiently for all the differences observed at present in the inhabitants of the different regions of the globe. If we were disposed to submit, in this question, to authority, the number and celebrity of the philosophers[20] who have contended for the influence of climate, and other physical and moral causes, would certainly compel our assent to their opinions. Our respect for their talents and labour will be sufficiently marked if we enter into a closer examination of the arguments which they have adduced on this subject.

That solar heat causes blackness of the skin is an ancient opinion, and must have appeared very probable, when the Negro natives of the torrid zone were the only black people known. "Æthiopas," says PLINY, "vicini sideris vapore torreri, adustisque similes gigni, barba et capillo vibrato, non est dubium[21]."

"The heat of the climate," says BUFFON, " is the chief cause of blackness among the human species. When this heat is excessive, as in Senegal and Guinea, the men are perfectly black; when it is a little less violent, the blackness is not so deep; when it becomes somewhat temperate, as in Barbary, Mongolia, Arabia, &c. mankind are only brown; and lastly, when it is altogether temperate, as in Europe and Asia, men are white. Some varieties, indeed, are produced by the mode of living. All the Tatars (Mongols), for example, are tawny; while the Europeans, who live under the same latitude, are white.

---

20   Among them are BUFFON, BLUMENBACH, SMITH (*Essay on the Causes of the Variety of Complexion and Figure in the human Species*, Philadelphia), ZIMMERMANN (*Geographische Geschichte des Menschen*, &c.); and FORSTER (*Observations made during a Voyage round the World*; chap. vi. sec. 3). The arguments of these writers are very ably combated by Dr. PRICHARD in his *Researches into the physical History of Man.*

21   *Hist. Nat.* lib. ii. 80.

This difference may safely be ascribed to the Tatars being always exposed to the air, to their having no cities or fixed habitations, to their sleeping constantly on the ground, and to their rough and savage manner of living. These circumstances are sufficient to render the Tatars more swarthy than the Europeans, who want nothing to make life easy and comfortable. Why are the Chinese fairer than the Tatars, though they resemble them in every feature? Because they are more polished; because they live in towns, and practise ever to guard themselves against the injuries of the weather; while the Tatars are perpetually exposed to the action of the sun and air.

Climate may be regarded as the chief cause of the different colours of men; but food, though it has less influence than colour, greatly affects the form of our bodies. Coarse, unwholesome, and ill-prepared food, makes the human species degenerate. All those people, who live miserably, are ugly and ill-made. Even in France, the country people are not so beautiful as those who live in towns: and I have often remarked, that in those villages, where the people are richer and better fed than in others, the men are likewise more handsome, and have better countenances. The air and the soil have great influence on the figures of men, beasts, and plants.

Upon the whole, every circumstance concurs in proving that mankind are not composed of species essentially different from each other; that, on the contrary, there was originally but one species, which, after multiplying and spreading over the whole surface of the earth, has undergone various changes by the influence of climate, food, mode of living, epidemic diseases, and mixture of dissimilar individuals; that, at first, these changes were not so conspicuous, and produced only individual varieties; that these varieties became afterwards more specific, because they were rendered more general, more strongly marked, and more permanent, by the continual action of the same causes; that they are transmitted from generation to generation, as deformities or diseases pass from parents to children; and that, lastly, as they were originally produced by a train of external and accidental causes, and have only been perpetuated by time, and the constant operation of these causes, it is probable that they will gradually disappear, or, at least, that they will differ from what they are at present, if the causes which produced them should cease, or if their operation should be varied by other circumstances and combinations[22]."

"In tracing the globe," says SMITH, "from the pole to the equator, we observe a gradation in the complexion, nearly in proportion to the latitude of the country. Immediately below the arctic circle, a high sanguine colour prevails: from this you descend to the mixture of red and white: afterwards succeed the brown, the olive, the tawny, and at length the black, as you proceed to the line. The same distance from the sun, however, does not, in every region, indicate the same temperature of climate. Some secondary causes must be taken into consideration, as correcting and limiting its influence. The elevation of the land, its vicinity to the sea, the nature of the soil, the state of cultivation, the course of winds, and many other circumstances, enter into this view. Elevated and mountainous countries are cool, in proportion to their altitude above the level of the sea[23]," &c. &c.

BLUMENBACH informs us how climate operates in modifying the colour of the skin, but does not attempt to explain its effects on the stature, proportions, and other points. He states that the proximate cause of the dark colour of the integuments is an abundance of carbone, secreted by the skin with hydrogen, precipitated and fixed in the rete mucosum by the contact of the atmospheric oxygen[24]. He observes further, that this abundance of carbone is most distinctly noticeable in persons of an atrabilarious temperament; which fact, together with many others, proves intimate connexion between the biliary and the cutaneous organs; that hot climates exert a very signal influence on the liver; and thus, that an unnatural state of the biliary secretion, produced by heat, and increased through many generations, causes the vessels of the skin to secrete that abundance of carbone, which produces the black colour of the Negro[25].

If any one can believe that the Negroes and other dark people, whom we see in full health and vigour, and with every organic perfection, labour under a kind of habitual jaundice, he may think it worth while to inquire further into this assumed

[22]   *Natural History*, by WOOD, vol. iii. pp. 443, 446.

[23]   *Essay*, pp. 8, 10.

[24]   Ibid. pp. 126, 137.

[25]   *De gen. hum. var. nat.* p. 124

secretion and precipitation of carbone. It will then be necessary to explain how this jaundice is produced in the numerous dark races which dwell in temperate climates; and why it does not occur in the white people who occupy hot countries.

It cannot be supposed that men of undoubted talents and learning would take up these opinions without any foundation at all; and accordingly we find that there is a slender mixture of truth in these statements; but it is so enveloped in a thick cloud of error, and so concealed by misrepresentation and exaggeration, that we do not recognize it without difficulty. The colour of Europeans nearly follows the geographical positions of countries: this part of the world is occupied almost entirely by a white race, of which the individuals are fairer in cold latitudes, and more swarthy or sunburnt in warm ones: thus, the French may be darker than the English, the Spaniards than the French, and the Moors than the Spaniards. In the same way, where different parts of a country differ much in latitude and in temperature, the inhabitants may be browner in the south than the north: thus, the women of Granada are said to be more swarthy than those of Biscay, and the southern than the northern Chinese, &c. For a similar reason the same race may vary slightly in colour in different countries. The Jews, for example, are fair in Britain and Germany, browner in France and Turkey, swarthy in Portugal and Spain, olive in Syria and Chaldea. An English sailor, who had been for some years in Nukahiwah, one of the Marquesas islands, had been so changed in colour, that he was scarcely to be distinguished from the natives[26].

These diversities are produced by the climate, as I have already explained. The effect goes off if the cause be removed: it terminates in the individual, and is never transmitted to the offspring, as I shall prove most introvertibly presently.

Moreover, the effect is confined to the parts of the body actually exposed to the sun and air. Those which remain covered retain all their natural whiteness. Mr. ABEL found this strikingly exemplified in his Chinese journey. "The dark copper-colour of those who were naked, contrasted so strongly with the paleness of those who were clothed, that it was difficult to conceive such different hues could be the consequence of greater or less exposure to the same degree of solar

[26] LANGSDORFF's *Voyages*, &c. v. i. p. 90.

and atmospheric influence: but all conjecture on this subject was set at rest by repeated illustrations of their effects. Several individuals, who were naked only from their waist upwards, stripped themselves entirely for the purpose of going into the water, to obtain a nearer view of the embassy. When thus exposed, they appeared at a distance to have on a pair of light-coloured pantaloons[27]."

On a superficial view, again, we observe that temperate Europe is occupied by a white race, and that the blacks, of whom we see and hear most, dwell chiefly under the burning suns and on the parched sands of Africa and Asia; the numerous whites who live in hot, and the greater number of dark-coloured people who are found in cold countries, are not taken into the account in these imperfect and partial comparisons.

I proceed to shew that climate does not cause the diversities of mankind; and in this consideration, my remarks are chiefly directed to the colour of the skin, as that is the part in which its operation has been regarded, by all the defenders of its influence, as the most unequivocal; the reasoning, however, will apply in general to the other points of difference, as well as to this.

The uniform colour of all parts of the body is a strong argument against those who ascribe the blackness of the Negro to the same cause as that which produces tanning in white people, namely, the sun's rays. The glans penis, the cavity of the axilla, the inside of the thigh, are just as black as any other parts; indeed, the organs of generation, which are always covered, are amongst the blackest parts of the body. Neither is the peculiar colour of the Negro confined to the skin; a small circle of the conjunctiva, round the cornea, is blackish, and the rest of the membrane has a yellowish-brown tinge. The fat has a deep yellow colour, like beeswax, at least in many of them, which may be distinguished by a very superficial inspection, from that of an European. The representation that the brain of the Negro is darker coloured than that of the white races, is not correct.

The developement of the black colour in the individual does not accord with the notion of its being produced by external causes. "Negro children," says Dr. WINTERBOTTOM, "are

[27] *Narrative of a Journey*, &c. p. 78

nearly as fair as Europeans at birth, and do not acquire their colour until several days have elapsed. The eyes of the new-born Negro children are also of a light colour, and preserve somewhat of a bluish tinge for several days after birth[28]."

CAMPER had an opportunity of observing the change in a Negro child born at Amsterdam. It was at first reddish, nearly like European children: "on the third day, the organs of generation, the folds of skin round the nails, and the areolæ of the breasts, were quite black: the blackness extended over the whole body on the fifth and sixth days; and the boy, who was born in a close chamber in the winter, and well wrapped up, according to the custom of the country, in swaddling-clothes, acquired the native colour of his race over the whole body, excepting the palms and soles, which are always paler, and almost white, in working Negroes[29]."

On the other hand, a black state of the skin is sometimes partially produced in individuals of the white races. In the fairest of women, towards the end of pregnancy, spots of more or less deep black colour have been often observed; they gradually disappear after parturition. "The dark colour of the skin," says WHITE, "in some particular parts of the body, is not confined to either the torrid or frigid zones: for in England the nipple, the areola round the nipple, the pudenda, and the verge of the anus, are of a dark brown, and sometimes as black as in the Samoiede women. It is to be remarked, that the colour of these parts grows darker in women at the full period of gestation. One morning, I examined the breasts of twenty women in the Lying-in hospital in Manchester, and found that nineteen of them had dark-coloured nipples; some of them might be said to be black; and the areola round the nipple, from one inch or two inches and a half in diameter, was of the same colour[30]." LE CAT mentions a woman near Paris, in whom the abdomen became black at each pregnancy, and afterwards recovered its colour; in another the same change occured in the leg[31].

CAMPER dissected at Groningen, a young woman who died in child-bed: her abdomen, and the areolæ round the nipples,

28   *Account of the Native Africans*, v. i. st. 1. p. 189.

29   *Kleinere Schriften*, b. i. st. 1. p. 44.

30   *On the Regular Gradation*, p. 114.

31   *Traité de la Couleur de la Peau Humaine*.

were of a deep black: the face, arms, and legs, were of a snowy whiteness[32].

The species of domestic fowls in the East Indies, with black periosteum, affords a further proof that the operation of the sun's rays is not a necessary circumstance to the production of colour in animal bodies.

If we take the trouble of examining the races in any particular division of the world, we shall quickly find that the opinion which ascribes their distinguishing characters to climate, must be given up; that the same race inhabits the most different regions, preserving in all an uniformity of character; that different races are found in the same countries; and that those, who have changed their native abodes for situations, in which, according to the hypothesis, they ought to have undergone a complete metamorphosis, still retain their original distinctions.

In the north of Europe, as also in the north of Asia and America, that is, in countries nearest to the pole, in which, according to the opinions above stated, the whitest races ought to be found, we have very brown and black people: they are much darker coloured than any other Europeans. The Moors in Africa, and the Arabs of the desert, are born with a white skin, and continue fair unless adventitious causes are applied. But the Laplanders and Greenlanders, the Eskimaux, Samoiedes, Ostiacs, Tschutski, &c., who hardly ever feel a moderate heat from the rays of the sun, are very dark. They appear to be all of the same race, who have extended and multiplied along the coasts of the North Sea, in deserts, and under climates which could not be inhabited by other nations. They have broad large faces and flat noses, the olive or swarthy colour, and all the other characters of the Mongolian variety.

It is curious to observe how easily the assertors of the power of climate in changing the human body get over an instance so fatal to their opinions: they tell us roundly, that great cold has the same effect as great heat: "when the cold becomes extreme, it produces effects similar to those of violent heat. The Samoiedes, the Laplanders, and natives of Greenland, are very tawny; we are even assured that some of the Greenlanders are as black as the Africans; thus the two extremities approach each other: great cold and great heat produce the same effect

---

[32] *Kleinere Schriften*, v. i. st. 1. p. 47.

upon the skin, because each of these causes acts by a quality common to both; and this quality is the dryness of the air, which, perhaps, is equally great in extreme cold and extreme heat. Both cold and heat dry the skin, and give it that tawny hue which we find among the Laplanders. Cold contracts all the productions of nature. The Laplanders, accordingly, who are perpetually exposed to all the rigours of frost, are the smallest of the human species[33]."

If this reasoning should not convince us, there are other arguments in reserve. The state of society is said to have great effect on the conformation and colour of the body. The nakedness of the savage, the filthy grease and paint with which he smears his body, his smoky hut, scanty diet, want of cleanliness, and the undrained and uncleared, country which he inhabits, not only, according to SMITH, darken his skin, but render it impossible that it ever should be fair[34]. On the other hand, the conveniences of clothing and lodging; the plenty and healthful quality of food; a country drained, cultivated, and freed from noxious effluvia, improved ideas of beauty, the constant study of elegance, and the infinite arts for attaining it, even in personal figure and appearance, give cultivated an immense advantage over savage society, in its attempt to counteract the influence of climate, and to beautify the human form[35]. What false notions must mankind have hitherto entertained on this subject! We can no longer believe travellers, who tell us that the finest forms and the greatest activity are to be seen in savage tribes, and that no ill-formed individuals can be met with amongst them, and as little can we trust the testimony of our own senses, concerning the frequency of deformity and disease in civilized society; since there are so many reasons why the former should be deformed, black, and ugly, and the latter well-proportioned, fair, and handsome. Unluckily, however, this theory does not correspond with a few plain facts. Most of the modern European nations existed in a more or less complete state of barbarism within times of which we have the most authentic records: some of these were seen and described by philosophers; yet the permanence of their characters is so remarkable after a greater progressive

---

[33] *Essay*, &c. p. 48–52.

[34] BUFFON, v. 3. p. 443. See also SMITH's *Essay*.

[35] SMITH's *Essay*, p. 53.

civilization than has happened in any other instance, that those descriptions are applicable, with the greatest exactness, to the same races of the present day. Instead, therefore, of accounting for the dark colour, peculiar features, and stature of the Greenlander, Laplander, and Samoiede, from their smoke, their dirt, their food, or the coldness of the climate, we can have no hesitation in ascribing them to the same cause that makes the Briton and the German of this day resemble the portraits of their ancestors, drawn by Cæsar and Tacitus, viz. their descent from a race marked by the same characters as distinguish themselves. These tribes owe their origin to the Mongols, and retain in the north those marks of their descent, which we find as strongly expressed in the Chinese, under the widely-different latitudes of the south. At the same time, the parent tribes live in the middle of Asia, equally removed from the former and the latter.

"With slight exceptions," says Dr. PRICHARD, "the different countries of Europe are now occupied by the same nations that have occupied them since the date of our earliest authentic accounts. Conquests have been made by small numbers, so that the races have been little changed by this cause. Then, when CLOVIS and his 30,000 Franks reduced the large and populous province of Gaul under their dominion, the bodily characters and the language of the conquerors were lost in those of the conquered. The nations which have inhabited Europe for the last 2500 years, consist of three great races, distinguished from each other by their bodily formation, character, and language.

"1. The Celtic race, with black hair and eyes, and a white skin verging to brown, occupies the west of Europe: to this belongs the ancient and modern inhabitants of France, Spain, Portugal, and the greatest part of Italy; the ancient Britons, Welsh, Bretons, Irish, Scotch, and Manks. The resemblance of the Silures to the Iberi was noticed by TACITUS; it is obvious to every observer in the present time; nor is the observation peculiar to the Welsh; it holds good of all other Celtic nations. Silurum colorati vultus, et torti plerumque crines, et posita contra Hispania, Iberos veteres trajecisse, easque sedes occupasse, fidum faciunt. That black hair and a browner complexion belonged to all the Celts is not only proved by many direct observations, but also because the marks of the sanguine constitution were universally considered as the distinction of the German race.

2. The great German race, characterized by its blue eyes, yellow or reddish hair, fair and red skin, occupies the middle of Europe, and includes the Swedes, Norwegians, Icelanders, Danes, ancient and modern Germans, Saxons and English, Caledonians or Pictæ, and the Lowland Scotch, who have sprung from them; the inhabitants of the Low Countries, the Vandals and Goths, &c. Historical records, and the similarity of language and character, both of body and mind, prove that all these people belong to the same race.

3. The east of Europe contains the Sarmatian and Slavonic tribes, characterized by dark hair and eyes, and a darker skin than the German, with perhaps larger limbs than the Celts. To this division belong the Russians, Poles, Croats, Slavons, Bohemians, Bulgarians, Cossacks and others who speak the Slavonic language[36]." He proceeds to shew from DIODORUS SICULUS, that the Sarmatians descended from the Medes, and were found on the banks of the Tanais, 700 years before the Christian era: by the authority of HERODOTUS, that they occupied the country between the Tanais and the Borysthenes, when DARIUS HYSTASPES invaded Syria; and from CLU-VERIUS, that the coasts of the Baltic, and the banks of the Vistula, Prussia, and the country as far as the situation of the Finni and Venedi, were the ancient seats of the Sarmatians. Since then, a people of very different race have existed in the neighbourhood of the Germans from the most remote times; how can we explain the differences of the European nations, by the operation of climate, by heat and cold? How does the same sky cause the whiteness of the German and Swede, and the comparatively dark complexion of the Pole and Russian?

But these European races are found also in Asia and Africa. All that part of the former region, which lies to the west of the river Ob, the Caspian Sea, and the Ganges; all the north of Africa, Abyssinia, and perhaps other parts still farther south, on the east, are occupied by a race agreeing nearly in character with the Sarmatians and Celts.

Thus it appears, that, excepting the Germans, and the Laplanders and Samoiedes, whom we deem of Mongolian origin, the same native or congenital constitution prevails over the whole of Europe, the western parts of Asia, and the north of Africa. Black hair, dark eyes, and a white skin, tending

36   *Diss. Inaug. de Variet.* p. 102–109.

rather to a browning tint than to the peculiar whiteness of the German tribes, belong to the French, Spaniards, Portuguese, Italians, and all the Celts; to the Russians, Poles, and others of Slavonic origin; to the Tatars, commonly confounded with the Mongols, the Armenians, Persians, Circassians, and Georgians, the Turks, Greeks, Arabians, Abyssinians, Syrians, Jews, and the inhabitants of Tripoli, Tunis, Algiers, and Morocco. That climate cannot cause similarity of character in nations spread over fifty degrees of latitude, and that food, dress, state of civilization, peculiar customs, or other moral causes, are equally inefficacious in accounting for the phenomenon, when we consider how various in all these points the nations are in whom it occurs, will be allowed by every unprejudiced observer.

The middle and northern parts of Asia, and most of its eastern portion, are occupied by tribes and nations, all of which possess the general characters of the Mongolian variety, although distinguished from each other by such modifications as usually characterize separate people. They are distinct in their conformation from all other races, and differ from Europeans quite as decidedly as the Negroes. History points out as their original seat, the elevated central table-land of Asia, from which they have spread in various directions, according to circumstances, every where preserving their peculiar traits of organization. The Mongols, Calmucks, and Burats are three great divisions, of which each includes many tribes, scattered over the middle of Asia, leading generally a pastoral life, sometimes practising agriculture, and devoted universally to the idolatrous lama worship. Their first distinct appearance in history is under the name of Huns (Hiong-nu of the Chinese), in the first century of the Christian era, when they were impelled towards the west by the progress of the Chinese power. Afterwards, three great conquerors appeared among them at distant periods, – the most conspicuous that the world has ever seen, who made all Asia and Europe tremble, but, happily, appeared and vanished like meteors; because, though powerful in conquest and desolation, they knew not how to possess and govern. ATTILA with his Huns, penetrated into the centre of Europe. Eight centuries later, ZINGIS or DSCHINGIS KHAN united not only the Mongolian but the Tataric tribes, and with this formidable mass reduced nearly all Asia. In two hundred years more, TIMURLENG or TAMERLANE appeared, and rendered himself the terror of western Asia and India, which latter country has been ruled by his descendants until very modern times. The Mantchoos or Mandshurs, the Daourians, Tungooses, Coreans, Kamschatkans, and perhaps other tribes, on the east; the Yakuts, Samoiedes, Kirgises, on the west; the people of Thibet and Bootan on the south; have a similar organization to that of the central tribes. The empires of China and Japan, the islands of Sagalien, Lewchew, and Formosa, are peopled by races of analogous physical and moral characters. Short stature, olive-coloured skin, deviating into lighter yellow; coarse, straight, and perfectly black hair; broad flat face, high and broad cheek-bones, flat nose, oblique eyes, entire deficiency or smallness of beard, are the common traits of the numerous people spread over this immense portion of the globe. Besides this general agreement of the tribes occupying countries so distinct and different from each other, it is important to observe that the Samoiedes, Kamschatkans, and others in the colder northern parts, are darker-coloured than the Chinese, Tunquinese, and Cochin-Chinese, in the warm southern regions.

"India," says Dr. PRICHARD, "is inhabited by a mixed race, made up of the aborigines, and of others, whom the pursuits of war and conquest have at various times brought there. The religion of BRAMAH seems to have been introduced from the north; and at later periods vast numbers of the Mongols have entered and conquered the country. These mixtures have effaced the peculiar characters of the original inhabitants; which we must, therefore, seek for in the islands protected by their situation from such visits. The islands of the Indian sea, as well as those of the Pacific, contain two races of men, differing in many respects. One of these approaches, and in some instances equals, the blackness of the Negro: the hair is curled and woolly, the body slender, the stature short, the disposition barbarous and cruel. The other is more like the Indians of the continent, has a fairer skin, larger limbs and stature, better proportions, and exhibits some marks of humanity and civilization. According to FORSTER, the former, who are aborigines, have occupied the middle and mountainous parts of many islands, leaving the coasts and plains to the more recent colonists. They occupy the highest parts of the Moluccas, the Philippines, Formosa, and Borneo; all New Guinea, New Britain, New Ireland, and New Caledonia, Tanna, Mallicollo,

New Holland, and Van Dieman's Land. The more recent nation occupies Sumatra and the other islands of the Indian Sea, Otaheite and the Society Islands, the Friendly Islands, Marquesas, Ladrones, Marian and Caroline Islands, New Zealand, Sandwich and Easter Islands. The language of all the latter resembles the Malay; and there can be no doubt that they arise from that race, and have spread by their ships over these distant spots. The black people are every where barbarous; and, according to FORSTER, have languages not agreeing with each other. In neither can we perceive any traces of the influence of climate. The latter race, scattered in various parts of the vast island of New Holland, which has such variety of temperature, every where retains its black colour, although the climate at the English settlement is not much unlike that of England: and in Van Dieman's Land, extending to 45° S. lat. (it is well understood that the cold is much more severe in the southern hemisphere, at an equal distance from the equator, than in the northern), they are of a deep black, and have curled hair like the Negroes[37]."

The same observations are applicable to the Malay race. The inhabitants of Otaheite are very fair; yellow hair is not unfrequently seen amongst them: those of New Zealand, and of Easter Island, twice as distant from the equator are much darker. "The fairness of the Sumatrans," says Mr. MARSDEN[38], "situated as they are under a perpendicular sun, where no season of the year affords an alternation of cold, is, I think, an irrefragable proof that the difference of colour in the different inhabitants of the earth is not the immediate effect of climate. The children of Europeans born in this island are as fair as those born in the country of their parents. I have observed the same of the second generation, when a mixture with the people of the country has been avoided. On the other hand, the offspring and all the descendants of the Guinea and other African slaves, imported there, continue in the last instance as perfectly black as in the original stock."

The foregoing statements authorize us in concluding, that in Asia, where we have countries with every variety of situation and temperature, at every distance from the equator, mountains, valleys, plains, islands, and continents, no effect of

---

37   *Dss. Inaug. de Variet.* p. 85–89.

38   *History of Sumatra*; ed. 3. p. 46.

climate can be traced on the colour, or on any other characters of the human race.

On the hypothesis, which assigns the varieties of mankind to the operation of climate as their cause, we should expect to find in Africa all tribes under the equator of the most intensely black colour; the tinge should become lighter and lighter as we proceed thence towards the south, and the complexion ought to be white when we arrive at regions which enjoy an European climate. This, however, is by no means the case. The Abyssinians, on the east, with dark-olive colour and long hair, are placed near the equator, and surrounded by Negroes. In the same part also, the Gallas, a great and barbarous nation, having, according to BRUCE, long black hair, and white skin verging to brown, occupy extensive regions under the equator itself. On the other hand, as we proceed from the equator towards the south, through tribes of Negroes, we find the black colour continued with undiminished intensity. It is known in the West Indies, that the Congo Negroes, in the blackness of their skin and woolly hair, equal any race of Africans. PATTERSON assures us that the Kaffers, within a few degrees of the Cape of Good Hope, where the climate is so far from being intolerably hot that the corn is often hurt by the winter frost, are of the deepest colour; and the same fact is familiarly known of the surrounding tribes.

The island of Madagascar, which is cooled by the mild breezes of the Indian Ocean, and ought, therefore, to contain a white race, has two kinds of natives: one of olive colour with dark hair; the other, true Negroes.

The Hottentots, at one or two degrees from the deep black Kaffers, are of a brownish-yellow colour: this distance can hardly account for the difference.

When we consider how large an extent of Africa is occupied by the black woolly-haired Negroes; and that these regions vary in their latitude, their elevation, and every other point; that they include sandy deserts, coasts, rivers, hills, valleys, and very great varieties of climate; the conclusion that these adventitious circumstances do not influence the colour or other properties of the race is irresistible.

It only remains for us to examine the continent of America; which, as it stretches uninterruptedly from the neighbourhood of the north pole to 55° S. lat. and includes regions diversified in every possible way, affords the most ample opportunity for the developement of all the changes that climate and position can produce: and to examine whether the facts ascertained concerning its inhabitants are more favourable to the hypothesis under consideration, than what we have observed in the other three divisions of the world.

The reports of travellers are unanimous concerning the identity of general character in the whole American race: copper-coloured skin: long and straight black hair, and a certain cast of features, are said to belong to all the inhabitants of this extensive continent. How remarkable this agreement is, may be collected from the statement sometimes made, that a person who has seen one may consider that he has seen all; which, however, in its full extent, must be regarded as an exaggerated or partial view. This Eskimaux are not included in this account; their colour is more of the olive cast; in which, as well as in other points, they betray their Mongolian origin. They retain in America the same characters which distinguish the Mongolian tribes, and natives of the old continent.

The most intelligent and accurate observers have informed us that nearly all the native tribes, whether of the northern, middle, or southern parts of America, have the skin of a more or less red tint; and some of them expressly state that its lighter or darker shades are entirely uninfluenced by any of the causes connected with geographical position.

"The Indians (Americans)," says ULLOA, "are of a copper colour, which, by the action of the sun and air, grows darker. I must remark, that neither heat nor cold produces any sensible change of colour, so that the Indians of the Cordilleras of Peru are easily confounded with those of the hottest plains; and those who live under the line cannot be distinguished by colour from those who inhabit the fortieth degrees of north and south latitude[39]."

HEARNE[40] and MACKENZIE[41] found the hunting tribes in the cold regions about Hudson's Bay and thence to the Frozen Ocean, copper-coloured and black-haired. LEWIS and CLARKE[42] describe those on the Columbia, and near its mouth,

---

[39] *Noticias Americanas*: cap. 17. p. 307; quoted in HUMBOLDT, *Personal Narrative*, 3,297.

[40] *Journey from Hudson's Bay to the Northern Ocean*: ch. 9. p. 305.

[41] *Travels through the Continent of North America*; prel. remarks: p. 92.

[42] *Travels*, 4to., p. 437.

as of the "usual copper-coloured brown of the North American tribes; though rather lighter than that of the Indians of the Missouri, and the frontier of the United States." WAFER[43] and DAMPIER[44] found the same tint in the isthmus of Darien; BOUGUER[45] and CONDAMINE[46] under the equator; STEDMAN[47] and others in Brasil; MOLINA[48] in Chili; WALLIS[49] and COOK[50] in Patagonia and Tierra del Fuego. HUMBOLDT, whose extensive opportunities for observation and philosophic spirit gave great weight to his statements, confirms these representations in the most ample manner.

"The Indians of New Spain bear a general resemblance to those who inhabit Canada, Florida, Peru, and Brasil: they have the same swarthy and copper colour, flat and smooth hair, small beard, squat body, long eye, with the corner directed upwards towards the temples, prominent cheek-bones, thick lips, and an expression of gentleness in the mouth, strongly contrasted with a gloomy and severe look. The American race, after the Hyperborean[51] race, is the least numerous; but it occupies the greatest space in the globe. Over a million and a half of square leagues, from the Tierra del Fuego islands to the river St. Lawrence, and Bering's Strait, we are struck at the first glance with the general resemblance in the features of the inhabitants. We think we perceive that they all descend from the same stock, notwithstanding the enormous diversity of language that separates them from each other. However, when we reflect more seriously on this family likeness, after living longer among the indigenous Americans, we discover that celebrated travellers, who could only observe a few individuals

43   *New Voyage and Description*, &c. p. 134.
44   *Voyage round the World*: v. i. p. 7.
45   *Acad. des Sciences*, 1744, p. 273.
46   Ibid. 1745. p. 418.
47   *Travels in Surinam*, v. i. p. 395.
48   *Natural History of Chili*, p. 274. Of the Araucans; *Civil History*, p. 54.
49   HAWKESWORTH's *Collection of Voyages*, v. i. 374.
50   Ibid. v. 2. p. 55.
51   The author probably means to include under this name the diminutive olive-coloured black-haired people, of Mongolian formation, who occupy the high northern latitudes of both continents; viz, the Eskimaux, Laplanders, Samoiedes, and Tungooses.

on the coasts, have singularly exaggerated the analogy of form among the Americans.

Intellectual cultivation is what contributes most to diversify the features. In barbarous nations there is rather a physiognomy peculiar to the tribe or horde than to any individual. When we compare our domestic animals with those which inhabit our forests, we make the same observation. But an European, when he decides on the great resemblance among the copper-coloured races, is subject to a particular illusion. He is struck with a complexion so different from our own; and the uniformity of this complexion conceals from him for a long time the diversity of individual features. The new colonist can at first hardly distinguish from each other individuals of the native race, because his eyes are less fixed on the gentle melancholic or ferocious expression of the countenance, than on the red-coppery colour, and dark, coarse, glossy, and luminous hair; so glossy, indeed, that we should believe it to be in a constant state of humectation.

The Indians of New Spain have a more swarthy complexion than the inhabitants of the warmest climates of South America. This fact is so much the more remarkable, as in the race of Caucasus, which may also be called the European-Arab race, the people of the south have not so fair a skin as those of the north. Though many of the Asiatic nations who inundated Europe in the sixth century had a very dark complexion, it appears that the shades of colour observable among the white race are less owing to their origin or mixture than to the local influence of the climate. This influence appears to have almost no effect on the Americans and Negroes. These races, in which there is abundant deposition of carburetted hydrogen in the corpus mucosum or reticulatum of Malpighi, resist in a singular manner the impressions of the ambient air. The Negroes of the mountains of Upper Guinea are not less black than those who live upon the coast. There are, no doubt, tribes of a colour by no means deep among the Indians of the new continent, whose complexion approaches to that of the Arabs or Moors. We found the people of the Rio Negro swarthier than those of the lower Orinoco, and yet the banks of the first of these rivers enjoy a much cooler climate than the more northern regions. In the forests of Guiana, especially near the sources of the Orinoco, are several tribes of a whitish complexion, – the Guaicas, the Guaiaribs, the Ariguas; of whom several robust individuals, exhibiting no symptom of the asthenical malady which characterizes Albinos, have the appearance of true Mestizos. Yet these tribes have never mingled with Europeans, and are surrounded by other tribes of a dark-brown hue. The Indians in the torrid zone, who inhabit the most elevated plains of the Cordillera of the Andes, and those who, under 45° S. lat. live by fishing among the islands of the Archipelago of Chonos, have as coppery a complexion as those who, under a burning climate, cultivate bananas in the narrowest and deepest valleys of the equinoctial region. We must add, that the Indians of the mountains are clothed, and were so long before the conquest; while the aborigines, who wander over the plains, go quite naked, and are consequently always exposed to the perpendicular rays of the sun. I could never observe that, in the same individual, those parts of the body which were covered were less dark than those in contact with a warm and humid air. We everywhere perceive that the colour of the American depends very little on the local position in which we see him.

The Mexicans, as we have already observed, are more swarthy than the Indians of Quito and New Granada, who inhabit a climate completely analogous; and we even see that the tribes dispersed to the north of the Rio Gila are less brown than those in the neighbourhood of the kingdom of Guatimala. This deep colour continues to the coast nearest to Asia. But under 54° 10′ of North latitude, at Cloak Bay, in the midst of copper-coloured Indians, with small long eyes, there is a tribe with large eyes, European features, and a skin less dark than that of our peasantry[52]."

How does it happen, that the same sun, which makes the African black, tinges the American of a copper colour? and that the dark hue, which might possibly be produced by heat, in the equatorial regions, should be found also in the cold and inhospitable tracts of Tierra del Fuego, and the most northern part of the continent? The absence of white races can surely not be ascribed to the want of sufficiently cold

[52] HUMBOLDT's *Political Essay on the Kingdom of New Spain*, v. i. p. 140–145.

climates. BOUGAINVILLE found the thermometer, in the middle of summer, 54½° in lat.. 52° S.; and Messrs. BANKS and SOLANDER, and their attendants, had nearly perished altogether from the cold, in an excursion in Tierra del Fuego, in the middle of the summer. Two of the servants were actually lost[53].

A very cursory survey of the globe will shew us that the same regions have been occupied by men of different races, without any interchange of characters, in many instances, for several centuries. The Moors and Negroes are found together in Africa; Europeans, Negroes, and Americans, in north and South America; Celts, Germans, and Slavons, in Europe, and even in the same kingdoms of Europe; Mongols, Afghans, and Hindoos in India; &c. &c. The distinctions of these different races, except where they have been confused by intermarriages, is just as easy now as it has been in any time, of which we have authentic records.

The permanency of the characters of any race when it has changed its original situation for a very different one, when it has passed into other climes, adopted new manners, and been exposed to the action of these causes for several generations, affords the most indisputable proof that these characteristics are not of the offspring of such adventitious circumstances. From the numerous examples, in every race which a slight knowledge of history will furnish, I shall select a few of the most striking.

In the earliest times, to which our historical records ascend, the west of Europe was occupied by Celtic people with a brownish-white skin, dark hair and eyes; the characters, in short, which are now visible in the Spaniards, most of the French, the native Welsh, the Manks, and the Highland Scotch. The German race, originally situated more to the north and east, have long ago obtained settlements by war and conquest in many of the countries previously peopled by the Celts; but their light-rosy skin, flaxen hair, and blue eyes, are now, after nearly two thousand years, just as strongly contrasted with the very different traits of the Celtic character, in those situations and those families where the blood has remained pure, as they were originally.

It was observed by CÆSAR, that the Germans had possessed themselves of the Belgic provinces of Gaul, and the contiguous

53 HAWKESWORTH's *Collection*, v. ii. ch. 4.

southern parts of Britain[54]. That the Caledonians or Picts (Lowland Scotch), were a German people is rightly represented by TACITUS, whose description of the natives occupying this island exhibits the same physical characters which exist in the present day: "Habitus corporum varii: atque ex eo argumenta; namque rutilæ Caledoniam habitantium comæ, magni artus Germanicam originem adseverant. Silurum colorati vultus, et torti plerumque crines, et posita contra Hispania, Iberos veteres trajecisse easque sedes occupâsse fidem faciunt: proximi Gallis, et similes sunt: seu durante origines vi, seu procurrentibus in diversa terris, positio cæli corporibus habitum dedit[55]." Under the names of Saxons, Angles, Danes, and Normans, numerous supplies of Germans successively arrived in England, and gradually drove the original Celtic population into the most distant and inaccessible parts of the island. An exposure to the same climate for so many centuries has not approximated the physical characters of the more recent German to those of the older Celtic inhabitants in the smallest degree; and both descriptions are equally unchanged after a progress from barbarism to the highest civilization. A similar permanence of the original distinctive characters is observable in France. "Among us," says VOLNEY, "a lapse of nine hundred years has not effaced the discriminating marks which distinguished the inhabitants of Gaul from the northern invaders, who, under CHARLES THE GROSS, settled themselves in our richest provinces. Travellers, who go from Normandy to Denmark, observe with astonishment the striking resemblance of the inhabitants of these two countries[56]."

The Vandals[57] passed from Spain into Africa about the middle of the fifth century: their descendants may be still traced, according to SHAW[58] and BRUCE[59] in the mountains of Aurez, by their white and ruddy complexion and yellow hair. "Here I met," says the latter writer, "to my great astonishment, a tribe, who, if I cannot say they were fair like the English,

54   *De Bell. Gall.* lib. 2 & 5.

55   *Agricola*, 11.

56   *Travels in Syria and Egypt*, v. i. ch. 6.

57   GIBBON; *Decline and Fall*, ch. 33.

58   *Travels*, ch. 3.

59   *Travels to discover*, &c. 8vo. ed. Introduction, p. 35.

were of a shade lighter than that of the inhabitants of any country to the southward of Britain. Their hair also was red, and their eyes blue." – "I imagine them to be a remnant of the Vandals. PROCOPIUS mentions a defeat of an army of this nation here, &c. They confessed their ancestors had been Christians." The change in the race produced by climate must be infinitely small, since it is not yet perceptible after a lapse of thirteen centuries.

The establishments of the Europeans in Asia and America have now subsisted about three centuries. VASQUEZ DE GAMA landed at Calicut in 1498; and the Portuguese empire in India was founded in the beginning of the following century. Brasil was discovered and taken possession of by the same nation in the very first year of the sixteenth century. Towards the end of the fifteenth, and the beginning of the sixteenth century, COLUMBUS, CORTEZ, and PIZARRO subjugated for the Spaniards the West-Indian islands, with the empires of Mexico and Peru. Sir WALTER RALEIGH planted an English colony in Virginia in 1584; and the French settlement of Canada has a rather later date. The colonists have, in no instance, approached to the natives of these countries: and their descendants, where the blood has been kept pure, have, at this time, the same characters as native Europeans. In the hotter situations, indeed, as in the warmer countries of Europe, the skin is swarthy in parts of the body which are not covered; but the children, at the time of birth, and women who are never exposed much to the sun's rays, have all their native whiteness. This observation admits of no exception: in the tint of the skin, the colour and other qualities of the hair, the features, the form of the cranium, the proportions and figure of the body, the European colonists retain all their original characters. The sanguine constitution, with its blue eyes, yellow hair, and fair skin, which is so remarkably different from that of the natives, is nevertheless transmitted, without the least alteration, from generation to generation.

Negroes have been introduced into the New World for nearly an equal length of time: in the West-Indian islands, in the United States, in the various parts of Spanish America, they live under new climates, and have adopted new habits: yet they have still woolly hair, black skins, flat nose, thick lips, and all the other characters of their race.

The inhabitants of Persia, of Turkey, of Arabia, of Egypt, and of Barbary[60], may be regarded in great part as the same race of people, who, in the time of MAHOMED and his successors, extended their dominions by invading immense territories. In all these situations the skin retains its native fairness, unless the tint be changed by exposure to the sun; and the children are invariably fair. "Il n'y a femme de laboureurou de paysan en Asie (Asia Minor) qui n'a le teint frais comme une rose, la peau delicate et blanche, si polie et si bien tendue, qu'il semble toucher du velours[61]." The Arabians are scorched by the heat of the sun; for most of them are either covered with a tattered shirt, or go entirely naked. LA BOULLAYE informs us, that the Arabian women of the desert are born fair, but that their complexions are spoiled by their being continually exposed to the sun[62]. Another traveller remarks, that the Arabian princesses and ladies, whom he was permitted to see, were extremely handsome, beautiful and fair, because they are always covered from the rays of the sun; but that the common women are very much blackened by the sun[63].

The Moors, who have lived in Africa since the seventh century, have not degenerated in their physical constitution from their Arabian progenitors: the sun exerts its full influence on their skin, but their children are just as white as those born in Europe. They are by no means confined to the northern

---

[60]   Africa, north of the great desert, has been always inhabited by races of Caucasian formation. The original tribes, called Berbers or Brebers, have given the name of Barbary to this division of the Continent. We know but little of their peculiar physical characters; which, however, probably were similar to those of the ancient Egyptians and Guanches (see p. 299.) These Berbers, which constituted the people known to the Roman writers by the names of Libyans, Getulians, Numidians, Mauritanians, Garamantes, have received accessions of Phœnicians (the Carthaginians), Greeks, Romans, Vandals, and Arabians. The latter particularly entered the north of Africa in great numbers, destroying or driving away the original inhabitants. The general prevalence of Mahomedanism and of the Arabian language, testifies the impression which they made on the country. The remnants of the aboriginal tribes are now principally found in the mountains. They may be traced, however, south of the great desert, and seem to form even considerable states between Tombuctoo and Upper Egypt; where they preserve their distinctive characters in the same climates with the Negro race.

[61]   *Obs. de* PIERRE BELON, p. 199.

[62]   *Voyages de* LA BOULLAYE LE GOUZ, 318.

[63]   *Voyage fait par Ordre du Roi dans la Palestine*, p. 260.

coast, but have penetrated, as the prevalence of the Mahomedan religion attests, deeply into the interior: here they dwell in countries, of which the woolly-haired Negro is the native, but have not acquired, in six centuries of exposure to the same causes, any of his characters. The intelligent and accurate SHAW informs us, that most of the Moorish women would be reckoned handsome even in Europe; and that the skin of their children is exceedingly fair and delicate; and though the boys, by being exposed to the sun, soon grow swarthy, yet the girls, who keep more within doors, preserve their beauty till the age of thirty, when they commonly give over child-bearing. "Les Maures," says POIRET, "ne sont pas naturellement noirs, malgré le proverbe, et comme le pensent plusieurs écrivains; mais ils naissent blancs, et restent blancs toute leur vie, quand leurs travaux ne les exposent pas aux ardeurs du soleil. Dans les villes, les femmes ont une blancheur si èclatante, qu'elles éclipseroient la plupart de nos Européennes; mais les Maur-esques montagnardes, sans cesse brulées par le soleil et presque toujours à moitié nues, deviennent, même dés l'enfance, d'une couleur brune qui approche beaucoup de celle de la suie[64]." The testimony of BRUCE is to the same effect.

That the swarthiness of the southern Europeans is merely the effect of the sun's action on the individual, whose children are born perfectly white, and continue so unless exposed to the operation of the climate, might be easily proved of the Spaniards and Portuguese, the Greeks, Turks, &c.; but the fact is too well known to render this necessary.

The Jews exhibit one of the most striking instances of national formation, unaltered by the most various changes. They have been scattered, for ages, over the face of the whole earth; but their peculiar religious opinions and practices have kept the race uncommonly pure; accordingly, their colour and their characteristic features are still the same under every diversity of climate and situation.

The advocates for the power of climate have made very erroneous representations respecting these people; asserting that their colour is every where modified by the situation they occupy. The Jews, like all the native people adjoining their original seats, have naturally a white skin and the other attributes of the Caucasian race. In hot countries they become

---

[64] *Voy. en Barbarie*, tom. i. p. 32.

brown by exposure, as an European does, but they experience no other influence from climate. Their children are born fair; and the countenance and other characters are everywhere preserved in remarkable purity, because their religion forbids all intermixture with other races. Dr. BUCHANAN met, on the coast of Malabar, with a tribe, who represented that their ancestors had migrated from Palestine after the destruction of the temple by TITUS, and who have preserved their native colour and form amidst the black inhabitants of the country, excepting in instances where they have intermarried with the Hindoos. Those of pure blood are called White Jews, in contradistinction from the others, who are termed Black Jews[65].

The foregoing facts sufficiently prove, that native differences in general, and particularly that of colour, do not depend on extraneous causes: I have an observation or two to make on some other points. That the curled state of the hair in the African is not produced by heat, appears from its being found in many situations not remarkable for high temperature, as in the Moluccas, New Guinea, Mallicollo, Borneo, New Holland, and even in the cold regions of Van Diemen's Land; as well as from the hot regions of Asia and America being inhabited by long-haired races.

The woolly appearance of the Negro hair is just opposite to that which hot climates have been said to produce in the covering of sheep in which it is represented that hair is produced instead of wool. When we contrast the hairy coat of the argali or mouflon with the beautiful fleeces of our most valuable sheep, we see a prodigious difference, which is probably owing more to cultivation and attention to breed than to climate. It does not appear, at least, that change of climate will convert the wool of an individual English sheep into hair; and it is equally incapable of conferring a woolly covering on the hairy sheep. Dr. WRIGHT[66], who lived many years in Jamaica, speaking of the opinion that the wool of sheep becomes more hairy in warm climates, says, that in the West-India islands there is to be found a breed of sheep, the origin of which he has not been able to trace, that carry very thin fleeces of a coarse shaggy kind of wool; which circumstance, he

---

[65]   *Christian Researches in Asia*; section, On the Jews.

[66]   Dr. ANDERSON *on the different Kinds of Sheep*; Appendix ii.

thinks, may naturally have given rise to the report. But he never observed a sheep that had been brought from England to carry wool of the same sort with those native sheep: on the contrary, though he has known them live there several years, these English sheep carried the same kind of close burly fleece that is common in England; and, in as far as he could observe, it was equally free from hairs.

The differences in stature, again, have been very confidently ascribed to adventitious causes. A temperate climate, pure air, copious food, tranquillity of mind, and healthy occupation, have been thought favourable to the full developement of the human frame; while extreme cold, bad and unwholesome food, noxious air, and similar causes, have been thought capable of reducing the dimensions of the body below the ordinary standard. That these causes may have some effect on individuals I do not deny, although I believe that it is very slight: but the numerous examples of large people in cold countries, and diminutive men in warm climes, induce me to deny altogether its operation on the race. The tall and large-limbed Patagonians, certain North American tribes, and some of the German races, inhabit cold situations: the Mongols, who are small in stature, live in warm countries.

The facts and observations adduced in this section lead us manifestly to the following conclusions: 1st, That the differences of physical organization and of moral and intellectual qualities, which characterize the several races of our species, are analogous in kind and degree to those which distinguish the breeds of the domestic animals; and must, therefore, be accounted for on the same principles. 2dly, That they are first produced, in both instances, as native or congenital varieties; and then transmitted to the offspring in hereditary succession. 3dly, That of the circumstances which favour this disposition to the production of varieties in the animal kingdom, the most powerful is the state of domestication. 4thly, That external or adventitious causes, such as climate, situation, food, way of life, have considerable effect in altering the constitution of man and animals; but that this effect, as well as that of art or accident, is confined to the individual, not being transmitted by generation, and therefore not affecting the race. 5thly, That the human species, therefore, like that of the cow, sheep, horse, and pig, and others, is single; and that all the differences, which it exhibits, are to be regarded merely as varieties.

If, in investigating the subject, we are satisfied with comparing the existing races of men to those of the domestic animals, and with bringing together the characteristic marks, on which the distinctions are grounded in the two cases, as I have done in several preceding chapters, we shall have no difficulty in arriving at the fifth conclusion. If, however, we should carry ourselves back, in imagination, to a supposed period, when mankind consisted of one race only – and endeavour to shew how the numerous varieties, which now occupy the different parts of the earth, have arisen out of the common stock, and have become so distinct from each other, as we find them at present – we cannot arrive at so satisfactory a decision; and we experience further embarrassment from the fact, that the races have been as distinctly marked, and as completely separated from the earliest periods, to which historical evidence ascends, as they now are. The same remarks, in great measure, are true, concerning animals; so that, on this ground, no difficulty prevents us from recognizing the unity of the human species, which is not equally applicable to them.

HISTOIRE NATURELLE
DES RACES HUMAINES

(Natural History of the Human Races of the North-East of Europe, Northern and Eastern Asia, and Southern Africa, from Researches into Antiquity, Physiology, Anatomy and Zoology). By A. Desmoulins. Paris. London. 1826

Anonymous

Source: Monthly Review, vol. 3 ns, 1826

Louis-Antoine Desmoulins (1794–1828) was born in Rouen. He studied medicine in Paris, taking his MD degree in 1817. Afterwards he delved into theoretical studies of the nervous system. Initially he was promoted by Georges Cuvier, who invited him to give papers at the Museum d'Histoire Naturelle. But his physiological theories were judged as eccentric and ill-founded. In the early 1820s he fell out with Cuvier. Having lost the favour of the faculty, he took to berating his former mentor and criticized him heavily in the Introduction to his work on the human races of 1826.

This is altogether a strange production; and not the least extraordinary part of it is, its prefatory matter, addressed, in the form of a very angry and vituperative epistle, to Monsieur le Baron Cuvier. That eminent naturalist has, it appears, unhappily for his fame, incurred the personal hostility, and provoked the indignation of the learned doctor Desmoulins; and his scientific and private character is accordingly destined, in this immortal work, to be branded with disgrace, not only during his own times, but to the latest posterity.

The indictment against the Baron displays several counts. In the first place, it declares that M. Desmoulins having made sundry important discoveries in physiology, the said baron took umbrage at the success of his young *rival*, and in his quality of reporter to the French Institute, avoided to notice the results of these valuable researches with suitable commendation;

being moved to this criminal omission, as it is broadly insinuated, by the evil passions of envy, hatred and malice. Secondly, the Baron is charged with having confounded the Urus (the Thur of the Sclavonic nations), with the Buffalo, until M. Desmoulins set him right by proving the difference between those animals; and with having then attributed to himself the merit of shewing this distinction. M. Desmoulins, however, disclaims the wish of insisting very much upon the enormity of this unjust appropriation of his labours; having, as he complacently confesses, himself made so many discoveries in that branch of science (which he may say that he has created), as to be well able to resign to M. Cuvier the honour of a single one of the number. 'Ayant fait peut être assez de découvertes en ce genre, que je puis dire avoir créé, je vous laisserais l'honneur de celle-ci, &c.' And, accordingly, by way of evincing his generous forbearance, he goes no farther than merely to tax the Baron publicly with this scientific theft.

Our doctor's third charge relates to the publication of his former work. In his "Anatomie des Systèmes Nerveux," he spoke of M. Cuvier in terms which, though composed, as he says, with "un luxe d'eloges," were so far from satisfying the great naturalist, as to induce him, when the author called on him after its publication, to *turn him out of his house*. Not having the good fortune to have read the Anatomie des Systèmes Nerveux, we are unable to decide on the just interpretation of that, which one party offered as a prodigal eulogy, and the other received as a mortal offence: – but this ultimate measure of M. le Baron in his own house does, we admit, incur the appearance of having been *un peu fort*. As the dimensions of quarrels and injurious proceedings ever grow in geometrical progression, this misunderstanding seems to have increased in an alarming ratio; and our author next accuses the Baron of having drawn down upon him the hostility of the whole Academy of Sciences; of having prevented his being put in nomination to succeed the Comte de Lacepède in the department of anatomy and zoology in that learned body; and finally, of having arbitrarily excluded him from the usual access to the museum of anatomy, of which the Baron is director.

Of all his charges, this last is the only one of which our exasperated author offers any proof; and here certainly M. Cuvier appears, by copies of his own letters, to have acted in a manner which we cannot but designate as betraying a mean and petty spirit of personal animosity. Such collections as a national museum of anatomy are intended, we presume, for the general advancement of knowledge, for the use of the whole republic of science; not for the exclusive benefit of a faction. In a memoir, "proving that the hippopotamos of Senegal differs more from that of the Cape than the latter differs from the fossil species," M. Desmoulins complained that he could not elucidate his subject by drawings, as he had been denied admission to the Museum. M. Cuvier first boldly pronounced this statement to be false: but he admitted its truth, and exposed the unworthy influence of private hostility, when he afterwards descended to make a quibbling distinction between the right of admission to the galleries, and to the use of the specimens.

This our author smartly and justly compares to allowing a man to look at the shelves of a public library, without permitting him to open the books; and he seems to be galled, with reason, at the reflection that, to the cases of specimens which were thus closed against him, "he has himself contributed some fifty anatomical preparations." Whereupon it is, that M. le docteur Desmoulins pours out the whole phial of his wrath upon the devoted head of the Baron. In his indignation and impotent rage, he is reckless how far he wanders from the matter in dispute: he assails the object of his vengeance with all the missiles of ridicule and abuse; from the filth of an indecent jest about the Hottentot Venus, to the more serious reproach of being destitute of all personal and political integrity. Having thus disposed of M. Cuvier, by "gibbeting him to fame," our magnanimous author protests that he shall not condescend to notice inferior antagonists, who have fallen under his displeasure; modestly applying to himself the injunction of Alfieri,

Va, tuona, vinci; e se fra pie ti vedi
Costor, senza mirar sovra essi passa;

that he should proceed, *thunder*, and conquer; and if he saw them under his feet, pass over them without deigning to regard them!

Having given a summary of this epistle introductory, as much to illustrate the general temper of the writer and his book, as for the mere sake of exhibiting so whimsical a compound of anger and vanity, we proceed to the immediate subject of the volume. The nature and design of the work may be very briefly explained: it is composed with the laudable purpose of proving, in opposition to the authority of Holy Writ, the absurdity of ascribing a common and single derivation to the several races of man.

Some partiality for researches into the origin of nations, we have upon a former occasion expressed[1]: we are convinced that such inquiries, if rationally conducted, may throw much light upon the physiology of human talent and disposition; and we can imagine few objects of intellectual speculation more interesting to an inquisitive mind, than the attempt to investigate the natural causes of the diversities of national character, as operating by difference in political and religious institutions, in prevailing occupations of industry, in climate and local position, and above all by the distinction and admixture of races. That all these causes, and especially the last, have had their share in the formation of national character, we presume no man of reflection is prepared to dispute; and it will scarcely be doubted, that there are physiological laws in the moral world, acting by principles as fixed and determinate, as those which regulate the operations of nature.

But while we confess the attraction, and feel the importance of inquiries into the origin of nations, as a part of this general subject, we are not the less disposed to deprecate the tendency and object of such researches, when they blindly abandon, or would presumptuously extinguish, the sure light of revelation and scriptural evidence. Any system of such philosophy, whatever be its range, which is not at least in accordance with sacred authority, we should be satisfied at once to reject as unsafe and untrue; and we can choose only between the feelings of pity for the error, or scorn for the purpose, which can have prompted its development. Not that the slightest fear or reluctance should in any case be entertained to meet the arguments of infidel speculation upon their own vantage ground: their regulation needs no *petitio principii*; and there will never be wanting some ray of truth, from mere reason and philosophy itself, to enable us to detect their fallacy, or destroy their dangerous implication.

The arrangement of M. Desmoulins' treatise is sufficiently systematic. He commences by an attempt to prove, from the

[1]   Monthly Review, No. viii, p. 279.

records of ancient history, that the existing varieties of the human species have been known from the remotest ages, by the same physical diversities which they exhibit at this moment, and that they have always been grouped, from time immemorial, in distinct regions of the earth. He next examines what he calls the anatomical characters of these different races of men, and particularly of those of eastern Asia and southern Africa. He then labours to establish 'an agreement of the laws which regulate the geographical distribution of the different species of animals and men;' and he concludes that it is equally impossible that these *different species of either* should have been produced from a common stock, or dispersed from a common centre of creation. He contends that each existing form must 'have had a primitive centre of existence, and in so much, of creation;' that 'in the creation of animals no unity of place can be admitted, from whence they could have been dispersed; that therefore the plurality of the centres of creation is evident;' and that, 'for the geographical distribution of the races and species of men, there are no other laws than for that of animals.'

In the plan of his work, as we have here given it, M. Desmoulins' first book is occupied with an account of the people known by the ancients under the names of Scythians, Huns, Turks, Alains, Khazars, &c., and according to physical characters given to them by historians. Here he professes to exhibit all the clear and precise facts, that history and the monuments of art have transmitted to us, on the physical character of the various people of Europe and of Asia, to the north east of Persia, the Euxine and the Caspian seas. Three chapters are devoted, successively, to a description of those people, as known by the Greeks and Romans, by the Armenians, Persians, Arabians, and Turks, and by the Chinese. The agreement of all writers which these chapters are to shew, will confirm the identity of each people described, and coincide with a physical principle of distinction between one race and another. This principle is the invariability of the colour of the skin and hair, and of the shape of the countenance in races and species not mixed: and M. Desmoulins felicitates himself upon having already given in his "Anatomie des Systèmes Nerveux" such proofs of it as to expose the imperfection or nullity of all former labours, and to demonstrate the precision and exactitude of his own!

On the execution of this portion of his labours, with which he is himself so well satisfied, we shall only observe, that M. Desmoulins has lavished a great parade of deep learning on a very small purpose. For he has not established a single historical fact or deduction which was not already familiar to every general scholar. Indeed, he seems himself to have been strangely ignorant of the present state of historical literature; or, it may be supposed that he would scarcely have engaged in the laborious researches which he has imposed upon himself in this part of his work, merely to establish some recognised conclusions, which can have novelty for few of his readers, and which no one of them will care to dispute. We never heard a doubt expressed by physiologists, that the existing nations of our northern continent, and some of the modern hordes of north eastern Asia, are of consanguineous races with those several barbarian swarms, which some fifteen centuries ago, however impelled, burst like successive inundations upon more civilized Europe, overthrew in their course the institutions and power of imperial Rome, and even in some cases swept from before them the mass of the ancient population.

Take, for one instance, the Huns, to fix whose identity our author has expended so much dissertation. Long before he wrote, the genealogical history and physical characteristics of no ancient people had been better determined than theirs. In the description of Attila, which the horror of his contemporaries has bequeathed to us, it is impossible that any one should fail to recognise the exaggerated portrait of a genuine modern Calmuck. No one has doubted, that the exterminating followers of that "scourge of God" were a true Mongolian race; and even their history anterior to their irruption into Europe, has been satisfactorily examined. Their original Asiatic seats, their earliest vicissitudes of fortune, their pristine conquests, and the subsequent flight before hostile and more powerful hordes, which finally precipitated them on the western world, have all been defined and related with remarkable accuracy. The ingenious and indefatigable De Guignes, by his knowledge of the Chinese language and literature, was enabled to throw the clearest light upon the remote fortunes of that people; and his Histoire des Huns, which we detect M. Desmoulins in consulting much oftener than he has acknowledged, is a prodigious monument of erudition and patient research. The labours of De Guignes have been used by a great historian in

our own language with a worthier spirit than by his countryman; Gibbon, in the admirable view of which he has given (c.
26), of the gradual western progress of the Huns from their
original seats, frequently confesses his obligations to the
learned Frenchman.

Nothing can be more lucid than Gibbon's narrative of this
early history of the Huns; his masterly and fearful picture of
their later career, of the reign, the exploits, and the destroying
course of the ferocious Attila, is too well known to every reader
to need any eulogy of ours. But it is singular, that M.
Desmoulins should have written as though he were ignorant of
the familiarity of the subject, and conceived he were illuminat-
ing the world with his profound 'discourses' in national history,
as well as in physiology. He seems (p. 153) to attach great
importance to the originality of his remark, that the barbarian
irruptions were merely the separation of the fugitive or
adventurous hordes from the mass of their race, and not whole
national emigrations. But even there the boast of a novel
observation cannot be permitted to him. Gibbon has distinctly
characterized the Huns, who invaded the empire, as a broken
fragment only (vol. iv., p. 368, &c.) of the national mass; and
that fragment, when its frightful impetus was exhausted, and
its cohesion destroyed, by the death of Attila, dwindled and
crumbled, in the divisions of civil war, until the very remains of
it were again lost in the Scythian deserts. The reader will not
require to be reminded, that the modern population of
Hungary are not the descendants of the people, who seem to
have given their name to that kingdom, but of a proper
Tatarian (and not a Mongolian) horde, who so late as the end
of the ninth century established themselves between the
Danube and the Carpathian mountains.

So much for the value of M. Desmoulins' pretensions. In
addition we must remark, that he has crowded this part of his
dissertation with such innumerable quotations and references,
and involved each chapter in such confusion, without the
slightest regard to arrangement or order, that it is by no means
easy to decipher and define the precise conclusions at which he
would arrive. But if it be his object to prove, that the extant
races of mankind have existed from the earliest authentic
periods of profane history, with the same physical varieties of
colour and features which they now display, he has, we repeat,
made a large shew of erudition to very small effect. The fact

was before well known; and these, his important premises, will be freely conceded to him. But they will avail him little in the superficial conclusions, which he would deduce from them. Whatever may have been the period at which these various races diverged from the parent stock of mankind, it was far more remote than the earliest times to which the obscure heathen knowledge of classical antiquity can ascend; and the epoch of the dispersion of the human species is lost in that awful gloom, which it has pleased the purposes of Infinite Wisdom only dimly to shadow out to our imperfect understandings, in the earlier books of the inspired Writings.

The concluding chapter of our author's first book is occupied with a sketch of the races of Europe and Asia, next of the Mongolian race or *species*, as it better suits his purpose to call it. He here recapitulates the successive locations in Europe of the Celtic (Keltic), the German, Slavonic, or Sarmatian, the Mongolian, the Arabian, the Tatar or Turkish, and again, a second time, of the Mongolian nation. This part of his inquiry – the only legitimate or useful object of any such inquiries, as explaining the original composition of modern nations, and assisting to develop the germs and causes of their distinctive characters – he might have rendered full of curiosity and interest. For much, both of amusement and instruction, might be gathered from an examination of the geographical strata, as it were, in which the various races of our European population will be found to lie, according to the direction in which the stream of national conquest and emigration has flowed in successive ages. Thus, in our own island, the remains of the more aboriginal Celtic population are to be found in its extremities of Cornwall, Wales, and the Scottish Highlands, according as they were driven before the overwhelming tide of the Saxon invasions; again, the irruptions of the Northmen upon the Saxons, and their well known settlement in some of our eastern counties, have covered that coast with a superincumbent layer of Danish race, of which the marks are still visible to antiquarian scrutiny in a variety of peculiar customs and etymologies; and finally, the conquest overspread the whole island with a tinge of Norman and Frankish character and blood.

Thus, also, in France: the original Celtic population were rolled westward by the succession of German invasions, until their remains were compressed into the peninsula of Brittany, the fastnesses of Auvergne, and the Pyrenean mountains: where the abundant traces of a different language and countenance still remain to confirm the assertions of history. Meanwhile layers of Gothic, and Frankish, and Norman generations successively passed over the rest of France, and gradually cemented into the compactness and strength of the modern nation. If M. Desmoulins should be inquisitive to examine further the composition of the French 'national strata,' the events of our own times may afford some fresh specimens for his curiosity. The long occupation of France by the invading armies of Europe has doubtless not been without its effects upon the eastern provinces; and the rising generation of that part of his country may exhibit the amusing admixture of our Celtic races of Ireland and Scotland, of the Slavonic breeds of Russia, and even of the genuine Calmuk visage of his 'Mongolian *species*.'

Such speculations, however, are probably less to M. Desmoulins' taste than some others of not quite so innocent a tendency; and he offers merely a rapid enumeration of the races which have formed the parent stocks of the European nations. In connexion with this superficial part of his volume, we may observe, that he has, (in a general table, reprinted from M. Majendie's system of physiology), swelled the primary classification of Blumenbach from five races of man to sixteen *species*. The enumeration is not worth repeating: but it seems inserted in his volume principally to mark the south African population (Hottentots, Boschismans, &c.) as a distinct species, both from the Ethiopian (or Negro), and from the Mongolian, under which a very few modern physiologists have proposed to class them. To assist in the maintenance of his precious system of 'various centres of creation,' he triumphantly adduces evidence that no Mongolian hordes are known, from the remotest antiquity, to have penetrated into Africa; and therefore, that the South Africans cannot have their descent from such an emigration. His negative proof is here no real proof at all: for the emigration might as well have occurred by sea as by land – from China, for example; and an observant traveller has actually remarked the resemblance in colour and complexion between the Mongolian Chinese and the Hottentots[2]. But we do not, in fact, believe that the

---

[2] Barrow's Travels in China, p. 185.

Hottentot tribes are of Mongolian race; they have more frequently and naturally been classed under the Ethiopian variety; and, besides their local position on the globe, their thick woolly locks, (so different from the thin straight hair of the Calmuck), constitute a proof of community of race with the negro, at least, as strong as can be urged on the other hand, from their similarity of colour with the Mongolians.

Having, in his first book, prepared a masqued attack upon Revelation, M. Desmoulins more boldly opens the second with an infidel motto from Micali: "La generazione umana non puo esser derivata da una sola provincia, ne da un sola clima" – that the human race can neither be deduced from a single province nor from one climate: and he here gives the natural history of the races of northern and eastern Asia, and southern Africa, for the sake of proving that they cannot have had their original derivation from a common stock. He begins with an inquiry into the causes of the variety of the skin, hair, &c., of the human races; and he argues at much length, that these cannot have been primarily produced by the influence of climate and situation. Here, again, he has expended needless labour on a point, upon which the best modern physiologists are already agreed. This matter also we freely concede to him; the fairest Europeans of the German race are found in the same parallels of latitude with the copper-coloured Indians of North America; the Esquimaux, who scarcely ever feel the sun, are very dark, while the Arabs of the scorched deserts of Asia are still born, at least, in the hundredth generation, with a white skin; the Kaffers are of the blackest human jet, and the Hottentot tribes who adjoin them are no more than of an orange tawny. But fifty such examples might be added, if any proof were required, that the mere influence of climate will not alter the colour of the race. The European is swarthened by a residence under the tropic, but his child is born not the less fair: the offspring of the negro, in the most temperate regions of the United States, is as ebony as if it were produced under the African equator. So also in the European nations of compound origin, there is observable a constant mixture of light and dark complexions of the skin, eyes, and hair. In our own population this variety of tint is to be found, derived probably from the ancient fusion of German and Celtic blood; while in the unmingled nations of a Mongolian or Ethiopian race – the Chinese or Negroes, for example – different shades of colour are rarely exhibited in individuals of the same tribe. Nay, almost in every English family this mixture of complexions is to be found; and the children of the same bed often alternate irregularly in two castes, of "blonde and brunette." Even where both parents are fair, the offspring will be dark-eyed, and *vice versâ*: paternal resemblances will disappear in the first, and be recovered again in the second and third generations; and children may be seen unlike their father and mother, and like their grand parents – for thus, in the language of Lucretius,

– Venus varias producit sorte figuras
Majorumque refert vultus, vocesque comasque.

Having elaborated these acknowledged facts – truisms we had almost said – that the various races of man have existed from antiquity with the same physical distinctions as at present, and that colour is not the result of climate and position, M. Desmoulins proceeds to his grand conclusion, that this *permanence of type* is what constitutes species: and that, therefore, the races of man are not merely varieties of the same species, but so many different species, created as such from the beginning of all things. It would be beyond our purpose and limits to offer the easy refutation of this pernicious system, by entering into minute and lengthened arguments: nor, fortunately, does the state of physiological science in the world require that we should waste time and words in opposing a conclusion so false, so gratuitous, and so decidedly opposed to the familiar results of all rational modern research. We shall be contented to enumerate only two or three among many well known and striking proofs, from analogy with the physiological laws of the lower animal world, which must afford a complete answer to this untenable hypothesis: even if it were not in itself obviously as repugnant to reason as to the authority of inspired Scripture.

And here we shall avowedly borrow our weapons from an armoury, in which they were assuredly tempered for far other purposes than the defence of the Christian dispensation. It is fortunate when the enemies of Revelation, by neglecting to observe an uniformity of error, enable us to play off their rival systems against each other; and the conclusions of a celebrated physiologist, who has utterly denied any weight to the Mosaic account of the creation, shall furnish a sufficient reply to those of M. Desmoulins. Mr. Lawrence considers the subject of the

origin of man to be open to the utmost freedom of discussion:
he examines it solely as a mere philosophical question; and he
arrives, after a most patient and full investigation, at a
conviction to which at least no partialities of opinion would
have led him, – that the different races of man can be no more
than varieties of the same species. His plan of reasoning from
the analogy of the animal kingdom is here so thoroughly safe
and satisfactory, that we shall do no more than give the
conclusions at which he arrives:–

> "The facts and observations addressed in this section, lead
> us manifestly to the following conclusions: 1st, That the
> differences of physical organization, and of moral and
> intellectual qualities, which characterise the several races of
> our species, are analogous, in kind and degree, to those
> which distinguish the breeds of the domestic animals; and
> must, therefore, be accounted for on the same principles.
> 2dly, That they are first produced, in both instances, as
> native or congenital varieties; and then transmitted to the
> offspring in hereditary succession. 3dly, That, of the
> circumstances which favour this disposition to the produc-
> tion of varieties, in the animal kingdom, the most powerful,
> is the state of domestication. 4thly, That external or
> adventitious causes, such as climate, situation, food, way of
> life, have considerable effect in altering the constitution of
> man and animals; but that this effect, as well as that of art or
> accident, is confined to the individual, not being transmitted
> by generation, and therefore, not affecting the race. 5thly,
> That the human species, therefore, like that of the cow,
> sheep, horse, and pig, and others, is single; and that all the
> differences, which it exhibits, are to be regarded merely as
> varieties." – p. 548.

Thus the apparent 'permanence of type' does not constitute
species, as M. Desmoulins would peremptorily conclude; nor
can the mere difference of colour which he has so confidently
upheld for that type, be received as indicating any thing more
than a variety of the same species. For it if did, it must involve
the palpable contradiction that a number of new species may be
produced. The proof *ex absurdo* is here simple and short. The
strongly marked tints in the human races have, for the sake of
classification only, been distinguished as five: white, yellow or
olive, red or copper, brown or tawny, and black; but between

all these there is every conceivable intermediate shade of colour. For example, the fair flaxen-haired German and the swarthy Portuguese are necessarily included alike under the white variety. The opposite extremes run into each other by the nicest and most delicate transitions; and the human skin exhibits every possible hue, in almost imperceptible gradation, from the clear snowy whiteness of our most beauteous females, to the deep ebony of a Gold Coast negress. If colour constituted species, how should we accurately define the number of human kinds already existing, and distingush them, as all species in the animal kingdom may easily be distinguished? But this is not all: the difficulty would be endlessly on the increase. The pairing of the European and the negro produces the well-known variety of the mulatto; and there can be no doubt, from all the laws of animal analogy, that if without any re-admixture of European or negro connection, mulattos were to match exclusively with each other for a few generations, this variety would be fixed as a permanent breed. Moreover, the same thing would be true in all races of such a single mixture of two bloods, uninterrupted by farther crosses. And thus in every such case, according to M. Desmoulins, a new permanent type being produced, a *new species of man would arise*!!

But after all, to what does this boasted permanence of type amount, when encountered by accidental interruptions? The Persians as a nation are of positive Mongolian origin; but their men of rank have for ages filled their harems with the women of Georgia and Circassia; two races which surpass all the world in personal beauty; and the consequent refinement of blood from this mixture, by the female line, has so completely washed out the stain of their Mongolian descent, that the Persians are become a well-grown and a handsome people. Are they still Mongolian? Say, what has then become of their permanent type, and how shall they be recognized for the same race of four centuries past? Have they been converted altogether into a new race or *species*? Then is this novel creation at least within the memory of history.

But it is little less than audacious presumption to declare any breed permanent, because it has existed since the earliest records of profane history: those records, even when most illuminated by human research, extend comparatively but a short distance back into the unfathomable darkness of time. If we have proved only that the common derivation of man from one stock, and therefore the Mosaic account of his creation, is not incompatible with the existing laws of physiology, we have ascertained enough for the humble inquirer to know. The established possibility of that common descent, is sufficient refutation of all the mere hypotheses which scepticism would invent to deny it. We are no more called upon to explain the physical incidents which might originally produce the variations of colour and feature in our species, than we are to scan the inscrutable designs of the Almighty, in gifting some races with superior intellect and beauty, and permitting the degeneracy of others from the primitive stock.

THE GERMANIC ORIGIN
OF THE LATIN LANGUAGE
AND THE ROMAN PEOPLE
By Ernst Jäkel.
Breslaw. 1831.

[J. G. Lockhart]

Source: Quarterly Review, vol. 46, 1831–2

The Scot John Gibson Lockhart (1794–1854) studied law at the University of Glasgow and afterwards at Balliol College, Oxford. In 1817 he began to contribute to learned journals. In 1820 he married the daughter of Sir Walter Scott, subsequently publishing a widely-acclaimed biography of his father-in-law. Between 1825 and 1853 he edited the *Quarterly Review*. Being fascinated by the modern discipline of comparative linguistics, Lockhart studied German philologists understanding national descent in linguistic terms. He preferred a philologist like Jäkel who followed the new methods, to his countryman Alexander Murray, whose learning was still in the eighteenth-century mould.

To enter into a full and systematic examination of the subject, one detached portion of which has been concisely treated in this volume, is obviously far beyond the scope and purpose of a periodical work; but were this otherwise, we should be reluctant to make the attempt. There is indeed no class of books in which we find more of interest and excitement, than in that to which Professor Jäkel has made an important addition; but to understand thoroughly, to say nothing of lucidly abridging, and expounding popularly, any one of them, would require the undivided labour of years in the first place, and the unbroken leisure of a cloister in the second. Such scantlings of information as to the archaic dialects of Europe and Asia, as may be picked up in tumbling over the leaves of vocabularies and lexicons, will no longer entitle any man to announce an opinion on questions which have occupied the lifelong toil of such minds as those of Adelung, Grimm, and Schmithenner. But, not only does the consciousness of the want of such information press on us, as might be supplied by patient study of existing literary monuments: we confess we shrink under a feeling of another kind – our dread of that fascinating but bewildering and exhausting species of mental exertion, which, were all the information we allude to in our hands, would be required in order to turn it to much account. We remember the case of the poor schoolmaster in the *Diable Boiteux*, who had gone mad on the *paulo-post-futurum*; nor is our alarm diminished when we cast our eyes on the *posthumous* and *unfinished* work of the late amiable and ingenious Dr. Alexander Murray, according to which the whole of the languages spoken between the Himalaya mountains and Ben Nevis, may be traced to nine euphonic primitive *verbs* – namely *ag*, *bag*, *dwag*, *gwag*, *lag*, *mag*, *nag*, *rag*, and *swag* –

'– and that's as high
As metaphysic wit can fly.'

To be serious – the philological researches of the last and the present age, more especially those of the Germans, have already so entirely revolutionized what before constituted this department of scholarship, and at the same time enlarged its boundaries so enormously, that much time must elapse before the mass of even what may be called accomplished readers can be expected to come, in a tolerable state of preparation, to the analysis of such a work as that now on our table. It is as if a new sense had been conferred on us; we are still puzzled and dazzled. In this country, in particular, very few minds have grappled effectually with these brilliant novelties – to the general run even of the students in our universities they remain the objects of at best a distrustful wonder.

We shall, after this apology, limit ourselves to a slight, we would fain hope to make it a generally intelligible, specimen of Mr. Jäkel's 'Essay on the Germanic *Early spring* of the Latin *speech* and the Roman *folk*.' As our own tongue and nation have undoubtedly their main sources in the quarters to which he would trace the blood and language of the masters of the ancient world, the subject of the inquiry ought, in the Professor's opinion, to be little if at all less interesting here than among our contemporaries of Berlin and Breslaw. But it may perhaps be as well to give, *in limine*, a rough outline of the theory now all but universally accepted by the learned, as to the population of the European continent.

The nations of Christendom, with the exception of one or two inconsiderable and isolated tribes, appear to be descended from five races, all of which, though originally from the same stock, had ceased to know or acknowledge their affinity at a period beyond the reach of history, viz.

1. The Celts, whom we find at the dawn of history in possession of the western extremity of Europe. Their name is taken from the forests in which they dwelt; *Caillé* signifying, in all the Celtic dialects, *wood*.[1] The most ancient and simplest dialect of Celtic is that spoken in Ireland, and in the highlands of Scotland – the population of which is *mainly* of Irish descent, and whose language is by themselves called *Erse*. The tribes using this primeval dialect had yielded, at a very remote period, in Gaul, in Spain, and even Great Britain, to a more powerful and civilized race of Celts, namely the *Cymri*: and in proof of this, it is sufficient to state that the Celtic names of rivers,. mountains, chiefs, &c., mentioned in the Roman accounts of these countries during their early intercourse with them, whether peaceful or hostile, are in general referable to the *Cymraic*, or more artificial, species of the *Celtic* genus. These Cymri, after expelling the elder Celts from Great Britain, or at least subduing and mingling with them so as to supplant their language, yielded in their turn to the arms of races more advanced than themselves: their descendants are the modern Welsh, and the British colony in Armorica. The Cymraig is the connecting link between the ruder Celtic of Ireland and the languages of the Gothic or Teutonic race.

2. These Teutons, in their gradual advance from the East, the Mother of Nations, had occupied Germany, which still bears their name, (Deutchland,) and were threatening the Celtic tribes beyond the Rhine, long before the Romans were masters of Italy. When Cæsar began his Gaulish campaigns, they were, under the name of Belgæ, in possession of one-third of Gaul, and of the eastern coasts of Great Britain. Their subsequent history is well ascertained; their language is still

---

[1]   From *Caillé* come also, of course, Gallia, Caledonia, and Wales; and Jäkel is probably right in connecting with the same root the German *wald* (wood), whence our *wold*, and *wood* itself. The north of Italy, the *Gallia Cisalpina* of the Romans, is still called by the Germans *Welschland*.

spoken, in various dialects, by much of the greater part of the European population, and can be distinctly connected, in essential points, with the Persic and the Sanskrit.

3. The Sclavonic race, the parent of the Poles, Bohemians, and Russians. The dialects of this great family have as yet been little studied; but they are undoubtedly separated from the Gothic genus, still more widely than is the Celtic.

4. The Laplanders and Finns, the descendants of a once great people, the primeval occupants of all Scandinavia, who were driven into the recesses which they now hold, by the progress of Gothic tribes, exactly as the Celts of Gaul and Britain were by others of the same family. Their dialects are the rudest and poorest in Europe, but Murray and Jäkel agree in recognising even in them sufficient indications of a remote connection with those of the Teutonic family.

5. The Greeks and the Romans, the latter of whom it was formerly the fashion to consider as *descended* from the former. This theory, however, is no longer maintained: although few doubt that Pelagic colonists, established in very remote times on the northern shores of Italy, may have mingled their blood with the tribes that formed the main root of the Latin nation, and of course had a share in the *construction* of their language, while it is universally admitted that the intercourse between the Latins and the comparatively polished inhabitants of Magna Grecia, had powerful influence on every stage of its *refinement*.

'The Latin (says Murray) is not a dialect of the Greek: it possesses many properties of an original and distinct character: it approaches, in a variety of peculiar and remarkable features, to what may be considered as the natural aspect of the Greek, while unmoulded by time into that form which is common to the Ionic, Doric, and Æolic dialects. If the Latins had been, like the Phocean and many other states, a colony from Greece, the resemblance of language must have been incomparably greater. It may be safely admitted that the Romans were related to the Greeks, and that their language, on that account, is an excellent commentary on the Hellenic dialects; but if the Latin be viewed as a *descendant* of the Greek, which has degenerated from a pure original, the conclusions drawn from that opinion will be ill-founded, and the philological reasonings erected on them fallacious.'

We quote Murray; but he is only abridging the language of Adelung. The Greek and Latin have for some time been considered by all competent scholars as two separate dialects, formed, each in its own peninsula, by a conquering race, of Gothic origin, planting itself, each among a conquered primeval population, and each adopting, of necessity, part of the language originally spoken by that population into the substance of its own. It is thus that the Celtic element, largely visible both in the Greek and the Latin, is accounted for; and one of the most curious branches of the whole of this inquiry is that which tends to confirm the radically separate formation of the two languages of classical antiquity, by showing that, though each has much of Celtic, the Celtic element of the one is not the Celtic element of the other. They have both borrowed, we are told, from the same vocabulary, but, generally speaking, they have not taken the same words. It is much to be wished that this very curious point should be made the subject of a separate and minute investigation; and we confess we should be mortified to see such a problem worked out by any other than a countryman of our own. It is to the scholarship of Wales, surely, or Ireland, or Scotland, that the world ought naturally to look for the ultimate elucidation of the *Celtic* part of this discussion; and we believe no one who has read Mr. Williams's Life of Alexander the Great, and Essays on the Geography of Central Asia, will dispute that we have amongst us at least one 'true Briton,' fully competent to such a task.

We must, with these few hints, leave for the present both the Greek and the Celtic parts of the controversy, and devote the little space we have to the proper subject of Mr. Jäkel's Essay, – which is to show that the words expressive of the first and simplest ideas are common, for the most part, to the Latin and the German; – that the mass of vocables, found both in the Latin and in the German languages, appear in simpler and more archaic shapes in the latter than in the former; – that many of them are found *insulated* and detached in the Latin, insomuch that the classical etymologists could never explain them satisfactorily, while in the German the corresponding vocable is part of a whole family of words, the root obvious, and the ramifications disposed in a natural order; and hence arrive at the conclusion that the Latin tongue is mainly and essentially the dialect of a Teutonic race that migrated from

Germany into Italy by the way of the Tyrol, at a period vastly more remote than Roman history reaches to.

We do not pretend to care whether Mr. Jäkel shall be thought to have established the precise conclusion at which he arrives; it signifies little, in our opinion, whether we should suppose Italy to have been mainly peopled from her coasts, or from the passes of the Alps. The details on which the professor builds his theory are far more important than the fate of that theory; they cannot be perused without throwing light on many hitherto obscure and unexplored features, both of the Latin language and of our own mother tongue: and if our notice of the book should be the first thing to turn one young mind towards the habit of looking below the skin of lexicographic etymology, our purpose will be sufficiently attained.

The historical dissertation appended to the philological essay of Jäkel would lead us into a world-wide field. The author combats, with great ingenuity, some of Niebuhr's notions as to the origin of the various Italian tribes who were ultimately merged in the Roman state: one, at least, of these he considers to have been of Sclavonic race; more than one of Celtic; but the far greater part of them, including the most important, pure Goths. The use he makes of the spelling of *names* in old inscriptions is particularly curious. Thus, for *Euganei* he finds on an antique vase *ausuganei*, and interprets it *ausgänger*, the outgoers (Scottish, *outgangers*), 'the people of emigrants.' He claims kindred for the modern 'Baiern' (Bavarians) with the Boii – and interprets 'the young men – *the boys*.' The *Volsci* are the *folk – the* people κατ' εϛοχην. But the *Etruscans* occupy much more space than any of these; *all* the names by which they are known are, he says, purely Gothic. The name by which they generally called themselves was *Rasena*: Livy (Book v. 33) tells us that the Ræti, an Alpine people, were, 'haud dubie,' of the same origin, and spoke the same mother tongue in a ruder form. Jäkel has no doubt, then, that the Rasenæ and the Ræti were originally branches of the same people, distinguished by the same name; and he finds their primeval seat in that great district of Germany which bore the name of *Rætia* – that is, the country of hills, the *raised land*. *Tyrrheni*, he proceeds, must have been a later appellation – it signifies the *tower-men*, the dwellers in fortified places. As for *Tusci*, that is nothing but a slight disguise of *Teutsche* (Teutonici): when Tacitus names the founder of the German race as *Tuisco*, he betrays exactly the same fashion of eliding the consonants. The names of the gods, borrowed by Rome from Etruria, confirm, he thinks, the same view: Neptunus being *naff*, lord, and *tunn*, water; Minerva, a compound of *man* (qu. maiden?) and *arf*, arrow; *Mars*, from *mar*, fame; (qu. Mavors – Germ: *machtig-fürst*, *i.e.* great prince, answering to the Hindoo Maha-Rajah?): Nortia, the Etruscan Fortuna, identical with the *Norne* of the Scandinavians, &c. Many other Etruscan vocables are traced to the same source: *Aruns* is *Ernst*, the serious, the *Earnest*, *i.e.* the brave, the determined; *Felsina* is the town built on the *rocks* (*felsen*, German): this was the Etruscan name for the city at the foot of the Apennines, of which the *Boii* afterwards made their capital, and to which they gave their own name – Bononia – now Bologna. Other Etrurian towns were *Cosa* or *Cossa*, identical with *haus*, dwelling-place; *Comum* (Como), with *heim*, German, our *home*, *ham*, hamlet, &c.; *Puteoli*, the town of excavations, *pits*, wells. The river *Auser* is the German *Wasser* (water); Statonia is *stadt* (German for *town*); and the *Armenia* (supposed to be the Fiore near Montalto) is the river flowing in the country of the *Hermans* – the *war men*.

In the *Oscic*, rocks were called *herna*: in some of the Swiss dialects *fern* still means rock – in others *horn*; as the Schreckhorn (the terrible rock), the Finster-horn (the dark rock), &c. *Petorritum* meant a four-wheeled carriage – from the Oscic *petor* (four), identical with the old German *fedwor*, and *rit*, old German for *wheel* (the modern *rad*). The Oscic termination was usually in *or* and *ur* (as Tyrren*or*, Latin*ur*) – this is the German *er*.

Latium is the *flat* country, according to Jäkel, and the *Romani* were the *men of ruhm*, *i.e.*, in almost all the German dialects, *fame*. On an Etruscan monument, still visible, we have *Ruemunes* for *Romani*.

We must leave untouched the professor's Teutonic interpretations of the names of the elder institutions, and magistrates, and ceremonies of Rome. We have done enough to direct the attention of those who have really a taste for such studies to his treatise, and we hope furnished the general reader with a little amusement and food for speculation.

PHYSICAL EVIDENCES OF THE CHARACTERISTICS OF ANCIENT RACES AMONG THE MODERNS

Anonymous

Source: Fraser's Magazine, vol. 6, 1832

Fraser's Magazine of Town and Country was founded in 1830 under the editorship of William Maginn. Its editorial guidelines emphasized the importance of theories and 'principles'. The article illustrates the great impact of William Frédéric Edwards's *Des caractères physiologiques des races humaines* (*The Physiological Characters of Human Races*, 1829). Edwards (1776–1842) was born as the son of a well-to-do Jamaican farmer and the brother of Henri Milne-Edwards who was to become a famous zoologist. Before the turn of the century, the family moved to Belgium. From 1808 William Frédéric studied medicine in Paris. In 1824 he published a volume on the physical influence of external agents such as light and heat: *De l'influence des agents physiques sur la vie* (*On the Influence of Physical Agents on Life*, transl. into English in 1832). He was well versed in the physiological aspects of environmentalism. His interest in racial varieties was stimulated, however, by his desire to take part in the historical discussions of learned French republicans. His *Des Caractères physiologiques des races humaines* was conceived as an open letter to the historian Amédée Thierry. As explained in the introduction to this volume, Edwards strove to furnish the physiological basis to Thierry's political argument.

Dr. Edwards of Paris, member of the Institute, has recently suggested a method of tracing the ancient races of mankind among the existing inhabitants of the globe, by the application of physiological science to written history, each being considered by him as corroborating the evidences derived by the other.

M. Thierry has endeavoured to follow up the people of ancient Gaul to the present era; and Dr. Edwards has sought to discover, what there is common to the Gauls of the earliest ages and the inhabitants of those territories formerly their proper abodes, with regard to physical distinctions which are usually admitted to mark the natural families of the earth in a prominent degree.

The great mixture of nations now existing upon the continent of Europe renders it very difficult for historians to procure accurate data; and Dr. Edwards has found his system hitherto of advantage in dispelling much of the confusion encountered. The types of different original races are involved with modern varieties, from the frequent changes which commerce and conquest have effected during many centuries, so that every country contains a variety of types; and it is not perhaps too much to advance, that physiological science may separate these more effectually than the best historical data, if there by any truth in the assumed permanency of varieties among human beings, as we know there is in the other species of animals, and in the vegetable creation.

Blumenbach divided the human races into five distinct original families, adopting the principle of Camper, as to the form of the head, for the purpose of characterising a special type, which is transmitted from the earliest epochs indefinitely. Thus the first variety in his system is the Caucasian, including the inhabitants of Europe and Western Asia, the finest examples of which are met with usually among the Georgians and Circassians. The second variety is the Mongolian, including the inhabitants of Northern Asia, the Kalmucks, Tartar tribes, &c. The third variety is the Æthiopian, or Negro; and these three varieties of peculiarly marked skulls possess also other physical characters, less permanent indeed, but well understood. The two last varieties are more allied, perhaps, to the former than equally distinct, as the Malay and South Sea Islander resemble the Æthiopian, and the American the Mongolian variety.

The peculiar characters of the Caucasian head lie in its superiority of symmetry and roundness, moderate forehead, narrow cheek-bones without projection, but depending downwards, the alveolar edge well rounded, and the front teeth perpendicular.

The face corresponding with this head is oval and straight; the features are moderately prominent; the forehead is arched; the nose narrow, and slightly arched; the mouth small; the lips turned out, especially the lower one, which in the present Austrian royal family is remarkably so; and the chin is full and rounded. This character constitutes the *beau ideal* of the fair daughters of Caucasus.

The Mongolian head is nearly square; the cheek-bones project out; the nose is flat; the space between the eyebrows is even with the cheek-bones; the superciliary arches are slightly developed; the nostrils are narrow; the alveolar edge is somewhat rounded forwards; and the chin projects slightly.

The face of the Mongol is broad and flat, with the features indistinct; the space between the eyes is flat and broad; the nose is flat; the cheeks are projecting and round; the narrow and linear aperture of the eyelids extends towards the temples; the internal angle of the eye is depressed towards the nose, and the superior eyelid is continued at that part into the inferior by a rounded sweep; and the chin is slightly prominent. The Siamese youths displayed this form of head and features very closely.

The Æthiopian, or Negro, head is narrow, and compressed laterally; the forehead is very convex, and vaulted; the cheek-bones project forwards; the nostrils are wide; the jaws are very long; the alveolar edge is long, narrow, and elliptical; the front upper teeth are turned obliquely forwards; the lower jaw is strong and large; and the skull generally is thick and heavy. This character will be observed to bear a striking affinity to the head of the ape and monkey tribes.

The face of the Æthiopian is narrow, and projects towards the lower part; the forehead is convex and vaulted; the eyes project; the nose spreads and is confounded with the cheeks; the lips are very thick; the jaws are prominent, and the chin retracted.

The aboriginal American head approaches to that of the Mongolian. The cheek-bones are prominent, but more arched and rounded than in the skull of the Mongol, and less angular and projecting at the sides; the orbits are usually deep; the skull is generally light. The upper part of the head is frequently altered in shape by artificial means in infancy.

The American face is broad, but not flat; the profile is prominent and deep; the forehead is low, and the eyes deep seated; and the nose is rather flat and prominent.

The head of the Malay and South Sea Islanders is slightly narrowed at the top; the forehead is a little arched; the cheek

-bones do not project; the upper jaw is a little pushed forwards; and the parietal bones are marked by a strong degree of prominence. The face associated with this head is less narrow than that of the Negro, advancing in profile towards the lower part; the nose is thick, full, and broad, or what is termed a bottle-nose.

This argument has not, however, been found to correspond with the great divisions of the world; and others have been adopted, which run into the other extreme, and are too complex for our purposes.

The figure of the skull has been observed to be by no means a constant and invariable sign of a single type; and recourse has been therefore had to the measurement of the facial angle, with reference to the projections of the principal features, in order to establish a regular grade of intellect, connected with the formation of the face. But so many contradictions occur in applying this principle, among many striking coincidences, that little faith can be put in it. It seems more probable, that the faculties both of our own and other species are not definable by such rules, and that nature has adapted the mental powers and perceptions in general to the different spheres in which the Creator has destined man and animals to move. Nor can we well assume any farther universal adaptation of intellect to structure, than that where the greatest relative preponderance of brain naturally exists, the species possesses the highest order of intellect; while in cases where the nervous development is large, and that of the brain small, the physical powers and animal perceptions are far superior to the intellectual faculties. And however great is the popular bias in favour of physiognomical distinctions, these do not appear to be by any means universally certain indications, any farther than is the altitude of the forehead, or the projection of the hind or fore part of the head, a criterion of talent or the reverse.

Blumenbach himself was aware of the objections to his arrangement, and that it presented too broad an outline, being, in fact, more useful as a general system of character among human beings, than as referable to family relations. On this account, the original arrangement of Camper answers equally well, and is, perhaps, more applicable upon the principle of general character. He takes the measurement of the horizontal section of the vertex as his guide, and according to the breadth of the vertex distinguishes three varieties of the skull.

The first variety is the most common, and assumes a mediate form, expressed by the term *mesobregmate*, in which the horizontal section of the vertex is oval, and the prominence of the cheek-bones moderate when regarded from above. With the probable exception of the Laplanders, all European nations possess this skull. It is also common in Asia, excepting the Mongols, the Chinese, &c., in the northern and eastern divisions. It is traced likewise in Africa, notwithstanding many aberrations towards the second variety.

In the next variety the section of the vertex is narrowed, and expressed by the term *stenobregmate*. The skull is compressed laterally, the forehead is depressed, and the lower parts of the face are long and protruding, with flat features.

The Negroes of Guinea possess this form of skull; and the Africans generally approximate more or less to it. It is found in Madagascar and throughout the South Sea, especially among the inhabitants of New Holland, the Papuas, and the Mallicolese. The Polynesian tribes also possess it in some degree.

In the third form or variety the section of the vertex widens, and assumes a square figure, and is expressed by the term *platybregmate*, the cheek-bones projecting beyond the outline of this section.

The Mongols, Chinese, and other Asiatics, indicate this form, and also the aboriginal Americans, who differ less from the people of Asia, and bear a more common resemblance to each other.

Of these three essential characters there are some variations in each division, of a subordinate description.

As to other physical distinctions of natural families, there is observed a great correspondence between the hair, the colour of the choroid coat of the eyes, and the skin. In albinoes among dark nations, the colouring matter of the hair, the choroid coat, and the skin, are each wanting.

The colour of the skin is entirely dependent upon a delicate tissue of mucous substance, interposed between the layers of the skin, the cuticle, and the cutis, but demonstrable only in dark tribes. It is an indelible mark, transmitted indefinitely through every generation possessing it, which neither change of climate nor temperature obliterates. Negro families in Europe continue black, unless they intermarry with whites, when the dark skin becomes ultimately lost, perhaps by repeated crossings of varieties. And Europeans in tropical climates equally preserve their cast.

That the blackness is not in proportion to the heat of climate, is indicated by the circumstance of there being some nations of a darker shade without, than others within the tropics; and as to forming a universal criterion by which we may distinguish one race or variety from another, this is liable to interruption, from the fact, that perfectly different nations are equally black, or white, or of intermediate fixed shades. The Cingalese and Malabars often appear as jetty as the Negro; and the Malabar colour glides, by imperceptible shades, into the olive tint of the northern Hindoo, without any material alterations of form or structure accompanying these variations. The embrowned Spaniards, Portuguese, Arabs, and Persians, however distinct otherwise, exhibit little variety of colour.

The mucous pigment is strongly developed wherever dark-skinned races are original inhabitants of countries exposed to elevated temperatures, without regard to original family distinctions.

As to *form*, as a distinguishing characteristic of separate families, it is assuredly hereditary, when naturally acquired. But some peculiarities of form are produced by art, such as the contracted feet of the Chinese ladies, and the flattened skulls of the Caribbees. Nor are our own more civilised ladies of modern Europe exempt from this barbarous custom of altering the natural form. The distortions occasioned by pressure on the yielding mechanism of the chest, are no uncommon sources of chronic visceral disease.

The hereditary characters of form are those which originally belong to the fœtus, and grow with its growth. But of all the peculiarities, the most striking and permanent is that of the head, of which Camper and Blumenbach availed themselves in arranging the natural divisions of the human species.

In the *figure and general proportions* of the body, we find some remarkable variations among different nations. The Negroes, the Australians (or New Hollanders,) and the Kalmucks, differ more than any others from the Europeans in this respect; and the Negro proportions less resemble those of the Europeans than the results of measurements among the ape and baboon tribes, although there are some exceptions to this general law.

Stature varies among the different races of mankind, and in such a manner as to hold out no probability of our being able to make any arrangement of families by reference to this distinction. The Patagonians are the tallest tribe, measuring from six to seven feet high. We have the tallest and the shortest specimens from America. The people of Terra del Fuego are a puny race, and the Eskimeaux still more so. Africa produces very small persons; and some Europeans have reached eight or nine feet, while others have not exceeded thirty inches or less; in the brute creation the same diversity occurs in distinct families.

Of the physical characters now detailed, that of *colour* offers the least difficulty of explanation; although, in fact, the varieties of mankind are less nearly analogous to other varieties, as to colour, than some other species. There is a more general agreement in the human form and structure, than among other species, although, as to most physical distinctions, we perceive a greater aberration from one common standard. It is therefore a rational conclusion, that the diversities of the *human* form especially are but deviations from *one primitive type*.

The other distinctions, such as the colour of the skin, the texture of the hair, the stature, and the relations of parts, afford a similar conclusion.

The notion once entertained, that there are distinct species among mankind, is contradicted by every appeal to physiology and zoology; for all the physical as well as the moral characteristics lead us in the end to so close an approximation of individual varieties to each other, as scarcely to admit of any other conclusion than, that the whole human species is referrible to one primary stock, of which several varieties, not yet entirely made out perhaps, have been created from the necessity of the original stock spreading over the earth, and separating into distinct families. And thus a certain number of types probably has been constituted; and where nations have been conquered and exterminated, their types may nevertheless exist to attest their ancient origin; and, from having been scattered abroad, they may transmit physiological evidences thus supported as to their identity and distinctness, although dead in traditional history.

The vegetable kingdom affords a similar example, for we find from geological investigations, that all kinds of plants originated, not in one common centre, but from different points forming so many centres of vegetation. Each province had its peculiar tribes, and these, with few exceptions perhaps, existed not elsewhere at the time of their formation.

The analogy of the animal kingdom furnishes the same conclusion, the various species of which could not have been created all in one province; nor can it be supposed, that the same individual species arose from several distinct countries, and had various origins. It is reasonable to infer that the different tribes of organised beings originated in certain regions adapted to them, each commencing in a single stock, or one pair; nor have we any traditional history which contradicts this supposition.

Many species now existing probably originated in countries distant from each other, and were created since the Noachian deluge, subsequently to which catastrophe, new regions apparently emerged from the subsiding waters, and the earth became fitted for the propagation of our own and other species. And as the means and opportunities of propagation increased, the original stock spread into distinct varieties of mankind, having certain fixed physical characters and languages; and hence we trace original tongues, through all the various idioms which intercommunication has engendered, and tended to confuse, since man's first appearance upon the earth, from the active and roaming habits peculiar to his species.

Much, however, as this intermixture of varieties has confounded them, distinct families approximate so closely as to indicate less variation than exists among the different species of the brute creation.

Dr. Edwards proposes to avail himself of this approximation in physical signs and language, by referring to the marked characters of the countenance peculiar to existing nations in conjunction with their political history; whence original families may be more easily traced than by mere historical data.

He supposes that many circumstances, hitherto unexplained in history, may thus be cleared up, by a general application of the principle.

A nation now consists of many stocks or families, and their different physical characters are insufficient for the purpose of tracing out their origins; for many evidently distinct exhibit some peculiarities of form, &c. in common. In language and moral and physical attributes, human races seem to possess a greater degree of variety than is expressed in Blumenbach's arrangement. A less broadly extended scale of division is therefore required.

The connexion between ancient and modern nations must be greatly interrupted. We see examples of this in the European colonies of the new world, where the aboriginal inhabitants are disappearing, and giving place to new languages and races. But, however much the ancient formation of languages is corrupted, careful discrimination may detect it amidst modern idioms, notwithstanding the associations of mixed nations.

Europeans take possession of equinoctial territories, and castes are formed by a medley of interconnexions. Nevertheless, the white population is not lost in its genuine characters, and each nation recognizes its proper offspring. People established in foreign climates preserve their types indefinitely, notwithstanding the modifications of temperature and climate, and social intercourse.

Even a mother country of ancient origin may have among its inhabitants many distinct types, distinguished by different physical characters, habits, and languages, of which the Jewish race is an example. The Jews certainly bear some general resemblance to the people among whom they live, but in every country their common character is strongly defined, and they are marked by one universal identity. More than seventeen hundred years have elapsed since the dispersion of the Jews, and their type is upwards of three thousand years old in history.

Some authors appear to think that our species was originally *black*, and became *white* by the influence of civilisation. This opinion does not, however, appear to be sustantiated. On the tomb of an ancient Egyptian king figures of dark-brown-complexioned men are drawn, but they have not the *hair* which peculiarly characterises the Negro race of the present age. Other groups of strangers appear also, of the Jewish character, resembling the portraits of our London Jews. Belzoni discovered three distinct groups portrayed upon an ancient tomb, representing Jews, Æthiopians, and Persians, as we now see them.

If we consult the natural and civil history of man, it will appear, that nearly the whole of the ancient families are now represented; and their antiquity is evidently no bar to their continuance indefinitely. Various circumstances of conquest, climate, &c. may cut off some, as the Guanches and others, which are said to exist no longer; but such influential causes must be very limited, in comparison with the ancient families retained. History goes a great way back to trace these, but physiological distinctions may go farther in developing the origin of nations, especially when conjoined with historical data.

Impressed with the idea now alluded to, Dr. Edwards travelled for the purpose of endeavouring to discover ancient types among the present mixed nations of Europe, taking for his guidance the signs exhibited in the form and proportions of the head and the features of the face, considering that all other modifications of form and figure are too precarious to be depended upon, while, in extreme cases, he thinks that an appeal may be made to the colour of the skin, the texture of the hair, and the general form and figure, where the mere bust is not sufficient to determine the antiquity of a family.

Upon the frontiers of Burgundy was noticed a multitude of forms of one peculiar type, from Auxerre to Châlons. And, on a market-day at Châlons, another variety appeared, quite distinct from any seen elsewhere on this route.

In the Lyonnais the predominant Burgundian type appeared again, accompanied with some change of colour, as it did from Savoy to Mount Cenis, with another shade of colour, and some other physical distinctions. Among so many mixed people, from Auxerre to the Alps, had *colour* been made a leading distinction, there would have been a confusion of types, rather than two strongly contrasted.

History tells us that the ancient Gauls possessed the territories of this route, and were conquered by the Romans, who thus became mingled with the vanquished; and notwithstanding the subsequent conquest of France, the type of the Gauls appears to be that recognised by Dr. Edwards upon their ancient soil.

The ruins of past ages are the chief objects of attraction to travellers in Italy. But this country affords abundant opportunities of studying the ancient authors of Roman monuments, by comparing their descendants with their known types. At Florence great facilities appear to present themselves in this investigation. The busts of the early emperors best indicate the true Roman type, because these personages represent true and ancient families. Their forms and proportions are too strongly marked to be easily neglected or forgotten. The vertical diameter being short, gives them a large visage, and a squareness of the head and face; and any deviation from this character would not resemble the bust of an ancient Roman.

On the route from Florence to Rome were noticed the busts of Augustus, Sextus Pompei, Tiberius, Germanicus, Claudius, Nero, and Titus, mingled, of course, with many other varieties. On entering the Papal territories this character is said to be very striking, from Péruge to Rome.

In Rome the mixture of the people is extremely various throughout all ranks; yet probably the Roman type exists among them, both as to bust and the stature, which is moderate.

This type appears in the kingdom of Naples to be almost exclusively confined to the higher territories. It exists, also, north and west of Rome, towards Sienna, &c., where it is described as very distinct.

These observations seem to agree with the political and civil history of Rome; shewing that in the Italian states the people are generally the same as in times past, and bear a very strong resemblance, in numerous instances, to the figures represented in bas-reliefs, and to busts of Roman soldiers and civilians.

Rome itself appears to have been originally peopled by strangers from adjacent countries, the Trojans, the Sabines, and a portion of the Etruscans, &c., among whom separations and divisions into independent communities seem to have deceived historians into an idea of a greater variety of stocks than really existed. Thus original languages may have become corrupted, but physical characters do not yield to such circumstances.

The language, arts, and institutions of the Etruscans render it uncertain whether they are indigenous or strangers. And, although much mixed, there exists a great resemblance among them to a portion of the ancient Etruscans.

Portraits of Dante, Petrarch, Ariosto, and Tasso, copied from monuments of their days, bear a great degree of common resemblance, in a long head, small high forehead, bent-down nose, and projecting chin.

Dante's portrait appears on the Tuscan frontier very frequently; and the features of the Medici family, as delineated at Florence, together with prototypes of figures of Etruscan bas-reliefs and busts, constitute a perfect type.

On the road to Venice by Bologna, Ferrara, and Padua, the Dante head again presented itself, and a *cicerone* drew attention to the resemblance which subsisted between the portrait of a Venetian saint and Dante. The portraits of the Doges also, in the ducal palace of St. Mark's, have the Etruscan character, as seen as far as Milan.

In a village of the Milanese, Dr. Edwards recognised the type which appeared in the market-place of Châlons, the conformity to which he represents as strongly marked as the general diversity elsewhere, excepting among the Cisalpine Gauls of Switzerland, and in Geneva, where both the Châlons type and that of the Burgundian country generally appeared.

In an immense population on the road to Châlons and Mâion, two well-marked types, it appears, attracted notice, one characterised by a head more round than oval, with rounded features, and middle stature; and the other by a long head, a large and high forehead, bent nose, prominent chin, and elevated stature.

The first continues along the course of the river to Mâcon, where it disappears; and the second prevails about Châlons. M. Thierry's historical remarks corroborate the observations of Dr. Edwards.

In the remaining part of ancient Gaul two great families existed, very far back in history, at one epoch, differing in language, habits, and social state, and forming the majority of the population. If we now examine the corresponding spread of France, as to its actual population, two distinct types predominate, resembling the ancient Gauls, although, having been conquered by strangers, they have become modified in many respects, yet are still to be recognised. The conquered are represented to have been a more considerable nation than their conquerors; and the Gauls and the Kimri were both anciently very populous tribes; Eastern Gaul, containing the Gauls proper to Cæsar, and Belgic or Northern Gaul, including the Kimri, Burgundy, the Lyonnais, the Dauphinnais, and Savoy, constituted the first, where the distinguished Gallic type is general, excepting one canton; while the second type occupies the other portions of this region.

Referring to the historical descriptions of these tribes, they approximate closely to Dr. Edwards's accounts of their physical characters.

M. Thierry observes, that central Britain contains people
chiefly referrible to the Kimri, or northern Belgic Gauls, who,
although historically dead as ancient Britons, exist in their
well-marked physical character sufficiently to prove their
ancient alliance, having a long head, elevated forehead, bent-
down nose, with the point low and the alæ elevated, the chin
projecting and strongly pronounced, with a high stature, much
as Dr. Edwards observed them in Burgundy, Picardy, and
Normandy: existing in England prior to the conquests of the
Saxons, historians consider them to be exterminated upon
insufficient grounds. They are said to have recovered their
rights after the middle ages, and, raised by the progress of
industrious habits, became members of all classes of society;
and probably in many cases where questions have arisen as to
Saxon or Norman descent, the true origin was in these ancient
Britons.

History shews that the Gauls predominated in the north of
Italy, between the Alps and the Appennines, subsequently
mingled with others, but anciently settled there, within the
period of early historical glimmerings. Ancient authors
depicted the Italian and Belgic Gauls as they now appear in
France, England, Switzerland, and Italy, and tall in stature as
the Kimri are described.

The two grand divisions of the Gauls occupy more than half
of Italy, and a portion of Switzerland, France, and England.

In Venetian Lombardy the emperor's troops consist of
Silesians, Bohemians, Moravians, Polonnais, and Hungarians,
serfs from eastern Europe. The type of the *Huns* appeared
among this medley, who spoke a sort of slave-language in
general, and had no distinct physical character. The Hunnish
head appears to be rounded, the forehead slight, and the eyes
obliquely placed, and bearing altogether such a general
resemblance to the Hungarians, that a painter may substitute
one of them for an ancient Hun. The ancient language of the
Huns is also to be recognised among this portion of the
Hungarians.

Part of Europe has been peopled from Asia, and the eastern
half of the latter country contains the Mongols, characterised
by a round head, small forehead thrown backwards, broad and
flat nose, projecting cheek-bones, mouth advancing, thick lips,
the chin slightly supplied with hair, and the stature small. The
stocks of the other half more nearly resemble those of Europe;

many, however, of each family are common to both divisions. Both their language and history tend to confirm these notices.

The Mongolian character extends to Russia and Hungary, where the Finnish language prevails without the physical character, the dialect being acquired before their establishment in Hungary.

Such are the principal points, slightly touched upon, of Dr. Edwards's application of physiological principles to history, in order to fill up the voids of the latter, confirm its data, and supply more than the mere divisions of heads into five types are capable of.

If physiology can thus be made to co-operate with natural and political history, by comparing the physical distinctions which characterise peculiar families with their ancient alliances, the origins of nations may not only be more fully and satisfactorily made out, but separated more readily from the confusion of mixed types around them; while the principle of the investigation opens a new field of inquiry to the traveller, of no ordinary interest, and such as may afford more general gratification than the severer study of searching among the pages of ancient lore for the traces of the original families of mankind, however valuable have been their results and additions to human knowledge.

The correctness of the principle regarding the permanency of types, appears to be one admitted generally by physiologists and naturalists; and it seems to be by no means likely to become a fruitless search, if the general association of the features of the face be taken into conjunction with the form of the head, and other physical distinctions, in cases where language, and shades of colour, &c. fail from their instability of attachment to most races, by which such signs become lost among descendants, or so confused as to furnish no positive evidence of origin or antiquity.

The inquiry to which Dr. Edwards has turned his attention in a recent pamphlet, written in the French language, is one fully worthy the notice of scientific travellers, in conjunction with historical accounts of the ancient tribes of people, and their modern distribution and existence. And among the objects of interest to the tourist of this country, few seem to possess more probable sources of intellectual occupation, while passing through populous districts and cities; where, among the busy assemblages of mixed races, it must be curious to recognise comparative relations to different forms and styles of features, known only to the existing inhabitants of the earth by history, painting, or sculpture.

NATURAL HISTORY OF THE NEGRO SPECIES PARTICULARLY

Julien-Joseph Virey

(Translated by J. H. Guenebault)

Julien-Joseph Virey (1775–1846) took his MD degree in 1814 at the faculty of medicine in Paris. Between 1794 and his retirement in 1813 he acted as pharmacist in military service. Most of his career he spent in Paris. His natural philosophy was characterized by a commitment to teleological principles. In his publications on the vital principle (1823) and the philosophy of natural history (1835) he tried to refute 'materialist' doctrines and the philosophy of sensationalism.

In whatever light we consider Negroes, we cannot deny that they present characteristics of a race distinct from the white. This truth, grounded upon incontestable facts of anatomy, is universally acknowledged. Now, in natural history, that which distinguishes a *species* from a *race*, is the permanency of characteristic features,[1] notwithstanding contrary influences of climate, food, or other external agents: whereas, *races* are but varied modifications of a sole and primordial *species*.

All the facts which have been collected, concur to prove how constant and indelible are the natural and moral characteristics of negroes in every climate, notwithstanding a diversity of circumstances. In natural history, it is then impossible to deny that they form not only a *race*, but truly a *species*, distinct from all other races of men known on the globe.

From the most ancient times, it has been generally admitted that the black color of negroes was the effect of light, or the heat of the Torrid Zone. It has been said that the closer nations were in the vicinity of the equatorial line, the more they became

---

[1] It is not useless to demonstrate, that in old times, negroes were exactly shaped as they are now. From ancient sculptures, in Caylus, *Recueil d'Antiquités Etrusques, Egyptiennes, Grecques, Romaines et Gauloises*, (*Supplement*, tom. 7, Paris, 1767, in 4to. Planche 81, nos. 3 et 4.) see the picture of a negro boy very well shaped, (*Description*, p. 285). His face is well characterized, and even the strong contraction of his hip, is faithfully represented.

dark. They have represented Germans more colored than Swedes and Danes; Frenchmen darker than Germans or Englishmen; Italians and Spaniards more swarthy than Frenchmen; the inhabitants of Morocco more so than Spaniards; finally, Moors and Abyssinians, presenting shades of brown color, which place them next to the black color of the inhabitants of Guinea.[2]

However conclusive this observation may appear, it is not certainly sufficient, and others contradict it. This gradation of colors is also remarked among other nations in quite a different order; for, according to the explanation given above, all nations of the Torrid Zone should be *black*; those of temperate zones of a *more or less dark color*, and those of cold zones *very white*. This is not the case. Indeed, nations found in the vicinity of the Arctic pole, such as Laplanders, Samoyedes, Esquimaux, Greenlanders, Tschutchis, &c. are *very tawny*; whereas, those nearer the tropics, as Englishmen, Frenchmen, Italians, &c. are *more white*. Moreover, all men have not the same color under the same parallel, and the same degree of heat. For instance, Norwegians and Icelanders are *very white*; on the contrary, Labradorians, Irokois of America, Tartars Kirguis, Baschkirs, Buriats, and Kamtschatdales, are *darker*. In the neighborhood of the white Circassian and beautiful Mingrelian women, are to be seen *brown* and ugly Calmucs and Tartars Naujiks, with a *dark* skin. The Japanese are *darker* than Spaniards, although the countries they both live in are situated under the same latitude, and the temperature nearly the same. Although it is perhaps as cold towards the Straits of Magellan as the Baltic, Patagonians are not *as white* as Danes. At Van Diemen's Land, towards the south cape of New Holland, we find men *as dark* as Hottentots, yet the climate is at least as *cold* as in England. New-Zealand, placed under the same south latitude, is inhabited by very *tawny* nations; and yet inhabitants of islands are generally not *so dark* as those of great continents.[3] Inhabitants of upper Asia, situated under the same

---

2   Spaniards, born at Chili, from European parents, remain white, and are even more so than in Europe; on the contrary, the natives of Chili are rather copper-colored than olive-colored like Mulattos, (Frezier, *Voyage*, p. 63). Negroes remain black, if they do not mix. (*Ibid.*) But at Brazil, and in European colonies, they are of a sallowish yellow complexion. (*Ibid.*)

3   2d *Voyage* de Cook et Forster, *Observations*, vol. 5, p. 234, traduction Française.

parallel as Europeans, and exposed to the same temperature, are *much darker*. If the shades of the color of the skin were caused by the heat of the climate, why should we see inhabitants of Sunda Islands, Malays, Maldiveans, Moluccans, in short, those of Guinea, and so many other nations of the Torrid Zone, *much less dark* than negroes? Yet, Negroes are to be found out of the Torrid Zone; such are Hottentots of the Cape of Good Hope: how could we meet at Madagascar, an *olive colored* race and a *black* one? How could *white nations*, according to travellers, be found in the heart of Africa, surrounded by a *black* population?[4] Why, in the very same country, inhabited by *negroes*, and under the same degree of heat, should some remain *white* or only *olive colored*? If climate blackens the negro, why does it not render also monkeys, quadrupeds, birds, &c. &c. of a black color? – Why should the same temperature color so differently men living under the same parallel on the earth?

Still more: amidst our own population, and in the same family, we see brown and light colored persons, some with a fair skin, others of a darker color, although living together in the same manner, and even under the same roof. Negroes born in European and American Colonies, do not lose their black color. Dutch settlers at the Cape of Good Hope, who live nearly after the Hottentot fashion, but without ever intermarrying with the natives, have retained their original *white* color for two centuries without any alteration.[5] Lord Kaimes (Sketches on Man) says: The *Moors* in Hindostan retain their natural color, though transplanted there more than three centuries ago; and the *Mogul family* continue white like

---

4 Buffon, *Supplément*, in 12mo. vol. 8, p. 271, maintains with Bruce, Voyage, vol. 5, p. 115, that white nations are to be found in the heart of Africa; under the equator, according to Demanet and Adanson. The different shades among black nations are very far from being in proportion to their remoteness from the Equator, (Halle, *Encyclop. méthod.*, vol. 1, p. 312). Arabians are of a brown olive color; Cabyles, inhabiting the mountains of Atlas and Fez are white. Those inhabiting Mount Auress, in the kingdom of Alger, are white, or red haired, so that Shaw believed they were the descendants of Vandals of old. – (See also Bruns, *Afrika*, vol. 2, p. 119, and Poiret, *Voyage en Barb.* vol. 1, p. 31.)

5 Ovington, *Voyage*, vol. 2, p. 196; Marsden, *Sumatra*, traduction Française, vol. 1, p. 80; Pechlin, *Æthiop.*; Cook, *Voy. Austr.* vol. 2, p. 245 et 325; Hugues, *Barbad.* p. 14; Cœrdenus, *Voy.*, vol. 2, p. 262; *Hist. Academ.*, 1724, p. 18, maintain that whites never become completely black under the Tropics.

their ancestors the Tartars, though they have reigned in Hindostan above four centuries. The *Southern Chinese* are *white*, though in the neighborhood of the Torrid Zone, and women of fashion in the Island of Otaheite who cover themselves from the sun, have the European complexion. Some authors have stated that the Portuguese inhabiting the vicinity of Gambia, and the Cape Verde Islands, from the fifteenth century down to the present time, had become black; the cause of such a change in the color must be attributed only to the connexions of those Europeans with the natives. It is known that almost all Portuguese women die in Guinea, owing to the excessive heat which causes a very dangerous hemorrhage. Miscarriages frequently follow their pregnancies, or their delivery is accompanied with fatal uterine hemorrhagies. The Portuguese have then been unable to propagate in that climate, except by marrying with native females. Such is the cause why they are nearly black.

Black children when first born, are of a reddish, or rather of a yellowish color. Some parts of their body only, as the circles round the nails of the hands and toes, and organs of generation have a brownish hue; a week after, they become by degrees *perfectly black*, either in a *cold or a warm climate, either exposed to the light*, or *kept in a dark place*; why do they not remain *white* in *cold* countries, and when kept *from the light*? If the blackness of their skin was produced by a cause entirely occasional and external, why should it be hereditary in all countries, and the same in all generations? The reason why all children both of blacks and whites, and of every intermediate shade are all born of a ruddy color, is owing to the cuticle and *rete mucosum*, being so exceedingly thin and transparent: the latter not having yet acquired any color, shows through it the color of the *cutis vera*, or true skin, which is an integument very full of blood vessels, and therefore nearly of the color of blood itself. The cuticle and *rete mucosum* grow gradually thicker and less transparent; and in Negroes the latter grows gradually darker colored and harder; but the former preserves its transparency in the face through life, which is evinced in white people, by the redness of the cheeks, and by blushing; and in negroes by the superior blackness of the face, the dark *rete mucosum* appearing more clearly through it there than in any other part. In negroes this black color is not confined to their skin. Anatomists of old have observed, and Doctor Virey has seen it himself, that the blood of that species of men *is darker* than that of white men; and their muscles and flesh of a red color approaching to the brown. The brain, which in white men is gray or ash-colored, and its exterior or cortical part, is especially black in Negroes.[6] Their *medulla oblongata* presents a yellow gray color, and the striated bodies have a brown hue.[7] – Their bile is also of a darker shade than in whites; the Negro, therefore, is not only black on his exterior, but is so in the inward parts of his body, even the most interior.

A still better proof of this, is that his conformation differs from ours by essential characteristics. Not mentioning the crisped and woolly hair of negroes, nor giving in detail a full account of all that distinguishes their physiognomy from ours, such as round eyes, a rounded and depressed forehead, a flat nose, thick lips, a luxuriant mouth, an awkward gait, flexed legs; their interior especially presents striking singularities. Sœmmering and Ebel, learned German anatomists, have proved that the brain of the negro was comparatively narrower than that of the white, and the nerves on the base of the brain, larger in the former than in the latter. Several other observers have remarked that in proportion as the face of the negro protruded, his skull lessened. This gives a difference of a ninth more between the capacity of the head of a white, and that of a negro. Palissot de Beauvois who travelled in Africa, and Dr. Virey, when they came to compare the quantity of liquids which the skulls of whites and blacks could contain, have observed in the latter as much as nine ounces less than in European skulls.

The skull of a negro is thick, and its sutures very closely united. It resists blows better than that of Europeans; but the hemispheres and cerebral circumvolutions of the brain, are not so voluminous, numerous, and deep, as in the white man. They have great "*Tubercula Quadrigemina,*" and a small round protuberance. The hinder part of the brain is proportionately very great; the occipital hole has a large opening; the *medulla oblongata* is large; their propensity to sensations and nervous excitements, is excessive. All these signs indicate a greater animal disposition than in the white.

[6] Meckel, *Mem. Acad. de Berlin*, vol. 13, p. 69, an. 1767.

[7] *Ibid*, p. 70.

Herodotus had already said, that the skulls of Ethiopians were harder than those of Persians, and the cause of such a difference in the latter was attributed to the custom of wearing always on their heads a mitre, "*cindaris*;" while, on the contrary, the rays of the sun acting on the uncovered heads of the Ethiopians had hardened their bones. It is notorious that all the bones of negroes are more compact, and contain more "phosphate of lime;" they are also whiter than those of the Caucasian race. Fernandez Oviedo relates, that skulls of Caribbeans compared with those of Spaniards, present the same distinction. All nations, whose skulls are as hard as ivory, have very little intellect; undoubtedly, because the ossification is completed too soon, and prevents the perfect development of the brain. Hardness of bone, of other textures, and of the cerebral capacity, generally betray a poor intellect, congenial to that of brutes, which arrive sooner at puberty.

Very important reflections arise from these remarks on the proportions between the skull and face of the negro, and the comparative volume of his brain and nerves. Indeed, the more an organ extends, the more powerful and active it becomes; in like manner, the more it contracts, the more it loses its activity and power. Hence it follows, that if the brain contracts, and the nerves emerging from it expand, the negro will be less inclined to think, than to abandon himself to sensual pleasures, whilst the reverse will be remarked in the white. The senses of taste and smelling of the negro, having more extension than those of the white, they will have more influence upon his moral qualities, than they have upon ours. The negro will be more inclined to the pleasures of the body, we, to those of the mind. In our white species, the forehead is projecting, and the mouth retreating, as if we were rather designed to think than to eat; in the negro species, the forehead is retreating, and the mouth projecting, as if he were made rather to eat than to think. Such a particularity is much more remarkable in inferior animals; their snout is protruding, as if about to reach the food; their mouth becomes wider, as if they were born for gluttony alone; the size of their brain becomes smaller, and is placed backwards; the faculty of thinking is but secondary. We may remark that persons given up to the pleasures of the table, those great eaters, intemperate epicures, who seem to live only to eat, have a stupid look; they know of nothing but good eating; always digesting, they become incapable of thinking.

The elder Cato said: "what good can we expect from a man who is but a belly from his mouth downwards" – it is certain that the power of thinking is weakened in proportion as the power of nutrition is stronger; thus, all men of genius have but a poor digestion.

The members and senses likewise become more perfect externally, at the expense of the mind. It seems as if the brain of the negro had been almost absorbed by his nerves, so much do his senses possess activity, and his fibres mobility. He lives only by sensations. Every one knows that they have a piercing sight, an acute smell,[8] very delicate ears for music; a sensual taste, and that almost all of them are gluttons. They feel keenly the power of love; in short, they are superior to all other men in agility, dexterity, imitation, as respects the body. They excel particularly in dancing, fencing, swimming and horsemanship. Their feats of agility are surprising. They climb, vault on a rope with wonderful facility, equalled only by monkeys, their countrymen, and perhaps, their eldest brothers in the rank of nature. When dancing, negresses set in motion, at the same time, every part of their body – they are indefatigable in it.

Negroes could distinguish a man, or a ship at sea, at such a distance that Europeans could hardly distinguish them with a spy-glass. They smell a snake at a great distance, and often follow animals by the track; they hear the least noise, and run-away slaves can smell and hear white men pursuing them. As they feel much, so they think little; – they live only by impressions. The fear of the most cruel punishments, even of death, cannot deter them from abandoning themselves to the impetuosity of their passions. To spend a few moments with the object of their love, has induced many to expose their lives to great dangers. The sound of a tam-tam, or any rough music, delights them. Some words, without connexion, which they sing with a monotonous tone, and repeat again and again, amuse them for whole days together. Such songs, if they can be called so, prevent their being tired; their rhythm assuages their labors, and gives them strength anew.[9] A moment of pleasure

---

8   I. Dan Metzger. *Die Physiolog.* &c.

9   In the month of March, 1835, a fire took place in Savannah, Ga. (every one knows that in Savannah, a squad of negroes is attached to each engine) – the blacks to keep up their spirits, began to sing, and for nearly four hours, during which the fire raged with fury, they repeated this childish burden, "*O, jolly pump go well* – *O, jolly pump go well*, &c." At each "*go well*,"

to them makes up for a whole year of pain. – Abandoned to the affections of the present, they care not for the past or the future, so, their sorrows are not lasting; they become reconciled with their misery, and believe it tolerable, when they can enjoy a moment of pleasure. – As they follow rather the impulses of their senses and impressions, than the dictates of reason, they are excessive in every thing; *lambs* when governed, *tigers* when they have the power. Their minds, according to the expression of Montaigne, are running from the cellar to the garret, (going from one extremity to another). Disposed to lay down their lives for those they love, (and many have done so for their masters) they are capable, when excited by revenge, of butchering their best beloved, disemboweling their wives, and crushing their infants with stones. Nothing can be more terrible than their despair; nothing more sublime than their devotion. Such excesses are the more transient, in proportion to their impetuosity. Hence results in negroes the rapid change of sensations, their violence opposes their duration. For such men, necessity is the only possible restraint – force, the only law: so decreed by their constitution and climate.

If we find fewer *moral relations* among negroes, such as arise from the mind, thought, knowledge, religious and political opinions; in return, they have more *natural relations*; their affections are more readily communicated; they are more easily impressed by the same feelings, more subject to emotions; they share in a moment the feelings of their black fellow-men, and take instantly their part. Whatever *impresses* their *senses*, has a power upon them; whilst that which *strikes* their *reason*, will find them indifferent.

As pusilanimity results from such a constitution, it was in the nature of the negro to be more timorous. A narrow mind is the source of knavery, lies, and treachery; all vices common to negroes, and weak intellects. As they cannot act openly by force, they make themselves amends by dark machinations and plots. They rob, because they are not permitted to possess much. They are envious, jealous, proud, cringing in adversity, insolent in prosperity. They are fond of vain show, spending money, gaming, good eating, gaudy dresses, and when fortune

there was such a pull, as to satisfy the by-standers, that the poor fellows had not lost any of their vigor. The writer of this book witnessed the fact himself.

has emancipated them, they carry on luxury, even to extravagance. Such vices are common to almost all southern and weak-minded nations, and the best testimony of it, is the superstition to which Africans are subjected: the fact is, they have no sort of religion, except a puerile fear of *evil spirits*, sorcerers and conjurors; they foolishly worship Marmosets called "Fetichs," gris-gris, or some other animals, as snakes, crocodiles, lizards, birds, &c. Several tribes of negroes practice circumcision, which has been taught to them by Arabians, and fancy they are of the Mahometan religion, whilst they do not even understand it. For a bottle of brandy, an inhabitant of Senegal will be of any religion whatever; and, the day after he will change it for the same reward, he does not know a better argument. A negro is not to be persuaded by what does not strike him immediately; he will repeat whatever you please: his mind is of too narrow compass to think of the future, or too lazy to have a care for it.

This natural indifference is also a consequence of the constitution of the negro; for, although the same is remarked among nations but little civilized, it is more striking in the former. In fact, civilization exciting our wishes, and multiplying our wants, inspires us with a perpetual restlessness, and that burning ambition which prompts us to surpass each other, and makes us discontented with our present fate. The savage, on the contrary, desires very little, and confines his wants to necessaries. The African carries still to a further extent his apathy and carelessness for the future. There are always musicians on board Guinea-men, which transport slaves, to reconcile their minds with their wretchedness. Now, let a European only think how much music could please him, were he chained down in the hold, abused, badly fed, and destined to spend all his life in servitude and misery. Moreover, very often negroes carried in slavery, are fully convinced that they will be devoured by the white men, and still they submit themselves to their fate: for them, *to-day* has no *to-morrow*, and, provided, they are not driven to a state of despair, they bear up well under the burden of their miseries. – Happy indifference, by which unfortunate men are made insensible to the sad reflections on their misfortunes; – in like manner, the poor white people forget their unfortunate condition, when they can get wine, brandy, or food; whereas, rich and mighty men must conjure up their fortitude and courage, to contest with adversity.

In our time, the question about the degree of intellect among negroes, has given rise to great controversy; we believe that some authors, according to the system they have embraced, have over-rated or depreciated it too much: in order to discover the truth, in such a matter, let us separate that question from any reference to the servitude or liberty of negroes.

The friends of negroes have endeavored to extol their genius. They maintain that the reach of their mind is equal to that of the whites, but that want of education, and the state of degradation in which they live, prevent them, as a matter of course, from displaying their intellect. They say, "*admit young negroes into our Colleges, give them all the advantages that fortune and a liberal education secure to our children, and then decide.*" In the mean time several authors have collected instances of negroes, who possessed a natural talent for poetry, philosophy, music, and who had more or less disposition for the fine arts. Blumenbach assures, that he saw Latin and English lines composed by negroes, and which many European learned men might have been proud to have written.[10]

Brissot saw, in North America, free negroes engaged successfully in professions which require intellect and knowledge, as medicine, &c.; a black man could instantly make wonderful calculations. The eminent Bishop Gregoire composed a treatise on the literature of negroes,[11] and amidst numerous proofs given to him of their proficiencies in every branch of learning, he mentions several negro women; among them, we remark especially, Phillis Whately, who was brought from Africa to America, and then to England, when she was seven years old: she learned very soon the English and Latin languages: at the age of nineteen, she published a collection of English poetry, very much esteemed. Doctor Battie[12] believes the negro not inferior to the white man in any thing: so does Clarkson. Wadstroem, a Swede, who observed negroes on the Coast of Africa, admitted they were capable of superintending manufactures of indigo, salt, soap, iron, &c. &c. Doctor Trotter says that their social virtues are, at least, equal to ours.

[10]   *Magaz. fur Physik. und Nat. Hist.* Gotha, vol. 4, Band 3, p. 5 and *Gœtting. Magaz.* 1. 4, p. 421.

[11]   *Traité sur la Litterature des Nègres.* Paris, 1808, in 8vo.

[12]   *Essay on Truth, &c.*

On the other hand, Thomas Jefferson, in his Notes on Virginia, says: is the difference in the color between the black and the white of no importance? Is it not the foundation of a greater or lesser share of beauty in the two races? Are not the fine mixtures of red and white, the expressions of every passion, by greater or less suffusions of color in the one, preferable to the eternal monotony which reigns in the countenances, that immovable veil of black, which covers all the emotions of the other race? Add to these, flowing hair, a more elegant symmetry of form, their own judgment in favor of the whites, declared by their preference of them, as uniformly as in the preference of the Orang-Outang for the black women over those of his own species. The circumstance of superior beauty, is thought worthy of attention in the propagation of our horses, dogs, and other domestic animals; why not in that of man? Besides those of color, figure, and hair, there are other physical distinctions, proving a difference of race. They have less hair on the face and body. They secrete less by the kidneys, and more by the glands of the skin, which gives them a very strong and disagreeable odor. This greater degree of transpiration renders them more tolerant of heat, and less of cold than the whites. Perhaps too, a difference of structure in the pulmonary apparatus, which a later ingenious experimentalist (Crawford) has discovered to be the principal regulator of animal heat, may have disabled them from extricating in the act of inspiration, so much of the fluid from the outer air, or obliged them in exspiration, to part with more of it. They seem to require less sleep. A black, after hard labor through the day, will be induced by the lightest amusements, to sit up till midnight, or later, though knowing he must be out with the first dawn of the morning. They are at least as brave, and more adventuresome. But this perhaps proceeds from a want of forethought, which prevents their seeing a danger till it be present. When present, they do not go through it with more coolness or steadiness than the whites. They are more ardent after their female: but love seems with them to be more an eager desire, than a tender delicate mixture of sentiment and sensation. Their griefs are transient. – Those numberless afflictions, which render it doubtful, whether Heaven has given life to us in mercy or in wrath, are less felt, and sooner forgotten with them. In general, their existence appears to participate more of sensation than reflection. To this must be ascribed their disposition to sleep, when abstracted from their divertions, and unemployed in labors. An animal whose body is at rest, and who does not reflect, must be disposed to sleep, of course. Comparing them by their faculties of memory, reason, imagination, it appears to me, that in memory they are equal to the whites; in reason much inferior, as I think one could scarcely be found capable of tracing and comprehending the investigations of Euclid; and that in imagination, they are dull, tasteless, and anomalous. It would be unfair to follow them to Africa for this investigation. We will consider them here, on the same stage with the whites, and where the facts are not apocryphal, on which a judgment is to be formed. It will be right to make great allowances for the difference of condition, of education, of conservation, of the sphere in which they move. Many millions of them have been brought to, and born in America. Most of them indeed, have been confined to tillage, to their own homes, and to their own society: yet, many of them have been so situated, that they have availed themselves of the conversations of their masters; many have been brought up to handicraft arts, and from that circumstance have always been associated with the whites. Some have been liberally educated, and all have lived in countries where the arts and sciences are cultivated to a considerable degree, and have had before their eyes samples of the best works from abroad. The Indians, with no advantages of the kind, will often carve figures on their pipes, not destitute of design and merit. They will crayon out an animal, a plant, or a country, so as to prove the existence of a germ in their minds, which only wants cultivation. – They astonish you with strokes of the most sublime oratory; such as prove their reason and sentiment strong, their imagination glowing and elevated. But never yet could I find that a black has uttered a thought above the level of plain narration; never see even an elementary trial of painting or sculpture. In music they are more generally gifted than the whites, with accurate ears for tune and time, and they have been found capable of imagining a small catch;[13] whether they will be equal to the composition of a more extensive run of melody, or of a complicated harmony, is yet to be proved. Misery is often the parent of the most affecting touches in

13   The instrument proper to them is the *Benjar*, which they brought hither from Africa, and which is the original of the guitar, its chords being precisely the four lower chords of the guitar.

poetry – among the blacks there is misery enough, God knows, but no poetry. Love is the peculiar œstrum of the poet. Their love is ardent, but it kindles the senses only, not the imagination. Religion indeed has produced a Phyllis Whately, but it could not produce a poet. The compositions published under her name, are below the dignity of criticism.

Although it appears unjust in some respects to trace out the limits of the mind, yet, it is the duty of a naturalist to examine thoroughly, so important a question. Hume,[14] Meiners, Sœmmering, and many others have maintained that the negro race was very inferior to the white, as to the mind. Their opinions agree with the observations of the distinguished anatomists Cuvier, Gall, Spurzheim, and Dr. Virey, since the cerebral capacity of all negroes who have been examined is generally smaller than that of whites. – Blumenbach remarked that the skulls of Calmucs, or the Mongrul race, and of Americans, (although smaller than Europeans',[15]) were still larger than those of Africans.[16] But independently of this fact so well proved, and the stamp of which is apparent on the depressed forehead of the negro, let us consult the history of this species on the whole earth.

What kind of religious ideas has he been able to form by himself on the nature of things? This question is the surest way to appreciate his intellectual capacity: we see him kneeling before roughly carved idols, worshiping a snake, a stone, a shell-fish, a feather, &c. without being able to reach even to the theological ideas of the Egyptians of old, or of other nations who worshiped animals, as a symbol of God.

In political institutions, negroes have been unable to invent any thing above the family government, and the absolute power; is there here any kind of combination?

In reference to social industry, they never made by them-selves any conquest. Did they ever build great monuments, large cities, as the Egyptians did, even to shelter themselves from the heat? Are they protected from the sun by light tissues, as the Indians? No huts, or the shade of palmetto trees are sufficient for them. Can they beguile by arts or inventions, the

14 *Essays*, xxi. p. 222, note m.

15 See his *Decad. Cranior. divers. gentium.*

16 Le Chevalier de Chastelux in his "*Voyage en Amérique*," and also Thos. Jefferson's *Notes on the State of Virginia*, London, 1787, p. 270, think negroes are very inferior to our species.

tedious hours they spend in laziness on so rich a soil? No, they do not even possess the ingenious game of chess invented by the Indians, or those beautiful tales produced by the fruitful and lively imagination of the Arabians. Negroes living in the vicinity of Moors and Abyssinians, nations whose primitive race was white, are despised by them as stupid and incapable. How often are they deceived in commercial exchanges? They are oppressed, subdued in the very presence of their own countrymen, who have not sense enough to unite in strong bodies to resist and to form regular armies. They have thus been always conquered by Moors, and obliged to give way to them. They know of no other fabrication of arms but the "*zagaies*" and arrows, poor weapons to oppose to the sword, cannon and powder.

In their languages, so limited and abounding in monosyllables, terms are wanting to express abstractions; they cannot conceive anything but what is material and visible; so, they do not *pry* into the *future*, and *forget* very soon the *past*. No historical records are to be found among them. They do not even possess hieroglyphics: the alphabet has been taught to many of them, and yet their languages hardly present any grammatical combinations.

Their music has no harmony, though they appreciate and feel it; it consists only in a few loud intonations, and cannot form a train of melodious modulations. Their senses are perfect, yet they want the attention by which they are displayed, and that kind of reflection by which we are induced to put objects into comparison, in order to establish relations between them, and to observe their proportions.

As long as negroes will not become civilized, by their own exertions, as did the white race, some private examples of remarkable intellect among them, (such are mentioned by authors,) will prove only exceptions. *Time* and *space* have not been wanting to the African, yet he remains in a stupid and brutish state; whilst the other nations on earth have approached more or less to social perfection. No political or moral cause of the same nature to that which bends the minds of the Chinese, can prevent the improvement of the negro in Africa. This climate has assisted the extension of the intellect among the Egyptians of old: we must then conclude, that the constant inferiority of the minds of negroes, results only from their conformation; for, in the Islands of the South Sea, where they are to be found mixed with the uncivilized race of Malays, they stand inferior, although they have not been conquered by them.[17]

Authors who pretend to explain this inferiority, by stating that a degeneration of the human species in Africa, is caused by the heat, and an unwholesome food, may go and see very robust and healthy negroes, either in Africa, in Colonies, or elsewhere, and never will they find in them a larger brain, or greater intellectual faculties.

Every thing serves to prove that negroes form, not only a *race*, but undoubtedly a *distinct species*, from the beginning of the world, as we see other species among other living beings. Some negroes have been brought up with care and attention, have received in schools and colleges the same education given to white children, and yet they have been unable to reach the same degree of intellect: besides, and we must acknowledge this fact, man governs over all animals by his understanding, and not by the mere strength of his body.[18] The state of civilization in our days, proves evidently that the most learned and industrious nations, every thing being equal, predominate over all other nations of the globe – that science and knowledge have given to the white race, more power and empire than to any other race, on account of their intellect and industry.

Negroes are exceedingly simple. As we have said, no laws nor fixed governments are to be found among them; every one lives as he pleases, and he who apparently displays more intellect, or is richer, becomes judge of every quarrel; he is often made a king; but his royalty is a mere shadow; for, although he may sometimes oppress, enslave, sell and kill his subjects, yet the poor fellows have no kind of loyalty towards him; they only obey through fear, and as they do not compose a state, so the mutual obligations between them are reduced almost to nothing: being very vain, they like to be distinguished by ornaments; they have created ranks among themselves; they are exceedingly fond of feasts and ceremonies, and wish to appear with magnificence; zealous of distinctions, and over-joyed when they can attract the notice of the multitude. It is generally the mark of minds which have no other merit than

17   See Forster, *Observ. sur l'espèce humaine*, Voyages de Cook.

18   The proof of it is in negroes having never tamed elephants, as Indians and Asiatic nations do. Negroes have never tamed the Elephant in Africa, although he is smaller and more timid than in Asia.

that which arises from riches and power. Their petty wars consist only in fighting with cudgels, pikes and arrows, and often a campaign begins in the morning and terminates in the evening by peace.

Negroes are fond of military display; but, if it is necessary to come to blows, they prove themselves the greatest cowards, unless they are driven to a state of despair, or rendered mad by revenge; in such a case they prefer to be cut to pieces, rather than to give way; they carry ferocity to an extent unknown in our mild climates; happily the heat of their passion subsides very soon. Conquests are of very little importance to them, because the conqueror is as simple and ignorant as the conquered, both living in the same state of stupidity as before.

A negro, who had been a factor in the negro trade during his youth, went to Portugal when he became older."What he saw, what he heard, says Raynal, inflamed his imagination, and he learned that often a great reputation is acquired by being the author of great misfortunes. When he returned to Africa, he felt a degration in being obliged to obey men very inferior to him in intellect. With a great deal of intrigue, he became a chieftain of the *Achanese*, and succeeded in exciting them against the neighboring tribes. Nothing could withstand his valor, and he ruled over more than one hundred leagues of coasting countries of which Annamaboe was the centre. He died, and nobody dared to succeed him; his power being broken, every thing returned to its former place."[19]

The nations of the coasts of Africa, who trade in slaves, live under several kinds of governments, either as an absolute power, or a sort of aristocracy. The kingdom of *Ashantee*, at the north of Gold Coast, is governed by a ferocious aristocracy, and the king is often obliged to yield to the nobles. The capital city in which he reigns with a savage magnificence, numbers more than one hundred thousand inhabitants.[20] Among *Fantees*, another aristocratic and very populous tribe, on the borders of the Zaire, examples of the greatest ferocity are to be found coupled with horrid superstitions; they impale human victims, even women. Individuals of both sexes are butchered, particularly at the death of nobles, to propitiate the Gods.[21]

[19]   *Hist. Philos. des deux Indes*, l. xi.

[20]   Bowdich, *Embassy to the Kingdom of Ashantee*. London, 1819, in 4to.

[21]   Capt. John Adam, *Remarks from Cape Palmas to the River Congo*. London, 1823, in 8vo.

It is then certain that negroes cannot be civilized by themselves.[22] Chiefs have an unlimited power over their lives, but condemnations to death, in criminal cases, are generally commuted for servitude, on account of the profit made by selling slaves to Europeans[23]. If the imperfections of negroes prevent the establishment of a lasting despotism among them, as among Indians, it is another gift which Providence in its kindness has granted them, since science and great intelligence among other men, are so often employed to create tyrannical institutions, and to weave a net of multiplied laws, to entangle nations with more cunning.

Negroes cannot be managed, except by captivating *their senses* with pleasures, or striking *their minds* with fear. They work only through necessity, or when compelled by force[24].

[22] "It is indisputable that the declaration of freedom to the slave population in Hayti, was the ruin of the country, and has not been attended with those benefits which the sanguine philanthropists of Europe anticipated. The inhabitants have neither advanced in moral improvement, nor are their civil rights more respected; their condition is not changed for the better. They are not slaves, it is true; but they are suffering under greater deprivations than can well be imagined; whilst slaves have nothing to apprehend, for they are clothed, fed, and receive every medical aid during sickness. The *free laborer* in Hayti, from innate indolence, and from his state of ignorance, obtains barely enough for his subsistence. He cares not for clothing, and as to aid when indisposed, he cannot obtain it. Thus, he is left to pursue a course, that sinks him to a level with the brute creation, and the reasoning faculties of the one, are almost inferior to the instinct of the other." – (James Franklin – *Present State of Hayti (St. Domingo)* p. 360, ch. xi. London, 1828.)

[23] *Edward's History of the West Indies*, vol. 2.

[24] It has been commonly asserted by the friends of Hayti, and I believe generally credited in Europe, that it preserves its agricultural pre-eminence solely by *free labor*. Now I think I shall be able to prove to a demonstration that this is not the case, and that it is too evident, from every document which has yet appeared on the subject, that agriculture has been long on the wane, and has sunk to the lowest possible ebb in every district of the republic, &c. I shall also be able to show that Hayti presents no instance in which the cultivation of the soil is successfully carried on, without the application of *force* to constrain the laborer. On the estates of every individual connected with the government, all the laborers employed work under the superintendance of a military police, and it is on these properties alone that any thing resembling successful agriculture, appears in Hayti. I am aware that this will excite the astonishment of persons who have been accustomed to think otherwise; but I shall state facts which cannot be controverted, even by President Boyer himself – nay, I shall produce circumstances which I have seen with the utmost surprise upon his own estate; circumstances which must show his warmest advocates that all his boasted productions have not been obtained without the application of

Satisfied with little, their industry is limited and their genius paralyzed, because they are not tempted by any thing but what satisfies their sensuality, or their natural desires. Their character being more indolent than active, they seem to be more fitted *to be ruled, than to govern*, in other words they *were rather born for submission, than dominion.* Moreover it is very seldom they know how to command; for it has been observed, that when they have power, they are capricious tyrants. This last character does not apply only to negroes; experience has taught us that the most *tractable slaves*, become always in every country the *worst masters*, because they wish to be indemnified in some measure for what they have suffered, by inflicting pain on others. It has been said of Caligula, a Roman Emperor, that he had been the best of servants, and the most cruel ruler.

that system, against which they so loudly exclaim: viz: *the* FREE LABORERS *working under the terror of the bayonet and sabre*!

The present condition of Hayti, arising from the events which have taken place, should render us exceedingly cautious how we plunge our own colonies into the same misery and calamity; by conferring on a rude and untaught people, without qualification, or without the least restraint, an uncontrollable command over themselves. However acutely we may feel for the miseries to which the West Indian slave was at one period subjected, yet I cannot conceive it possible that any one is so destitute of correct information on the subject, as not to know, that at this moment the slave is in a condition far more happy, that he possesses infinitely greater comforts and enjoyments, than any class of laborers in Hayti, and that, from the judicious measures which have been already adopted by the colonial legislatures, and from others which are in contemplation, for improving the condition of the slaves, it is rational to conclude that before long, slavery will be only considered as a name, and that were it to receive any other designation, it would furnish no peg on which the European philanthropist might hang his declamations against slavery. – (James Franklin: *Present State of Hayti, (St. Domingo)* p. 6–9, London, 1828.)

ON THE NATURAL HISTORY OF MAN
Marie-Jean-Pierre Flourens

Source: *Edinburgh New Philosophical Journal, vol. 27, 1839*

Marie-Jean-Pierre Flourens (1794–1867) was born into a humble family in Montpellier. He studied medicine in Paris. As soon as he had taken his MD degree (1819) he abandoned medicine to venture into experimental physiology. He became a protégé of Cuvier, started lecturing in 1821, became a member of the Paris Academy of Science in 1828 and Professor of Comparative Anatomy in 1832. He was a fervent opponent of Franz Joseph Gall's phrenology, insisting that the brain acted as a whole in its operations.

The study of man, viewed in the light of natural history, has a peculiar importance, which no other branch of this science can pretend to. The physical characters which distinguish the *human races* from one another, are, perhaps, the *fact of natural history*, which has at all eras most struck the imagination of men. We know the great astonishment of the first Portuguese, who, in the fifteenth century, penetrating into the interior of Africa, found there men absolutely black, with curled hair, flat noses, and thick lips. This astonishment was renewed at the epoch of the discovery of the New World. Historians relate, that, on the first return of Columbus, the Europeans could not withdraw their eyes from the unknown plants and animals he had brought back, *and above all from the Indians, so different from all the races of men they had hitherto seen.*

Notwithstanding this lively interest which the physical study of man inspires, and has at all times inspired, this study is very little advanced. And first, with regard to the ancients, one can scarcely collect any thing else concerning the natural history of man, properly so called, in Herodotus, Strabo, even Galen, &c., than certain erroneous opinions about the nature and causes of the colour of the Negroes. The true founder of this new science is Buffon. His treatise on the *Varieties of the Human Species* is the first important step made in this department of study. But, for want of sufficiently sure *anatomical characters*, Buffon did not arrive at the precise determination of these *varieties*. He admitted a transition from the *negro* to the *white*; he believed that the *heat of the climate* was the only cause of the black colour; and he came to this conclusion, that all the physical differences which at present distinguish the varieties of the human species have only been, *originally*, the effect of *external and accidental causes*.

Camper is the first who sought *precise anatomical characters*. His observations on the profile of the *Negro* compared with that of the *white*, were a real advance; and Blumenbach, the venerable father of present naturalists, made a farther step, by extending to the entire conformation of the cranium and of the face this study of precise characters, which Camper had only applied to the *facial line*.

On the other hand, Malpighi, Albinus, Meckel, Cruikshank, Gautier, &c., endeavouring to determine the seat of the colour of the Negroes, opened a way which has been much more successful, although its full results have only been obtained in our own days, as we shall now shew.

Malpighi supposed that the layer of the skin, which he called the *corpus* or *rete mucosum*, was the seat of the colour of the blacks. Albinus and Meckel believed they demonstrated it; but from new anatomical research, to which I have lately subjected the whole structure of the skin, it is evident that Malpighi, Albinus, Meckel, &c., had very confused ideas concerning the nature of the *corpus mucosum*.

In the *first* place, they supposed it arranged as a *network*; it forms, however, a continuous lamina. In the *second* place, they supposed it to be chiefly in the skin; it exists, in reality, only in the *mucous membranes*. *Lastly*, they supposed that this *corpus mucosum*, white in the white race, black in the black race, determined, by its colour alone, the colour of the men of these two races; it does no such thing.

There are in the skin of the *white* race three distinct laminæ or membranes – the *derm*, and two *epiderms*; and in the skin of the *black* race there is, besides the *derm* and the two *epiderms* of the *white* race, a particular apparatus, an apparatus which is altogether wanting in the man of the *white* race, an apparatus composed of two layers, the external of which is the seat of the *pigmentum* or colouring matter of the Negroes.

There is, then, in the skin of the *black* race, an apparatus which is wanting in that of the *white* race. The two races, the *white* and the *black* therefore, form two essentially and *specifically* distinct races. And these two races are not only distinct by a *character of form*, as the characters drawn from the conformation of the cranium and face are; they are so by a *character of structure*, by a special and very complicated apparatus, by an apparatus which exists in one of the two races, and is wanting in the other.

Buffon supposes that the black colour is only the effect of climate. He supposes, that *originally* the *Negro* was white. All these suppositions fall before the better known anatomy of the skin. The effect of climate can neither give nor take away an apparatus or tissue.

The individual, indeed, of the white race, may assume that swarthy dark complexion which is the effect of hot weather; but anatomy informs us, that the seat of this *swarthy complexion* is the *second epiderm*, and not a peculiar and distinct apparatus. On the other hand, the *Mulatto* results from the crossing of the *black* and *white* races; and the *colouring apparatus* of the Negro is always found in the *Mulatto*.

The *white* race and the *black* race are then, I repeat, two essentially distinct races. The same is true of the *red* or *American* race. Anatomy discovers, under the second epiderm of the individual of the *red, copper-coloured, Indian, or American* race (for this race is called indifferently by all these names), a *pigmental apparatus* which is the seat of the *red* or *copper colour* of this race, as the *pigmental apparatus* of the Negro is the seat of his black colour.

M. Cuvier says of the American race, "that, although it has not yet been clearly reduced to any of the races of the Old Continent, it does not possess *at once a precise and constant character*, which can make a particular race of it;" and he adds, that the *copper-red complexion is not a sufficient one*. He would assuredly have been of a quite contrary opinion, if he had known that the *copper-red tint* is owing to a special determinate apparatus, an apparatus which anatomy detaches and isolates from all the other parts of the skin.

In considering, I do not say *the characters of form*, but the *characters, the differences of structure*, there are then three specifically and primarily distinct races – the white or *Caucasian* race, the Negro or *Ethiopian* race, and the red or *American* race.

Such are the results which I have explained in my lectures of late years in the Museum. It is true that, for want of favourable opportunities, I have not yet been able to extend these researches of structure to the other races, and particularly to that which, among all others, appears most important, I mean the *yellow* or *Mongolian*. I have hitherto been reduced to characters of the second order, *characters of form*, viz. characters taken from the conformation of the cranium and of the face.

I call these last characters of the *second order*, and by this are explained the differences which exist among naturalists regarding the determination of the *human races*, a determination which, in truth, has been hitherto founded only on these characters. M. Blumenbach fixes the number of these races at five – the *Caucasian*, the *Mongolian*, the *Negro*, the *American*, and the *Malay*. M. Cuvier reduces these five races of Blumenbach to three – the white or *Caucasian*, the yellow or *Mongolian*, and the Negro or *Ethiopian*, and nevertheless he confesses, that "neither the *Malays* nor the *Americans* can be clearly referred to one or other of these three races." Lastly, a more recent author, the learned M. Pritchard [sic], raises, and always by regulating himself according to the form of the crania, the number of the *human races* to seven. The first four are, the *Caucasian*, the *Mongolian*, the *Negro*, and the *American* (except the *Esquimaux*, who form a separate tribe); the fifth is that of the *Hottentots* and *Boschismans*; the sixth that of the *Papuans*, or the people with curled hair of *Polynesia*; and the seventh that of the *Alfourous* and *Australians*.

As for ourselves, by adhering to the authentic crania alone which our Museum possesses, we think we can establish ten distinct forms or types of human heads – the *Caucasian* type, the *Mongolian*, the *Negro*, the *American*, the *Malay* or *Javanese*, the *Hottentot*, the *Boschisman*, the *Papuan*, the *Alfourou*, and the *Zealandic*.

I shall recapitulate, in a few words, the principal characters of these types.

The *Caucasian* type is distinguished by the oval head, the height of the cranium, the prominence of the forehead, that of the nose, &c; the *Mongolian* type by the lateral prominence of the cheek bones, the square form of the cranium, &c; the *Negro* type by a compressed forehead, a flat nose, oblique incisor teeth, &c.; the *American* type by the volume of the posterior part of the cranium, the prominence of the nose, the width of the orbits, &c. &c.

M. Pritchard has suppressed, as we have just seen, the *Malay* type. This type wants indeed, even in Blumenbach who established it, precise characters. I think I have found these characters on two heads in our Museum, one of a *Javanese*, the other of a *Madurais*; two heads whose type is quite similar, and both of which are distinguished by the projection which the vary large parietal protuberances make behind, and above all by the manner in which the occipital bone is abruptly flattened below these protuberances.

The cranium of the *Hottentots* evidently forms a particular type, beside the general type of the *Negroes*; this cranium is long and narrow, but it is proportionally very elevated; and by this also it is distinguished, in a marked manner, from the cranium of the *Boschismans*, which is, on the contrary, singularly flattened, and as it were crushed from above downward.

The *Papuans*, carefully described by MM. Quoy and Gaimard, and the *Alfourous*, described with no less care by M. Lesson, are two distinct types. The *Papuans* are remarkable for the flatness and the depression of the forehead and the face; the *Alfourous* have a long and narrow cranium. I add, that, if the sinking which the parietal bones on each side of the sagittal suture present, on the two heads from Van Diemen's land, in our museum, was found constant, it would be sufficient to indicate a variety in the type of the *Papuans*.

Finally, the last of the types which I propose, the *Zealandic*, is marked by the height and narrowness of the cranium, especially in front, by the extent of the temporal fossa, by the anterior prominence of the apophysis of the chin, &c.

All of these types are only founded on secondary characters; and, consequently, they have not the importance of the three *primitive races*, founded, as we have seen, on the characters of structure. It follows also, from the circumstance of the characters which constitute them being only secondary, that many of these types ought to enter as *subraces*, either into one of the three *primitive races* already established, or into some other of those *races* which may hereafter be established.

However this may be, I have made use, in my lectures, of these types, provisionally admitted to refer to fixed and determinate groups, the observations which have been collected concerning different people by travelling naturalists, such as Forster, Bougainville, Peron, &c., and more recently, Lesson, Quoy, Gaimard, Garnot, &c.

Besides, to these characters, drawn from the cranium and the face, all those other characters, the union of which constitutes their force, are to be added: – the colour of the hair, the prominence of the lips, the opening of the eyes, &c., and even the habits of those savage tribes which may be regarded as primitive, and consequently as a more immediate effect of their organization itself. I do not speak here of the characters drawn from the languages, characters of a very elevated order, but the development of which we must derive from another science.

Our business here is to establish *anatomical characters*. I have proposed, therefore, in my lectures, three principal objects: – the first, to seek *anatomical characters* which distinguish the human races from each other; the second, to follow the modifications which these *characters* experience in the filiations of these races, from the *primitive race* to the *sub-race*, and from the *sub-race* to the *tribes* and *families* derived from it; and the third, to go back to the particular laws which preside over the distribution of the particular branches of the human species on the different points of the surface of the globe.

The study of these three parts of the physical history of man, formed the subject of my lectures of late years. But I cannot finish this article, without examining a question which is at this day much controverted; – I mean, if the *different races* of men form a single *species*, or if, forming different species, they constitute what is called in natural history a *genus*. A simple glance at the definition of the word *species* will be sufficient to cause all difficulty on this point to vanish.

Buffon defines species, – "A succession of similar individuals which reproduce each other." M. Cuvier also defines species, – "The union of individuals descended from each other or from common parents, and of those who resemble them as much as they resemble each other." Now, it is easy to see that this definition, given by Buffon and M. Cuvier, is complex, and that it unites two very distinct facts, viz. the fact of *reproduction* or of *succession*, and the fact of *resemblance*.

Here the fact of the *resemblance* is completely subordinate to that of the succession; and Buffon and Cuvier afterwards agree in this themselves. "The comparison of the *resemblance* of individuals is only," says Buffon, "an *accessory idea*, and often independent of the first (the idea of constant *succession* by generation)." "The apparent differences of the races of our domestic species," says M. Cuvier, "are stronger than those of any savage species of the same genus."

Besides, the appreciation of *resemblance* is always more or less arbitrary. One naturalist often finds a *resemblance* important which another naturalist considers slight. The foundation of all natural history (for the foundation of all the natural history of organized beings is the positive determination of the species) would only repose, then, on an arbitrary appreciation.

The idea of *resemblance*, as Buffon says, is only an *accessory idea*. It is, in other words, a *subsidiary means* which naturalists employ for want of the only *decisive means*, the fact of the *succession*; but when the *decisive means*, the fact of the *succession* is known, the *subsidiary means* ought to be excluded.

The fact of the *succession*, therefore, and of the *constant succession*, constitutes alone the *unity of the species*. Thus, *unity*, *absolute unity*, of the human species, and *variety* of its races, as a final result, is the general and certain conclusion of all the facts acquired concerning the *natural history of man*.[1]

---

[1] Annales des Sciences, Nat. t. x., Dec. 1838, pp. 361, &c.

INAUGURAL LECTURE
Thomas Arnold

Thomas Arnold (1795–1842) studied Classics at Corpus Christi
College, Oxford. In 1828 he was appointed master to Rugby
School where he stayed until his death. Arnold's pedagogical
ideas annoyed some Tories, and his theological thoughts
irritated the Archbishop of Canterbury. His historical learning
was greatly influenced by the German historian Barthold
Georg Niebuhr. In 1841 he was appointed Regius Professor of
History at Oxford University. In his *Introductory Lectures on
Modern History* he stated that history 'is the biography of a
society'. His personalized view of nations linked up with his
fear that all contemporary nations were either 'exhausted' or
'incapable' of developing the 'seed' of history any further.

I have thus far spoken of history in the abstract; at least of
history so far as it relates to civilized nations, with no reference
to any one time or country more than to another. But, as I said
before, I must not forget that my particular business is not
history generally, but modern history: and without going
farther into details than is suitable to the present occasion, it
may yet be proper, as we have considered what history in
general has to offer, so now to see also whether there is any
peculiar attraction in modern history; and whether ancient and
modern history, in the popular sense of the words, differ only
in this, that the one relates to events which took place before a
certain period, and the other to events which have happened
since that period; or whether there is a large distinction
between them, grounded upon an essential difference in their
nature. If they differ only chronologically, it is manifest that
the line which separates them is purely arbitrary: and we might
equally well fix the limit of ancient history at the fall of the
Babylonian monarchy, and embrace the whole fortunes of
Greece and Rome within what we choose to call modern; or,
on the other hand, we might carry on ancient history to the
close of the fifteenth century, and place the beginning of
modern history at that memorable period which witnessed the

expulsion of the Moors from Spain, the discovery of America, and, only a few years later, the Reformation.

It seems, however, that there is a real difference between ancient and modern history, which justifies the limit usually assigned to them – the fall, namely, of the western empire; that is to say, the fall of the western empire separates the subsequent period from that which preceded it by a broader line, so far as we are concerned, than can be found at any other point either earlier or later. For the state of things now in existence, dates its origin from the fall of the western empire; so far we can trace up the fortunes of nations which are still flourishing; history so far is the biography of the living; beyond, it is but the biography of the dead. In our own island we see this most clearly: our history clearly begins with the coming over of the Saxons; the Britons and the Romans had lived in our country, but they are not our fathers; we are connected with them as men indeed, but, nationally speaking, the history of Cæsar's invasion has no more to do with us, than the natural history of the animals which then inhabited our forests. We, this great English nation, whose race and language are now overrunning the earth from one end of it to the other, – we were born when the white horse of the Saxons had established his dominion from the Tweed to the Tamar. So far we can trace our blood, our language, the name and actual divisions of our country, the beginnings of some of our institutions. So far our national identity extends, so far history is modern, for it treats of a life which was then and is not yet extinguished.

And if we cross the channel, what is the case with our great neighbour nation of France? Roman Gaul had existed since the Christian era; the origin of Keltic Gaul is older than history; but France and Frenchmen came into being when the Franks established themselves west of the Rhine. Not that before that period the fathers of the majority of the actual French people were living on the Elbe or the Saal; for the Franks were numerically few, and throughout the south of France the population is predominantly, and much more than predominantly, of Gallo-Roman origin. But Clovis and his Germans struck root so deeply, and their institutions wrought such changes, that the identity of France cannot be carried back beyond their invasion; the older elements no doubt have helped greatly to characterize the existing nation; but they cannot be said by themselves to be that nation.

The essential character, then, of modern history appears to be this; that it treats of national life still in existence: it commences with that period when all the great elements of the existing state of things had met together; so that subsequent changes, great as they have been, have only combined or disposed these same elements differently; they have added to them no new one. By the great elements of nationality, I mean race, language, institutions, and religion; and it will be seen that throughout Europe all these four may be traced up, if not actually in every case to the fall of the western empire, yet to the dark period which followed that fall; while in no case are all the four to be found united before it. Otherwise, if we allow the two first of these elements, without the third and fourth, to constitute national identity, especially when combined with sameness of place, we must then say that the northern countries of Europe have no ancient history, inasmuch as they have been inhabited from the earliest times by the same race speaking what is radically the same language. But it is better not to admit national identity, till the two elements of institutions and religion, or at any rate one of them, be added to those of blood and language. At all events it cannot be doubted, that as soon as the four are united, the national personality becomes complete.

It cannot be doubted then that modern history so defined is especially interesting to us, inasmuch as it treats only of national existence not yet extinct: it contains, so to speak, the first acts of a great drama now actually in the process of being represented, and of which the catastrophe is still future. But besides this personal interest, is there nothing in modern history of more essential difference from ancient – of difference such as would remain, even if we could conceive ourselves living in some third period of history, when existing nations had passed away like those which we now call ancient, and when our modern history would have become what the history of Greece and Rome is to us?

Such a difference does characterize what we now call modern history, and must continue to characterize it for ever. Modern history exhibits a fuller development of the human race, a richer combination of its most remarkable elements. We ourselves are one of the most striking examples of this. We derive scarcely one drop of our blood from Roman fathers; we are in our race strangers to Greece and strangers to Israel. But morally how much do we derive from all three: in this respect their life is in a manner continued in ours; their influences, to say the least, have not perished.

Here then we have, if I may so speak, the ancient world still existing, but with a new element added, the element of our English race. And that this element is an important one, cannot be doubted for an instant. Our English race is the German race; for though our Norman fathers had learnt to speak a stranger's language, yet in blood, as we know, they were the Saxons' brethren: both alike belong to the Teutonic or German stock. Now the importance of this stock is plain from this, that its intermixture with the Keltic and Roman races at the fall of the western empire has changed the whole face of Europe. It is doubly remarkable, because the other elements of modern history are derived from the ancient world. If we consider the Roman Empire in the fourth century of the Christian era, we shall find in it Christianity, we shall find in it all the intellectual treasures of Greece, all the social and political wisdom of Rome. What was not there, was simply the German race, and the peculiar qualities which characterize it. This one addition was of such power, that it changed the character of the whole mass: the peculiar stamp of the middle ages is undoubtedly German; the change manifested in the last three centuries has been owing to the revival of the older elements with greater power, so that the German element has been less manifestly predominant. But that element still preserves its force, and is felt for good or for evil in almost every country of the civilized world.

We will pause for a moment to observe over how large a portion of the earth this influence is now extended. It affects more or less the whole west of Europe, from the head of the Gulf of Bothnia to the most southern promontory of Sicily, from the Oder and the Adriatic to the Hebrides and to Lisbon. It is true that the language spoken over a large portion of this space is not predominantly German; but even in France and Italy and Spain, the influence of the Franks, Burgundians, Visigoths, Ostrogoths, and Lombards, while it has coloured even the language, has in blood and institutions left its mark legibly and indelibly. Germany, the Low Countries, Switzerland for the most part, Denmark, Norway, and Sweden, and our own islands, are all in language, in blood, and in institutions, German most decidedly. But all South America is peopled with Spaniards and Portuguese, all North America and all Australia with Englishmen. I say nothing of the prospects and influence of the German race in Africa and in India: – it is enough to say that half of Europe, and all America and Australia, are German more or less completely, in race, in language, or in institutions, or in all.

Modern history, then, differs from ancient history in this, that while it preserves the elements of ancient history undestroyed, it has added others to them; and these, as we have seen, elements of no common power. But the German race is not the only one which has been thus added; the Sclavonic race is another new element, which has overrun the east of Europe, as the German has overrun the west. And when we consider that the Sclavonic race wields the mighty empire of Russia, we may believe that its future influence on the condition of Europe and of the world may be far greater than that which it exercises now.

This leads us to a view of modern history, which cannot indeed be confidently relied on, but which still impresses the mind with an imagination, if not with a conviction, of its reality. I mean, that modern history appears to be not only *a* step in advance of ancient history, but *the* last step; it appears to bear marks of the fulness of time, as if there would be no future history beyond it. For the last eighteen hundred years, Greece has fed the humanist intellect; Rome, taught by Greece and improving upon her teacher, has been the source of law and government and social civilization; and what neither Greece nor Rome could furnish, the perfection of modern and spiritual truth, has been given by Christianity. The changes which have been wrought have arisen out of the reception of these elements by new races; races endowed with such force of character that what was old in itself, when exhibited in them, seemed to become something new. But races so gifted are and have been from the beginning of the world few in number: the mass of mankind have no such power; they either receive the impression of foreign elements so completely that their own individual character is absorbed, and they take their whole being from without; or being incapable of taking in higher elements, they dwindle away when brought into the presence of a more powerful life, and become at last extinct altogether. Now looking anxiously round the world for any new races which may receive the seed (so to speak) of our present history into a kindly yet a vigorous soil, and may reproduce it, the same and yet new, for a future period, we know not where such are to be found.[1] Some appear exhausted, others incapable, and yet the surface of the whole globe is known to us. The Roman colonies along the banks of the Rhine and Danube looked out on the country beyond those rivers as we look up at the stars, and actually see with our eyes a world of which we know nothing. The Romans knew that there was a vast portion of earth which they did not know; how vast it might be, was a part of its mysteries. But to us all is explored: imagination can hope for no new Atlantic island to realize the vision of Plato's Critias: no new continent peopled by youthful races, the destined restorers of our worn-out generations. Everywhere the search has been made, and the report has been received; we have the full amount of earth's resources before us, and they seem inadequate to supply life for a third period of human history.

I am well aware that to state this as a matter of positive belief would be the extreme of presumption: there may be nations reserved hereafter for great purposes of God's providence, whose fitness for their appointed work will not betray itself, till the work and the time for doing it be come. There was a period, perhaps, when the ancestors of the Athenians were to be no otherwise distinguished from their barbarian neighbours than by some finer taste in the decorations of their arms, and something of a loftier spirit in the songs which told of the exploits of their warriors; and when Aristotle heard that Rome had been taken by the Gauls, he knew not that its total destruction would have been a greater loss to mankind than the recent overthrow of Veii. But without any presumptuous confidence, if there be any signs, however uncertain, that we are living in the latest period of the world's history, that no other races remain behind to perform what we have neglected, or to restore what we have ruined, then indeed the interest of modern history does become intense, and the importance of not wasting the time still left to us may well be called incalculable. When an army's last reserve has been brought

---

[1] What may be done hereafter by the Sclavonic nations, is not prejudged by this statement; because the Sclavonic nations are elements of our actual history, although their powers may be as yet only partially developed.

into action, every single soldier knows that he must do his duty to the utmost; that if he cannot win the battle now, he must lose it. So if our existing nations are the last reserve of the world, its fate may be said to be in their hands – God's work on earth will be left undone if they do not do it.

ON THE UNITY OF THE HUMAN SPECIES

Marcel de Serres

Source: Edinburgh New Philosophical Journal, vol. 39, 1845

Born into a rich family of drapers in Montpellier, Marcel Pierre Toussaint de Serres (1780–1862) studied law. In 1805 he became deputy public prosecutor at the court of Montpellier. After the sudden financial ruin of his family, Serres moved to Paris where he became acquainted with the teachings of Cuvier, Lamarck and the transcendental anatomy of Geoffroy Saint-Hilaire. In 1809 he acquired a chair as Professor of Mineralogy and Geology at the University of Montpellier. Serres conducted his geological and zoological researches with the intention of reconciling science and the Bible. This goal is also the reigning principle of his essay on the unity of mankind.

When we follow the progress of the sciences, and compare them with the facts contained in the most ancient of existing books, presented by religion to the respect of nations, we are struck with their uniform agreement with all this Book teaches us. It seems as if God permitted man to make discoveries, and bring his knowledge to perfection, only for the purpose of confirming the truth of the Sacred Writings. The observation of natural phenomena, moreover, cannot lead us to conclusions opposed to the faith. The truth requires the most brilliant lights to be shed upon it, in order that it may shine with all its lustre; it cannot, accordingly, reject them, as they are calculated to render it more obvious to every eye.

Among the facts recorded in the Bible, there is one connected with the foundations of our belief, which has not yet been demonstrated in a manner sufficient to solve the doubts it has produced in certain minds, – I refer to the unity of the human species. This delicate question of natural philosophy has, at all periods, occupied the attention not only of savants properly so called, but also of philosophers, historians, and philologists.

The solution of this question appeared, to some authors, so clear, and so contrary to the accounts given in Scripture, that Voltaire has not hesitated to assert, that none but one that was blind could admit that the Whites, the Negroes, the Chinese, the Hottentots, the Laplanders, the Americans, and, finally, Albinos, are men of the same species, and have a common origin.

It is true that all persons of candour now know with how little consideration, and, it may even be added, with what a degree of ignorance, this otherwise eminent man judged of questions of the most momentous and eternal importance. Not less than a century, however, has been necessary to overturn and destroy all the systems and assertions which Voltaire and the philosophers of his day had accumulated against religion, and particularly against the Sacred Writings. Thanks to its all-powerful influence, aided by the progress of knowlege, truth has at last triumphed. New lights have recently been shed on the question of the origin of the human species; and it is these new facts that we are about to explain to those who seek the truth in sincerity.

The identity of the human species has been attempted to be demonstrated by two different methods. The first, which was partially pointed out by Buffon, consists in directing attention to the circumstance, that species very different from each other avoid sexual connection, while those that are very nearly allied produce sterile mules by crossing. The diverse races of one and the same species can alone have offspring capable of as indefinite reproduction as their parents. In other words, species remote from each other can neither reproduce nor perpetuate themselves; nearly allied species may be productive, but they cannot perpetuate their race; the most diverse *races* both reproduce and perpetuate themselves.

If we apply these facts to the varieties of the human species, we are led to the conclusion that they form only one true species; for the most dissimilar races of men give birth, by crossing, to individuals who transmit their own qualities to their descendants. The European colonies in America present all possible examples of crossing in different degrees, the effects of which render this conclusion obvious.

By the second method, that of Blumenbach, we arrive at the same results. On a great number of animals, whether wild or domestic, we may produce very considerable variations under the influence of external agents. These are, in many cases, much greater than those which distinguish the most dissimilar human races.

The observations of modern naturalists have thrown a flood of light on these questions, by shewing the influence which climate, and a return to a free state, exercise on the races of animals, – first subjected to the empire of man in Europe, then exported to America, and allowed to run wild in the vast savannahs of the New World. In this point of view, the labours of M. Roulin possess a high degree of importance, and ought to be classed in the first rank.

In order to explain the variations which man has undergone, these observers have thought it necessary to establish a much greater number of races than had been previously admitted. They have even subdivided the principal of these races, that is to say, the White or Circassian, the yellow or Mongolian, the Black or Negro, and, finally, the Red or American. We shall not follow them in their researches, but confine ourselves to a single observation on this point. This great variety, which recently observed facts compel us to recognise in the human species, is a striking proof of the number of transitions which unite them, and the difficulty of separating them by precise characters. We may perceive in it a new proof of the impossibility of admitting the parcelling out of the human race into many species.

It is the same with the physiological differences existing between the principal races; although real, these differences are less essential than they at first sight appeared. In fact, the medium duration of life is nearly the same among all the races, because they are affected by the same diseases, and their functions operate in the same manner. If some slight differences exist among them, they are easily explained by the prolonged influence of climate and habits.

No doubt the contrasts between the modes of life of different nations appear, at first view, very great; but if we look to the motives of their actions, and their exterior manifestations, in races the most distinct, we shall find that they are nearly the same. The necessity for preservation, and the desire of happiness, are as universal as the knowledge, or, at least, the idea, of a superior power, or a God. All nations, even the most degraded, have their fêtes, their ceremonies, and a respect, more or less profound, for the dead. In general, the means of carrying their acts into execution are more diversified than the motives which cause them. These considerations, as well as a multitude of others which might be easily added, are still further proofs of the unity of the human species.

We might believe even in more numerous variations, when we consider that man possesses a wonderful faculty, *intelligence*, of which the brain appears to be the material organ. Such, however, is not the case, notwithstanding the immense progress which civilization has made among certain nations, and the development of the encephalon, which is the consequence of it. We know that this organ implicates the exterior forms in its movements, and that these express its variations.

According to this new consideration, the modifications of the human species should be dependent on the material organ of intelligence. Accordingly, among the inferior races of men, the more the brain is exercised, the nearer man approaches the White race; when, on the contrary, he is deprived of the blessings of civilization, his nervous system is under the sway of his other parts. Greatly altered in a physical point of view, man becomes, in some measure, assimilated to the brutes, from which he is so far removed by his type and his future destiny.

A great portion of the human species has thus descended in the scale of life. It is to this departure from the primordial type that we owe those innumerable races, the lowest of which cannot be recognised by those who seek for some traits of the primitive beauty of man. A new experiment is in progress on the American continent, which will soon enable us to perceive the causes of all these alterations. The Negroes, who, up to our times, had never united themselves into a nation, nor possessed a regular form of government, have all of a sudden made surprising improvements in these respects, and are advancing with rapid steps, in the New World, to the possession of that knowledge which is now concentrated in the heart of Europe.

In proportion as intellectual labour causes the vital energy to predominate in the head, men of deeply coloured complexion, with crisped or woolly hair, or with short hair, will shew an obvious tendency to approximate to the White race; they will advance along with it in the path of improvement.

The proof of this has only begun; but even now the effects are perceptible; and they will become more and more conspicuous in future, if, in consequence of the vicissitudes which are inseparable from our destiny, men of colour do not abandon the new path they have opened up for themselves. This path will become to them more plain and easy to be followed, if they connect themselves with the White race, which are their elders in civilization.

If this latter has become degenerate, in proportion as it receded from its point of departure, future ages will be furnished with the proof that certain varieties of the human race, after having been subjected to degradations more or less marked, may yet reascend, by continued intellectual efforts, to their first origin. It will not be without surprise that they shall be seen to resume the beauty of their primordial type, after having reconquered, so to speak, the intelligence, whose precious light they had allowed to be extinguished. This view, like the preceding, tends to establish the unity of the human species, and to justify us in assigning the same cradle to the most elevated as well as the most degraded of the human species.

This consideration leads us to the examination of another fact, not less important, and which arises in some measure from the preceding. If man constitutes only a single species, he must have been placed on a single point, whence he has radiated, as from a centre, and extended his tribes over the whole surface of the earth. Here history agrees with the information we obtain from the study of man, considered without reference to his primitive abode. It teaches us that Adam was created alone, with a consort; that he was placed in the centre of Asia, with the injunction to people the earth, and that his posterity have extended from this central point, the one most favourable for its dispersion over all parts of the globe where the conditions were found requisite for his existence. The study of languages, as well as that of history, leads to the same conclusion; by mutually supporting each other, philology and historical documents import a striking character of truthfulness to this inference. It is confirmed by facts independent the one of the other; and this agreement is the most manifest proof of its justice and accuracy.

Such are some of the facts which prove that, on this question, science goes hand in hand with religion and historical traditions. In fact, all traditions represent nations as deriving their origin from a single stock, and as emanating from one individual.

The observations by means of which we have supported the beautiful opinion of the primitive unity of the human species, do not, however, demonstrate it in a direct manner. M. Flourens comes to our aid and supplies this deficiency: by a comparative study of the different structures of the human organism, he has arrived at the same result which has been reached by following another path.

He has commenced this study by an examination of the skin, considering it among the races where this organ is coloured, and among such as present no sensible colour. In the first, there is found a pigmental membrane or *pigmentum*, which is not seen in the second, except on certain parts of the body. This membrane, discovered by Ruysch in Negroes, had been considered, from the observations of that author, as characterising certain races, just as its absence distinguished others. But it is far from possessing the importance which was at first assigned to it.

The skin of a White man, by exposure to the sun, acquires a very thin layer of *pigmentum* between the second epidermis and the true skin, that is to say, in the same place as in the Negro. It may be said that the accidental coloration, produced by the sun, alters the cellular tissue and produces the pigmental substance peculiar to the coloured races. But it must be further observed, that the white man is not exempt from the common law. Even in his natural state his skin has its *pigmentum*, very inconsiderable, indeed, but still sufficiently perceptible. That part of the breast, which is named the nipple, is, as is well known, of a dark colour, in the male, and more particularly in the female of the white race. We there find a pigmental apparatus, so that this part of the skin exhibits, in the white race, the structure existing in that of the coloured races.

This membrane, connected with the coloration of the skin, is not therefore essential to the nature of the races; it cannot be considered as characterising them, since the skin of the fœtus in the negro shews not the least trace of it. So far is it from being essential, that we do not perceive the slightest indication of it in those individuals of the coloured races who are affected with partial albinism. In such cases the organ presents a great number of white spots; by the side of these spots, the skin preserves its ordinary colour, black, red, brown, or some other shade; but, what is remarkable, the points where the skin is not coloured, are destitute of the pigmental membrane.

M. Moreau de Jonnès has, in like manner, observed among the negroes of the Antilles, individuals of both sexes whose skin was spotted with white. These spots, which appear very conspicuous on the black surface of the body, are rather greyish or of a greyish-white colour, than pure white. The number of individuals in whom this appeared was very limited.

Other travellers affirm that they have witnessed similar facts in the island of Cuba, not only among the black population, but also among individuals of mixed blood. This discoloration of certain parts of the skin, in races which usually have it coloured, shews that the non-secretion of the pigmentum may be the effect of a morbid alteration, but cannot be regarded as characteristic of the different human races.

These researches will lead to certain others, of not less interest; for they are connected with the question we are now considering. According to the preceding statements, the pigmental substance disappears in all the parts of the skin which are discoloured, and remains only in those whose shades do not vary from a more or less sombre tint. Hence, individuals of the Negro race, who, by crossing with Whites, acquire tints more and more faint, ought to have the pigmentum but little developed; this organ should even almost wholly disappear, when the negro has in a great measure acquired the characters of the white race.

It would, therefore, be curious to follow the various degrees of alteration the pigmental membrane undergoes, and to ascertain whether they coincide with the varieties sprung from the Black or White races, which are commonly designated by the name of *quadroons* or *demi-quadroons*.

We wish we were in a situation to undertake these researches, which, we doubt not, would concur in establishing the identity of the human species, equally with the facts we have recounted. The lively interest this subject excites, leads us to hope that American observers, who have such facts under their eyes daily, will profit by the advantage of their position, and enlighten us on a point so important in the history of humanity.

When we compare at once, and without any intermediate series, the skin of the white man with that of the black or the red man, we are tempted to assign a distinct origin to each of these races; but if we pass from the white man to the black or the red, through all the intermediate varieties, it is no longer the difference, but the analogy, which strikes us.

The researches of which we have given an outline are far from being entirely new, but they lose nothing on that account of their merit and importance. In fact Aristotle, that great genius of ancient times, had stated, long before Camper, that the black colour of the skin in Negroes and Moors, was probably produced by the rays of the sun. This opinion, erroneous though it be, does much less violence to the truth, than the idea adopted by Pliny, on the authority of ancient writers. This naturalist mentions, as a certain fact, that the waters of a river in Thessaly had the property of staining the skin of men and animals black, and making the hair frizzle. Thus, according to him, the particular characters of certain human races had their origin in a circumstance, a belief in which nothing could authorize.

Such absurd or imperfect notions are widely removed from the present state of science; but we may perceive in them the germ of this essential fact, that the colouring matter exists more or less in all the races, and that external agents can render it more or less apparent.

The comparative anatomy of the skin affords, then, by the complete and universally prevailing analogy in the structure of this organ, a direct proof of the common origin of the human races, and of their primitive unity.

Thus, the European, with his graceful and elegant forms; the Negro, characterised at once by the colour of his skin and the peculiar contour of his head; the American Indian, with a red skin and herculean form; and, lastly, the Chinese, with a yellow tint and oblique eyes; are all derived from the same stock, and form a single chain, of which Adam constituted the first link.

Such is the solution science gives of this interesting question of the primitive unity of man; such is that which has been given in a book written upwards of 3500 years ago. Let us bow, therefore, before the Sacred Writings, in which such important knowledge is embodied; and let us not forget that, while they contain all the moral truths essential to our happiness and future destiny, they likewise present to us the greater number of the important physical facts, of which we formed no idea till after long-continued and toilsome labours.

If these researches interest our readers, we shall return to this question; and we shall make them more particularly acquainted with the works of M. Flourens on the study of the skeleton and the cranium of man. These investigations will be found to confirm a conclusion which was propounded by

Moses, and, in modern times, has been adopted by the majority of physiologists, at the head of whom stand Blumenbach, Camper, and Cuvier.

We shall likewise enumerate, in detail, the researches recently undertaken with the view of resolving the doubts of natural philosophers, respecting the truth of one or the other hypothesis proposed to explain the phenomena of light. We may state beforehand, that, as the facts related by the Hebrew legislator seem more favourable to the theory of undulations than to that of emission, we doubt not that the experiments by which the means of deciding between these two opposite theories are sought for, will confirm what this extraordinary man had already announced upwards of thirty-five centuries ago.

We thus see this admirable Book acquiring greater importance from age to age, at the same time that the sciences are making new conquests. The Bible, a rich and inexhaustible mine, will send forth into the world, treasures always becoming more valuable, in proportion as the progress of our knowledge shall furnish us with more perfect instruments for drawing from its bosom the truths, which the Supreme Intelligence has deposited there from the earliest period.[1]

---

[1] From the *Bibliothèque Universelle de Genève*, No. 107, 1845.

THE NATURAL HISTORY OF MAN
By James Cowles Prichard, M.D.
London. 1842

Anonymous

Source: Ecletic Review, vol. 12, 1848

After the first edition of the *Researches* had appeared, J. C.
Prichard published two further editions, one in 1826
(extended to two volumes), and one between 1836 and 1847
(five volumes). He strove to take new scientific discoveries
and further ethnological observations from travellers into
account. *The Natural History of Man*, published in 1842, was
his attempt to furnish a popular version of his ethnological
endeavours. He discounted the term 'race' as a meaningful
category. As the review illustrates, he stuck to his classification of mankind into differing varieties. *The Eclectic Review*,
which understood itself as a decidedly Christian journal,
agreed fervently with Prichard's monogenism.

This is a very beautiful work, illustrated with many coloured
plates engraved on steel, and interspersed with numerous
woodcuts. It supplies what had long been a desideratum in our
language, as there existed no previous work adapted to readers
not versed in anatomy and physiology, containing a general
survey of the various races belonging to the great human
family. The French have several treatises of this kind, which
are well known, and have had an extensive circulation. Those
of MM. Virey, Bory de St. Vincent, and Desmoulins, are the
most celebrated. None of these works are recent, or contain the
latest observations, and they are all founded on the position,
assumed without proof, *that there exist many distinct species
of men*; an hypothesis very convenient to the writer, since it
saves him the trouble of attempting to account for the
phenomena of varieties displayed in the different human races,
by at once cutting a knot, the solution of which requires a
diligent research. We are very happy to say that, as might be

expected from the name of the respected author, the object of the present work is to demonstrate the groundless nature of this unscriptural assumption, and at the same time to afford a general view of the principal characteristics, both physical and moral, which distinguish the various races spread through the different regions of the world.

This is, of course, not a religious work; nor is the question taken up in its religious bearings. The greater weight will, therefore, be generally allowed to its testimony to the Scriptural doctrine, that 'God hath made of one blood all nations of men,' and that the whole human family is descended from the man Adam and the woman Eve. Works of the class with that now before us, we receive as evidence of the good understanding which has now for many years subsisted between Science and Revelation. If only for the sake of the young, who were formerly beset by great dangers before their judgment could be matured, we are profoundly thankful that it is no longer deemed decent, or even witty, to be profane; nor any longer philosophical to pit science against Moses and the prophets. It seems to us, among the most satisfactory evidences of our intellectual advancement, since the peace – nay, within the last ten or fifteen years – that revelation has no avowed enemies in any quarter requiring the respect of an answer; that it receives a degree of homage, more or less sincere, from mere men of the world, mere men of science, mere politicians – among whom, generally speaking, sneers and witticisms upon any of the facts or doctrines of Scripture are received with coldness, as marks of, at least, bad taste, if not of ignorance and inexperience. Nor is this homage confined to what are called the educated classes. We happen to have had occasion to pay much attention to the history and progress of what is called 'cheap literature,' as understood chiefly of the weekly publications designed for circulation among the working classes. Some eight or ten years back, a very large proportion of those works were of an infidel tendency, not perhaps on the whole, but whenever occasion offered for a reference to the Bible or to religion; and a general disposition was manifested to confound the corruptions of religion with religion itself. This is not now the case. We had the curiosity, a few weeks back, to procure a collection of the cheap publications now current; and comparing the results with some notes on this subject which we made nearly ten years since, we find that – 1. Above three-fourths of all the cheap publications which then existed have disappeared. 2. Among these are *all* the avowedly infidel publications. 3. The survivors are either religious, or such as treat religion with respect. 4. No religious publication, which was in hopeful circulation at the former period, has since disappeared; and the *increase* in such works has been nearly three-fold. 5. The avowedly neutral publications, or such as studiously eschewed religious topics and allusions, have found it expedient to relax their rules. The 'Penny Magazine,' for instance, has been observed, for the last two or three years, to unbend somewhat of its stiff and guarded neutrality, and has furnished many satisfactory references to, or illustrative of, biblical facts and circumstances. 6. The licentious, as well as the infidel publications, have fallen; and no fresh ones have risen in their places. 7. Hence, the cheap literature of the present day, is not only more harmless, and much *cleaner*, but more entertaining and wholesome at the present than at the former period. Certainly, taken in the mass, it is not such as a heart-Christian would care much for, or would admit into his family; but rather because it has much *useless* than much decidedly objectionable matter.

But we would chiefly call attention to the gratifying fact that in publications addressed to what, we fear, may be described as 'the discontented classes,' there is generally a broad distinction now chosen between religion and its abuses. It begins to be seen that it is not Christianity, but priestcraft, which is unfriendly to liberty of thought and action, and bears hard on the poor and the oppressed; it begins to be felt that the Bible religion is, indeed, full of mercy and good fruits, full of sympathies for the afflicted and the wronged, and that its leanings and partialities are far less to those who have their portion in this life, those who are clad in purple and fine linen and fare sumptuously every day, than to the sons of toil, the poor, the afflicted, the destitute; to those who if in this life only they have hope, are of all men the most miserable. We are not now speaking of the higher influences of religion. But besides its saving influences, religion has many others; and we are endeavouring to show that some of these, of which there was, a few years ago, no sign, are now in full and vigorous operation; and that this operation is strongly manifested in the external marks of respect to the Bible which the current cheap literature finds it at least expedient to adopt; and in the disposition which is often indicated to try public men, public measures, public conditions, and religious bodies, by the standard which it offers. We know full well that there is nothing very *vital* in all this; but it is something, that those who do regard religion as a vital thing, are no longer exposed to the pain of seeing that which they love treated with frequent disrespect; and night and morning do we pray God that public feeling may advance in the direction which it seems to have taken, until the mass of society is leavened.

Again we ask, who would now deem such attacks on the Bible as those of Voltaire and Tom Paine worthy of an answer? What attention would they now attract? Works of that class, *and the answers to them*, are equally unknown to, and unheeded by, the new generation; and the honest man who should now, in the simplicity of his heart, sit down to furnish new answers to these old things, to rout the thrice routed, and to slay the thrice slain, would too soon find that he has mistaken his day and generation, and that he has only been providing for the chandler and the trunkmaker. It is much the same in Germany, where the danger is rather from rationalism than from infidelity. But in France, although of late years there has been much improvement of *tone* in that country, there old matters are still reproduced, and new answers are still deemed necessary. No one in this country who takes up such a work as M. Reghellini's *Examen du Mosaisme et du Christianisme*, which, in this country, would, *on all hands*, be deemed too paltry for even contempt, can fail to wonder that the state of public feeling should allow it to take the imposing form of three handsome octavo volumes, with a superior paper for the title-page, that the precious copy-right may be rendered the more secure by the sign-manual of the author. This work, which, from its form and cost, must be addressed to the higher classes in France, would, in this country, have no chance, even among the working classes, in a form the most inexpensive.

This reference to France brings us back to the book of Dr. Prichard. For, as we stated at the outset, the unscriptural tenet of a plurality of human species is still upheld by the French physiologists, long after it has been abandoned in this country and in Germany. Indeed the question was, long ago, so satisfactorily settled by Blumenbach, that his views could not but be adopted by such men as Mr. Lawrence (*Lectures*) on the one hand, and by Dr. John Mason Good (*Book of Nature*) on the other; who, above twenty years since, equally advocated the unity of the human species.

We do not know that Dr. Prichard has thrown much new light on the matter; but he has arranged the argument in a clear and satisfactory shape, and has thrown into it all the corroborative illustration which recent researches have accumulated. After some introductory observations, the writer thus states the

Bearings of the Question. The sacred Scriptures, whose testimony is received by all men of unclouded minds with implicit and reverential assent, declare that it pleased the Almighty Creator to make of one blood all the nations of the earth, and that all mankind are the offspring of common parents. But there are writers in the present day who maintain that this assertion does not comprehend the uncivilized inhabitants of remote regions; and that Negroes, Hottentots, Esquimaux, and Australians, are not, in fact, men in the full sense of that term, or beings endowed with like mental faculties as ourselves. Some of these writers contend that the races above mentioned, and other rude and barbarous tribes, are inferior in their original endowments to the human family which supplied Europe and Asia with inhabitants; that they are organically different, and can never be raised to an equality in moral and intellectual powers, with the offspring of that race which displays in the highest degree all the attributes of humanity. They maintain that the ultimate lot of the rude tribes is a state of perpetual servitude; and that, if in some instances they should continue to repel the attempts of the civilized nations to subdue them, they will at length be rooted out and exterminated in every country on the shores of which Europeans shall have set their feet. These μεξόθκρα, half men, half brutes, do not belong to what M. Bory de Saint Vincent terms the 'Race Adamique.' They were made to be the domestic slaves of the lordly caste, under whose protection they are susceptible of some small improvement, comparable to that which is attained by our horses and dogs. Nothing, in the opinion of persons who maintain this doctrine, can exceed the folly manifested by the people and parliament of England, when, under a mistaken impulse of what was termed philanthropy, or an erroneous notion of rights which have no existence, they committed the absurd act of emancipating from the precise condition which was most appropriate to their nature a tribe of creatures incapable of governing themselves, and of combining for objects of mutual interest in a civilized community. If these opinions are not every day expressed in this country, it is because the avowal of them is restrained by a degree of odium that would be excited by it. In some other countries they are not at all disguised. Nor is it easy to prove any of the conclusions unreasonable, if only the principal fact be what it is assumed to be. If the Negro and the Australian are not our fellow-creatures, and of one family with ourselves, but beings of an inferior order, and if duties towards them were not contemplated, as we may in that case presume them not to have been, in any of the positive commands on which the morality of the Christian world is founded, our relations to these tribes will appear to be not very different from those which might be imagined to subsist between us and a race of orangs. In the story of a pongo slaughtered by some voyagers in the Indian Archipelago, an account of the cries and gestures of the animal in its mortal agony, so like the expressions of human sufferings, was read, not without pity, and many persons censured the wanton commission of an outrage for which there appeared no adequate motive. But the capturing of such creatures with the view of making them useful slaves, even if some of them were occasionally destroyed in the attempt, would be scarcely. We thus come near to an apology for the practice of kidnapping, at which our forefathers connived, though it did not occur to them to defend it on so reasonable a ground. The kind-hearted Abbé Grégoire tells us with indignation, that on the arrival of blood-hounds from Cuba, in the island of Saint Domingo, 'On leur livra, par manière d'essai, le premier Négre qui se trouva sous la main.' He adds, 'La promptitude avec la quelle ils dévorèrent cette curée réjouit des tigres blancs à figure humaine.'[1] Those who hold that the Negro is of a distinct species from our own, and of a different and inferior grade in the scale of organized beings, smile at the good abbé's simplicity, and observe that it cannot be much more criminal to destroy such creatures when they annoy us, than to extirpate wolves or bears; nor do they strongly reprobate the conduct of some white people in our Australian colony, who

---

[1]   Abbé Grégoire, 'Sur la Littérature des Nègres.'

are said to have shot occasionally the poor miserable savages of that country as food for their dogs.

'I shall not pretend that in my own mind I regard the question now to be discussed as one of which the decision is a matter of indifference, either to religion or humanity. But the strict rule of scientific scrutiny exacts, according to modern philosophers, in matters of inductive reasoning, an exclusive homage. It requires that we should close our eyes against all presumptive and extrinsic evidence, and abstract our minds from all considerations not derived from the matters of fact which bear immediately on the question. The maxim we have to follow in such controversies is, "fiat justitia, ruat cœlum." In fact, what is actually true, it is always most desirable to know, whatever consequence may arise from its admission.' – pp. 5–8.

It is next shown that *species* are simply tribes of plants or animals, which are certainly known, or may be inferred on satisfactory grounds, to have descended from the same stocks, or from parentages precisely similar, and in no way distinguished from each other. And permanent *varieties* are races now displaying characteristic peculiarities which are constantly and permanently transmitted. They differ from species in this circumstance, that the peculiarities in question are not coeval with the tribe, but sprang up in it since the commencement of its existence, and constitute a deviation from its original character. It seems to be the well established result of inquiries into the various tribes of organized beings, that the perpetuation of hybrids, whether of plants or animals, so as to produce new and intermediate species, is impossible. But unless these observations are erroneous, or capable of some explanation that has not yet been pointed out, they lead, with the strongest force of analogical reasoning, to the conclusion that a number of different tribes, such as the various races of men, must either be incapable of intermixing their stock, and thus always fated to remain separate from each other, or if the contrary should be the fact, that all the races to whom the remark applies are proved by it to belong to the same species. At this point of the argument Dr. Prichard enters into a variety of curious details, which establish beyond dispute that mankind of all races and varieties are equally capable of propagating their offspring by intermarriage, and that such connexions are equally prolific, whether contracted between individuals of the same or the most dissimilar varieties; and this is regarded as a conclusive proof, *unless there be in the instance of human races an exception to the universally prevalent law of organized nature*, that all the tribes of men are of one family. Dr. Prichard rightly thinks that the solution of the problem which he has undertaken to discuss might very safely be rested on this issue. But as further light may be thrown on the subject by a careful analysis of the facts which can be collected relative to the organization of varieties, he proceeds to take a very interesting survey of the phenomena of variation in tribes of animals and plants.

Our readers will anticipate that the main object of the illustrations derived from this source, is to show that among the varieties of plants and animals known to be of the same species, and descended from the same stock, the diversities are very far greater than exist between any of the races of mankind. In this branch of the inquiry we are glad to see that the argument deducible from the very marked differences in the varieties of the dog is employed by Dr. Prichard with great skill and effect. It has often occurred to us that this common and familiar illustration was one of the very strongest that could be brought to bear on the question; for the most casual observer cannot but be at once cognizant of the fact, that the difference is infinitely greater between a greyhound and a spaniel, between a Dutch pug and a Newfoundland dog, than between any races of men to be found in the wide world.

From the survey of the phenomena of variation in the tribes of animals, and of the circumstances under which these appearances are displayed, the following general inferences are deduced by our author:–

'1. That tribes of animals have been domesticated by man, and carried into regions where the climates are different from those of their native abode, undergo, partly from the agency of climate, and in part from the change of external circumstances connected with the state of domesticity, great variations.

2. That these variations extend to considerable modifications in external properties, colour, the nature of the integument, and of its covering, whether hair or wool, the structure of limbs, and the proportional size of parts; that they likewise involve certain physiological changes or variations as to the laws of the animal economy; and lastly, certain psychological

alterations or changes in the instinct, habits, and powers of perception and intellect.

3. That these last changes are in some cases brought about by training, and that the progeny acquires an aptitude to certain habits which the parents have been taught; that psychical characters, such as new instincts, are developed in breeds by cultivation.

4. That these varieties are sometimes permanently fixed in the breed so long as it remains unmixed.

5. That all such variations are possible only to a limited extent, and always with the preservation of a particular type, which is that of the species. Each species has a definite or definable character, comprising certain undeviating phenomena of external structure, and likewise constant and unchangeable characteristics in the laws of its animal economy, and in its psychological nature. It is only within these limits that deviations are produced by external circumstances. Races of men are subjected more than almost any race of animals to the varied agencies of climate. Civilization produces even greater changes in their condition than does domestication in the inferior tribes. We may therefore expect to find fully as great diversities in the races of men, as in any of the domesticated breeds. The influence of the mind must be more extensive and powerful in its operations upon human beings than upon brutes; and this difference transcends all analogy or comparison. *A priori* we might expect to discover in the psychological characters of human races, changes similar in kind, but infinitely greater in degree.' – pp. 74, 75.

The argument which we have thus reported, forms a sort of introduction to the body of Dr. Prichard's work, which is occupied with a very able ethnographical survey of the various races of men who occupy the surface of the earth. Of this we shall say little further than that there is no other work in the English language which will supply the same amount of popular information on this very interesting subject. The pictorial illustrations are of a superior description, and are of the greatest use in facilitating comparisons, by embodying the details.

ON THE RELATIONS OF ETHNOLOGY TO OTHER BRANCHES OF KNOWLEDGE

James Cowles Prichard[1]

Source: Journal of the Ethnological Society of London, vol. 1, 1848

In his capacity as President of the Ethnological Society of London Prichard gave the Anniversary speech of 1847. It was published in the *Proceedings* of the Society and in the *New Edinburgh Philosophical Journal*. By the 1840s, ethnology was established as a proper discipline. But within the British Association for the Advancement of Science it was, to Prichard's regret, still incorporated into the zoological section. By 1847 Prichard was an old man. In 1845, he had moved to London to serve as a Commissioner in Lunacy. He had grown disillusioned about mankind. To his youthful theory on the improving impacts of civilization he had added a theory of environmentalism. On the whole, however, Prichard retained many theories which he had put forward as a young man.

The anniversary address delivered at the last meeting of this Society by our late excellent President Sir Charles Malcolm, gave so lucid and extensive a survey of the recent progress of Ethnology, that I should find little to offer on the present occasion, were I to follow the same path. The achievements of one year, taken by themselves, would appear fragmentary, and without results. It has, however, occurred to me, that there is a different course by which I may hope to fulfil the task allotted to me more to the satisfaction of the Society. The idea has been suggested to me by a proposal made lately to the British Association for the Advancement of Science, to appoint in that Society a distinct Section for the Cultivation of Ethnology.[2] In

---

[1] Read before the Ethnological Society, June 1847.

[2] This proposal was made at the meeting of the Association at York by Dr King, secretary of the Ethnological and Statistical Societies. It was negatived by the Committee of the Association.

some parts of the Continent, and in the United States of America, societies have for some time existed exclusively devoted to this pursuit, and supported by men highly distinguished in science and literature. In the meetings of the British Association alone, Ethnology claims but a subordinate place in the Section of Natural History. The reason assigned for this arrangement is, that the natural history of man is a part of the natural history of living creatures, and that there is an obvious propriety in referring to one division, the history of all organised beings, namely, of all those beings which exist in successive generations, destined one after another to rise, flourish, and decay – a lot to which are alike subjected the lords of the creation, and the worms on which they tread – and the plants and animals which they consume for their daily food. But though the natural history of man may, in a technical arrangement, be made a department of zoology, it is easy to shew that the main purport of ethnological inquiries is one distinct from zoology; and the reference of both these subjects to one section of the British Association can only have arisen from inadvertence. Of this I shall be able to convince the members of the Society now present, if they will allow me to call their attention for a brief space to the position which Ethnology ought to hold, and which it is destined hereafter to maintain, among the various divisions of human knowledge.

Ethnology is the history of human races, or of the various tribes of men who constitute the population of the world. It comprehends all that can be learned as to their origin and relations to each other. It is distinct from natural history, inasmuch as the object of its investigations is not *what is*, but *what has been*. Natural history is an account of the phenomena which Nature at present displays. It relates to processes ever going on, and to effects repeated, and to be repeated, so long as the powers of Nature, or the properties of material agents, remain unchanged. Ethnology refers to the past. It traces the history of human families from the most remote times that are within the reach of investigation, inquires into their mutual relations, and endeavours to arrive at conclusions, either probable or certain, as to the question of their affinity or diversity of origin. All this rather belongs to archæology than to natural history. It may, indeed, be truly said that the investigations, by means of which we endeavour to arrive at conclusions in Ethnology, involve many topics which are within the province of natural history. The facts and analogies which natural history presents, are the data on which a great part of the proofs or arguments adopted by the ethnologist are founded. But these contributions to natural history are only a part of the resources by the aid of which we carry on the investigations belonging to our favourite pursuit; and we shall find that it borrows fully as much from other departments of knowledge, quite separate from the study of Nature and her productions. The results at which the ethnologist arrives, do not fall within any department of natural history. They are archæological or historical. It may then be admitted, that there are some grounds for the opinion of those who would even deny us any place in the great system of scientific inquiries, which the British Association has established.

We are saved from apprehension as to the consequence of this admission, by remarking, that Ethnology stands exactly on the same ground, in this point of view, as one of the most popular of the studies which are cultivated at the British Association; and that it is impossible, with any shew of reason, to deny a place to one of these sciences in the arrangement of sections, without refusing the claims of the other. By compar-ing the position of ethnology to that of geology, we shall be enabled to survey, in a clear point of view, the relations of each of these sciences to other branches of knowledge.

Geology, as every one knows, is not an account of what Nature produces in the present day, but of what is has long ago produced. It is an investigation of the changes which the surface of our planet has undergone in ages long since past. The facts on which the inferences of geology are founded, are collected from various parts of natural history. The student of geology inquires into the processes of Nature which are at present going on, but this is for the purpose of applying the knowledge so acquired to an investigation of what happened in past times, and of tracing, in the different layers of the earth's crust – displaying, as they do, relics of various forms of organic life – the series of the repeated creations which have taken place. This investigation evidently belongs to *History* or *Archæology*, rather than to what is generally termed *Natural History*. By a learned writer, whose name will ever be connected with the annals of the British Association,[3] the term

---

[3] The Rev. Dr Whewell.

Palæontology has been aptly applied to sciences of this department, for which Physical Archæology may be used as a synonym. Palæontology includes both Geology and Ethnology. Geology is the archæology of the globe – ethnology that of its human inhabitants. Both of these sciences derive the data on which they found conclusions from the different departments of natural history. But ethnology likewise obtains resources for pursuing the investigation of the history of nations and of mankind from many other quarters. It derives information from the works of ancient historians, and still more extensively from the history of languages and their affiliations. The history of languages, indeed, greatly extended as it has been in late times, has furnished unexpected resources to ethnology, which could hardly have advanced a few steps without such aid. As geology would have been a barren and uninteresting study, and uncertain in most of its results, without the aids which the study of organic remains has unexpectedly brought, serving often to identify geological formations, and to connect particular series of rocks with periods in the world's history; so the discoveries of Glossology have enabled us to trace alliances between nations scattered over distant regions of the earth, of whose relation to each other we never should have had an idea without such evidence.

I shall now endeavour to point out, in a brief and cursory manner, what assistance each department of knowledge has contributed to the cultivation of ethnology. But here I must crave the indulgence of those who are conversant with the history and progress of this science, since I shall not be able to accomplish the task proposed without saying much that must to such persons be already well known and familiar.

The branches of natural history and science which furnish aids in the promotion of ethnology, are anatomy, physiology, zoology, and physical geography.

The first attempt that deserves notice to distinguish races of men was made by Camper, an anatomist. The distinction adopted by Camper is well known. It is founded on the shape of the skull. It is the facial angle, or the measurement of an angle included between two lines, one of which is drawn from the passage of the ear to the basis of the nose; and the other a line slanting off from the forehead to the mouth, or rather to the most advanced point of the upper jawbone. This angle was thought to afford a measure of the capacity of the anterior part of the skull, and of the size of the corresponding portion of the brain. Camper, who had within his reach very few skulls for examination, thought that he found this angle of different extent in different classes of human heads. He found that skulls of Europeans, when thus measured, gave an angle of 80°, the skull of a Kalmuck one of 75°, and the skull of a Negro one of 70° only. There are forms of the head in which the angle has been found to be greater than in the European, and others in which it is less than in the Negro. Those which have it greater than in the European, and in which it amounts to 90°, are the ideal heads of Grecian gods, forms not existing in nature; and the skulls in which this angle is less than in the Negro, are those of apes. In these last, the angle was estimated by Camper at 64°, 63°, or 60°. Camper accordingly thought that he found in the skulls of negroes a type intermediate between the cranium of the European man and that of the Orang. But in this he was mistaken. The supposed gradation exists only when skulls are compared which have the infantine form, or before the first dentition is complete. After the period of the first dentition, the difference in the facial angle in the heads of apes, and in those human skulls in which it is of the smallest measurement, becomes enormous. In the adult Troglodyte it is 35°, and in the orang or satyr it is only 30°, as we learn from the observations of Professor Owen.

Professor Blumenbach was, in reality, the founder of ethnology. He was the first person who made any considerable collection of human skulls, or possessed the materials requisite for an inquiry into the anatomical differences which exist in various tribes of men. Blumenbach divided the forms of the human head into five departments. He designated them, not as it would perhaps have been better to have done in the first instance, by epithets descriptive of forms, but by the names of the races of people to which they belonged, or of the regions of the world whence these races were supposed to have originated. The Caucasian form was so termed from Mount Caucasus, to which Blumenbach observed that ancient traditions refer the origin of many celebrated nations. He supposed this to be the primitive type of the human skull, and regarded the other forms as so many degenerations from it. These were the Mongolian, the American, the Ethiopian, and the Malayan. The five forms were supposed to belong to five divisions of mankind, comprising collectively the whole human family. This distribution was complete as far as the ethnographical knowledge of the time allowed it to be; but it would be necessary in the present day to enumerate many additional varieties in the shape of the skull, and to constitute additional human races, if we would follow the same method, and adapt it to the actual state of our acquaintance with distant regions of the earth and their inhabitants. For example, besides the Ethiopian race of Blumenbach, by which he meant the Negroes, we must reckon in Africa two other woolly-haired races, each having a form of the head different from the Ethiopian type of Blumenbach. I allude to the Kafir and Hottentot races. Again, among the nations termed collectively by Blumenbach the Malayan race, meaning the native people of all the islands of the Great Southern Ocean, we now distinguish several different forms which have little or nothing in common, and appear to belong to several distinct races. Among these are the Papuas, who resemble the Negroes in many respects, but have skulls of a form very different from any of the African nations, and the Australians having a peculiar type, and forming a very distinct race. The Polynesians are not so distinct in the form of their heads as Blumenbach supposed the Malayan race to be; and the true Malays approach in features, and apparently in their general physical character, to the other native races of the Indo-Chinese peninsula, who are described as nearly resembling the Chinese, and who probably belong to the class of nations termed by Blumenbach Mongolian. Blumenbach's delineations of skulls are admirable, and his descriptions of the forms which appeared to him the most prevalent and the most constant, are invaluable. There is, however, one very important view of the shape of the head which he seems to have overlooked; I allude to the form of the basis of the skull. The importance of this view of the cranium in comparing the heads of the human species and those of apes, in which it displays the immense difference between them in a very striking manner, was first pointed out by Professor Owen. It is a character by no means to be neglected in the comparison of human races with each other.

The latest scheme devised for the classification of human skulls, and the distribution of human races according to their forms, is that proposed by Professor Retzius of Stockholm, a very ingenious and able anatomist, and a very estimable man, who has lately devoted his talents to this subject. Professor

Retzius' researches are well known, and I shall not occupy the time of the Society by stating to them his results. They are particularly interesting in one point of view, probably not contemplated by the excellent author. I allude to the fact, that he seems to have established distinctions in the form of the skull among nations, who, though for many ages separate, are known, if I am not mistaken, historically, to have descended from the same original stock.

The head is not the only part of the body which displays different forms in different human tribes. Varieties in stature and in the proportion of limbs – in the form of the pelvis and other parts of the body – as well as in the texture of the skin, the hair, and other structures, are well known to distinguish races from each other. With respect to all these differences, anatomical researches have been made which have an obvious bearing on ethnology.

When we advert to the resources which physiology affords for the cultivation of ethnological science, we find that there are many relations between these studies. One series of inquiries is, whether the great laws of animal economy are the same in respect to all human races; whether any particular race differs from others in regard to the duration of life, and the different periodical changes of constitution, and, generally speaking, in the laws of the animal economy, and whether such diversities, if found to exist, can be explained by reference to external causes, or imply original difference, and form, therefore, specific characters. Another physiological inquiry connected with ethnology is, whether variations of form, colour, &c., can be explained by reference to any known principle, and how far, and under what conditions, they are transmitted to posterity, and may tend to account for the origination of particular breeds or tribes marked by some hereditary and permanent characters?

Zoology and the whole study of natural history opens a field to several inquiries highly interesting to the ethnologist.

We must take an account, for example, of the varieties of form and organization to which the different species of animals are subject, in order to solve the question, Whether the differences observed in human races, and the physical characters of any particular race, belong to the category of natural varieties, or indicate an entire distinction which must have existed from the creation, and therefore proves the species to be distinct?

Another question connected with zoology has been made a matter of great moment in these investigations. I allude to the theory of Hybridity, or to the general observations made with respect to mixed breeds and their supposed sterility. The bearing of these questions on the physical history of mankind is very obvious. I shall not enlarge upon it at present.

Physical geography has a very obvious bearing on ethnology, since physical geography comprises the localization of those agencies of climate which are supposed to modify the organization of living tribes, and which oppose limits to the sphere of their existence. We may observe, in connection with this subject, that great numbers of species, both animal and vegetable, are only to be found within certain latitudes, and in particular regions of temperature, and under particular local conditions. Those tribes in the animal kingdom which approach the human form, viz., the apes, are confined by nature to very narrow limits, while men live in all climates. This striking difference suggests several inquiries as to its causes, which have a bearing on physical geography.

One series of facts connected with physical geography, and having a bearing on ethnology, comprises the effects produced upon climate by elevation of the surface of the earth. It is well known that, in the ascent of mountains, changes of climate and of vegetation are perceived, analogous to those observed in passing from a lower to a higher latitude. Plants of the frigid zone reappear in equatorial countries near the summits of Alpine mountains. An inquiry is suggested, how far this may tend to explain the phenomenon, that the xanthous, or very fair complexion, with red hair and blue eyes, is often seen in the inhabitants of alpine regions. For example, if we begin from the eastern parts of the world, we find xanthous people on the Himalaya, in the Hindu families who reside near the sources of the sacred rivers at Jumnotri and Gangotri. Even the Rajpoots in Rajast'han, are known to be much fairer than the people of lower plains in Bengal and elsewhere. Passing the Indus, we find the Eusofzyes in the high tracts of Afghanistan, a fair xanthous people, while the Ghiljis of the lower country are dark, and the Jauts of the plain of the Indus nearly black. Then, again, we find on the high mountains of Hindu-Khu that curious people the Siah Posh, who speak a dialect allied to the Sanskrit, and are supposed by Bopp and Ritter, and other learned men, to be descendants from the ancient Brahman race who conquered India some thousands of years ago, and probably left these people behind them in Central Asia. Far westward in Arabia, according to Bruce, a similar phenomenon is displayed among the inhabitants of the cold mountains of Raddhua; and in Africa, the Kabyles, the natives of Mount Aurasius, behind Tunis and Algiers, are so fair, and red-haired, that they have been conjectured, without a shadow of proof, to be descendants of the ancient Vandals, as if it were possible for Vandals to have made their way to the tops of all the mountains in the world. Even in America, among the Ioways, and other tribes inhabiting the Rocky Mountains, similar facts have been observed. The rationale of this phenomenon is plainly connected with the physical conditions of so many moutainous regions. It admits a comparison with changes of complexion, discovered as we proceed from the country of black races under the equator, to that of the fair people of Northern Europe.

Another observation to which I shall briefly advert, will serve to indicate the bearing which researches in physical geography may possibly have upon the studies of the ethnologist. The phenomena of vegetation probably indicate conditions of climate which are inappreciable by thermo-meters, hygrometers, and all our instruments; and when we advert to the fact illustrated by that great botanist Mr Robert Brown, that the equatorial distribution of the great families of plants is extended to a considerable degree through the Southern Hemisphere, or that the Austral regions approximate much more to the equatorial in this leading character of vegetation than the northern climates of corresponding latitude, we are at liberty to infer, that the sum-total of those agencies of climate which affect organized beings is much more similar to that which exists under the equinoctial line in these countries than in the northern latitudes. I shall merely mention this conclusion in connection with the well-known fact, that the varieties of the human race which exist in the great southern continents, have much greater resemblance to the tribes who are natives of the torrid zone, than any of the aboriginal people inhabiting the northern parts of the world.

I have now gone over the branches of natural science which principally give assistance to students of ethnology, and it remains for me to make some remarks on the resources which history and archæology may be expected to furnish in aid of the same inquiries.

When we speak of historical inquiries as contributing to the promotion of ethnology, the meaning of the expression is not limited to information to be collected from historians. Much, indeed, is to be found in the works of such writers as Herodotus, Aristotle, Diodorus, Cæsar, Pliny, Strabo, and Tacitus, that is useful for investigating the history of those nations in Europe and Asia, which came within the knowledge of the Greeks and Romans; but all such information would be not only confined, but disjointed and fragmentary, without some more comprehensive method of investigation that may serve to bring the notices scattered through ancient writers, into a distinct and evident connection with the history of people actually known to us. Historical researches that may be applicable to ethnology, must occupy a wide field. They must collect all the different lights that can be brought to bear on the history of nations, whether from the testimony of ancient writers, or from manners, customs, and institutions – from old popular traditions, poetry, mythology – from the remains of ancient art, such as architecture, sculpture, inscriptions – and from sepulchral relics discovered in many countries, consisting of embalmed bodies, or more often the mere skulls and skeletons of the ancient inhabitants, which furnish the most authentic testimony, where it can be procured, as to the physical characters of various races of people. Besides all these, there is another source of information more extensively available than either of them; I allude to the history of languages and their affinities.

The history of mankind is not destined, like the facts on which geology is built, to be dug out of the bowels of the earth, though some of the ancients thought otherwise, if we may judge from the abundance of sculptures and inscriptions with which they covered the sides of caverns and excavations. Curious documents have, however, occasionally been discovered in various countries beneath the soil, which have brought evidence of historical facts otherwise unknown. We may allude, for example, to the great collections of silver money of the coinage of the early caliphs of Bagdad, which have been dug up in various places on the shores of the Baltic, marking out the path of an extensive traffic between the East and North, at a time when the northern people of Europe are generally supposed to have been in a state of extreme barbarism. But the discoveries most interesting in relation to ethnology are those of sepulchral remains, which, in various regions of the world, have preserved the most authentic records of the physical characters and the state of arts that belonged to many ancient races. I need hardly allude to the discoveries in the Egyptian Thebaid, – a vast sepulchre, where the successive generations of thirty centuries lie embalmed beneath their dry preserving soil, expecting vainly the fatal time, now long since passed, when they were to be summoned before the tribunal of Sarapis. Another African race exists only in mummies. I allude to the insular Guanches, the ancient inhabitants of the Fortunate Islands, who now, falsifying this name, exist only in the caverns of Teneriffe, or in the European museums to which they have been transported. Over the vast wildernesses in the northern regions of Asia, along the banks of the Irtish, and beyond the remote Jenisei, innumerable tumuli are scattered, containing the remains of ancient, and, perhaps, long extinct races of men; and it is a remarkable fact, that in this wintry region where living nature seems to struggle against the elements for a precarious existence, even the arts of decoration were studied in those times of yore, which witnessed the erection of these tombs. Implements of silver, gold, and copper, girdles of the precious metals, bracelets decked with pearls, and fragments of porcelain, have surprised the travellers who have seen a few of these tumuli excavated. Whole nations lie perhaps yet buried in these regions, and with them may be found some relics that may hereafter throw light upon their history. Similar tumuli spread over the north of Europe, contain the remains either of the same people, or of races more barbarous than the Asiatics. Hundreds of them have been rifled by treasure-hunters, or by mere antiquaries little more enlightened, who have sought to make collections of curiosities without any view to promote ethnology or history. Of late years, Eschricht, Nilsson, and Retzius, have attempted, in Denmark and Sweden, to identify in these remains the relics of different races, supposed to have inhabited the northern region of Europe in early times. Their example has been followed by Dr Wilde in Ireland, and more recently by MM. Eugène Robert, and Serres in France. It is too early to collect general results from these researches. I shall only observe, that, in the opinion of the learned Swedes who have devoted themselves to the investigation, the sepulchral remains of northern Europe belong to three different eras. They display three different physical types, and three successive stages of advancement in art and civilization. The oldest are the relics of a people with round heads, having the transverse diameter of the cranium large in proportion to the longitudinal. The implements and ornaments which are found in the tombs of these people, indicate the greatest rudeness of art. They consist of tools and the heads of lances and arrows made of stone and bone, but nothing indicating a knowledge of the use of metals. Whether these oldest sepulchres were the tombs of a Celtic race, is a question not yet decided. It seems to be the opinion of Professor Retzius, and of Nilsson, who has written a learned work on the Aborigines of Scandinavia, that they were the burial-places of a people more ancient than the Celts. Similar remains discovered in France, are supposed by MM. Robert and Serres to have belonged to the Cymrian or Welsh branch of the Celtic race; and these anatomists suppose a second class of heads of a larger shape, found in tombs containing metallic implements, to have been those of a people allied to the Irish or Gaelic branch. A third set of monumental relics are referred by Retzius to a superior race, supposed to have been Swedes or Saxons, or some branch of the Teutonic family.

It is much to be regretted that the ancient nations of Europe, those races from whom Englishmen, Germans, and Frenchmen are descended, were so obstinate in their barbarism, that they despised the use of letters, and remained for centuries in intercourse with the cultivated Massilians, and with Roman colonies, without adopting this art; and that all the sepulchral remains of the northern regions are without inscriptions, or a single name that may be a clue to their various history. On the other hand, parts of Asia and Africa, now the seat of barbarism, are covered, if we may use the expression, with inscriptions. Numerous and long inscriptions scattered over all India on rocks, the sides of caves, and on various monuments, in Cabul, through the ancient empires of Iran and Assyria, through Hadramaut and Oman, the remotest districts of Arabia, and through the North of Africa, to say nothing of the more celebrated relics of Egypt, prove that the use of letters was well known in these countries at a time when Europe was barbarous. In all those countries inscriptions, which have been gazed at with stupid wonder by the descendants of the people who composed them, and have been regarded as the workmanship of genii and imps, have been at length read and explained for the first time after twenty centuries. All this has been done within a few years. The discovery began, as every one knows, with the deciphering of the Egyptian hieroglyphics. The efforts of Dr Young and Champollion gained the clue, unravelling mysteries in a field where it has been reserved for a distinguished scholar of the present day (the Chevalier Bunsen) to erect the edifice of the most ancient history of the world, – a monument of the intelligence of modern Europe more exalted than the royal pomp of the Pyramids, whose real builders now, for the first time, come forth to our view after having been concealed in the rubbish of 4000 years. Scarcely less remarkable is the achievement of our illustrious countryman Mr Prinsep, in the East, who has read and interpreted the inscriptions spread over India and Afghanistan. It is a curious fact, that these most ancient records of the furthest East preserve not the victories of warriors, but the decrees of Buddhistical sovereigns, commanding throughout the provinces of their great empire the establishment of hospitals for the cure of men and brute animals. Many curious facts in history have been preserved by these inscriptions, and among others the extension of a Macedonian empire over a great part of India, and the conquest of the Island of Ceylon by a sovereign of Hindustan three centuries before the Christian era. Not less remarkable are the inscriptions cut in letters composed of wedge-shaped strokes which are spread through the empire of the great Cyrus, and have been lately read. These were engraved by the subjects of the Persian kings. Another set of these cuneiform inscriptions belonged to the older Assyrians and Babylonians. The clue to all these discoveries was obtained by Dr Grotefend, Lassen, and Burnouf; and by its aid our countryman, Major Rawlinson, has succeeded in reading the history of the Achæmenidæ engraven on their own monuments in a language which was doubtless spoken at the courts of Susa and Persepolis, but has not been heard since the overthrow of the last Darius. Even the old Assyrian inscriptions are now partially understood, and the name of Nebuchadnezzar has been found on the walls of his palaces.

Many ethnological facts may be collected from these inscriptions. I shall instance the supposed existence of the Affghans among the nations subject to Darius, and who, doubtless, contributed to form the armies that fought at Marathon and Thermopylæ. It would be curious to find the ancestors of Akhbar Khan among the invaders of Europe 2000 years ago.

The inscriptions spread through Arabia and Ethiopia will probably throw light on the most ancient relations between Asia and Africa. We may expect to find in them the history of those queens of Ethiopia who reigned successively under the name of Candace, known to the generals of Augustus Cæsar, and one of whom is mentioned by St Luke the Evangelist.

I shall only refer to another set of inscriptions deciphered within a few years in several of the ancient Italic languages, by means of which we have gained some knowledge of the languages spoken in Italy before the ascendancy of Rome. They have afforded an ethnological result, which is also of some importance in relation to classical history. It seems from them that the old Italic nations, the Latins, the Umbrians, the Opici or Oscans, the Ausonians, the Siculians, the Samnites and Sabines, all the old Italic nations except the Tuscans, were not, as the older writers, Frêret, Larcher, and even as Niebuhr supposed, partly Celtic or other barbaric tribes, and partly Greeks, or at least Pelasgi, but a distinct and particular branch of the Indo-European family of nations, and that they all spoke dialects of one language, which may be termed the old Italic, and of which Latin is but one variety.

The most important aids to historical researches into the origin and affinity of nations is undoubtedly the analytical comparison of languages. This may be considered as almost a new department of knowledge, since, although long ago sketched out, and followed to a certain extent, it has been wonderfully augmented in recent times, and it is only in its later development that it comes to have any important relations with ethnology. Leibnitz is considered to have been its originator. The Adelungs, Vater, Klaproth, Bopp, Frederick Schlegel, and Jacob Grimm, have been among its most successful cultivators; and lastly, to William von Humboldt it owes its greatest extension and the character of a profound philosophical investigation. But it is not, in this point of view that I contemplate the results of philological researches. It is as an auxiliary to history, and as serving in many instances to extend, combine, and confirm historical evidence, that the comparison of languages contributes to the advancement of ethnology. Great caution is, however, requisite when we attempt to draw inferences as to the relationship of nations from the resemblance or even identity of their language. We know that conquests, followed by permanent subjugation, have caused nations to lose their original languages and adopt those of their conquerors. The intercourse of traffic between neighbouring countries, the introduction of a new religion or of new habits of life, especially when rude and barbarous tribes have been brought into near connection with civilized ones, have given rise to great changes in the original idioms of nations, and have caused languages originally different to approximate. It is only when we have good reasons for believing that no contingent event has interfered to change the original speech of any particular race, or supplant it by the idiom of a different tribe, that we can be justified in founding on such ground an argument as to affinity in descent. Evidence may be collected on this point sometimes from historical facts, or from considerations founded on the known condition of particular nations. When we learn from history that two nations have been remotely separated from each other from a very distant age, and have never been brought into habits of intercourse, we may presume, that marks of affinity discovered in their languages can bear no other explanation than that of an original unity of descent. In other instances, phenomena are discoverable in languages themselves which enable us to determine whether traits of resemblance have been the effect of later intercourse between nations, or arose in the original development of their languages, and thus prove a common origin in the tribes of people who speak them. A careful analysis will often detect analogies of such kind as to afford undoubted evidence of primitive affinity between languages which have acquired in the lapse of time and the course of events great differences, and when each dialect has become unintelligible to people who speak another of the same stock. The investigation of affinity between languages has lately assumed the character of a scientific study, and when pursued with reference to certain general principles, has led to striking and important results. I shall briefly advert to some of these principles which have not yet been stated, as far as I know, in a systematic manner.

It is the prevalent opinion of philologists, that the most extensive relations between languages and those which are the least liable to be effaced by time and foreign intercourse, are the fundamental principles of construction. Grammatical constructions, or the laws which govern the relations of words in sentences, appear to be very enduring and constant, since it extends to whole classes of languages which have few words in common, though it is supposed that they originally had more. But beyond this, there is a cognate character in words themselves which pervades the entire vocabulary of a whole family of languages, the words being formed in the same manner, and according to some artificial rule. This may be exemplified by the monosyllabic structure of the Chinese and Indo-Chinese languages, and by the principle of vocalic harmony pervading the languages of High Asia, to which I shall have occasion again to advert. Of grammatical analogy, or correspondence in the laws of inflection and construction, we have a specimen in the Aboriginal languages of the New World, whose structure is known to be very complicated and artificial, and at the same time common to all the idioms of America which have been examined.

Another example of a more definite character is afforded by the grammatical structure of the language of High Asia and Great Tartary, and a still more striking one by that of the Indo-European idioms.

Connected with the subject of the formation of words is the remark, that in the various branches of particular families of languages which spring by gradual development from the same root, the elements of words, consonants and occasionally vowels, are found to undergo changes according to certain rules. Particular classes of consonants in one language are substituted for other classes in another language of the same family. One European idiom, for example, substitutes palatine letters for sibilunts; another rejects them both, and substitutes labials in their place. When corresponding phenomena can be traced through a great part of the vocabulary of two languages, we recognise a proof that the languages so related must have been derived from one root, the ramifications of which have been differently developed.

The existence of similar words in several languages, even when such resemblances are very numerous, does not, in all cases, afford proof that the languages in question belong to the same family, since intercourse between different nations often gives rise to the adoption of expressions by one tribe for the language of another, as the English have adopted a great many words from the French, and the Welsh a still greater number from the English. The question, whether a considerable number of common or similar words in two languages affords evidence of original connection between them, may be solved by adverting to the particular sorts of words which are found to resemble. Even when one nation has derived from another a considerable proportion of its entire stock of words, there often, and indeed generally, remains an indigenous or aboriginal vocabulary, if I may be allowed the expression, or a home-bred speech, consisting of such words as children learn in early infancy, and in the first development of their faculties. This domestic vocabulary consists of words of the first necessity, such as those denoting family relations, father, mother, child, brother, sister; *secondly*, words denoting parts of the body, and material objects, for which children have names; *thirdly*, personal pronouns, which are found to be amongst the more durable parts of language; *fourthly*, the numerals, especially the first *ten*; *fifthly*, verbs expressive of universal bodily acts, such as, to eat, drink, sleep, walk, talk, &c.; *sixthly*, names of domestic animals. As no human family was ever yet without its own stock of such words, and as they are never changed, within the narrow domestic circle, for other and strange words, they are almost indestructible possessions; and it is only among tribes who have been entirely broken up and enslaved, so that family relations have been destroyed, that this domestic language can have been wholly lost. Tribes and families spread abroad have preserved them for thousands of years, in a degree which has allowed an easy recognition of this sign of a common origin.

A second class of words, which are common to nations who had attained some degree of refinement before the era of their separation, consists of terms connected with simple arts such as simple nations early acquire, as, to plough, to weave, to sew; names of metals, of weapons, tools, articles of dress. It may be observed, that words of this class are often common to nations whose domestic vocabularies are different; and, on the other hand, often different when the domestic vocabulary is nearly the same.

A careful investigation of the phenomena of resemblance or analogy, which discover themselves on comparing different languages, on the principles to which I have now adverted, will go far towards an elucidation of the question, whether such phenomena of resemblance belong to the primitive and original parts of language, and therefore prove a common origin in the nations to which they belong, or are of later date, and are referable to intercourse, or conquest, or some secondary and contingent cause. Such an investigation will, at least, greatly aid and confirm the conclusions which we may draw from historical evidence of a different kind as to the history of tribes, and their mutual relations to each other.

I shall now advert to some of the principal instances in which ethnology has been extended through the medium of researches into the affinities of languages confirmed by historical facts.

Nearly the whole continent of Asia and Europe is divided between four great classes of languages; and in this instance history affords reason to conclude, with great probability, that the affinities of language really mark out as many races or great families of nations. These four sets of languages alluded to are, 1. The Indo-European Languages. 2. The Northern Asiatic, which, for reasons to be explained, I shall term the Ugrian or Tartarian Languages. 3. The Chinese or Indo-Chinese, or the Monosyllabic or Uninflected Languages. 4. The Syro-Arabian or Semitic Languages.

1. The name of Indo-European was first given some years since (by the writer of a review of Adelung's Sprachenkunde, in the Quarterly Review) to a group of languages which includes a great many of the principal idioms of Europe and Asia. It may be divided into several different groups. The first group, or the Classical (as it may be termed, for the sake of distinction), includes those languages in which are the chief remains of ancient literature; and these are more perfectly inflected, and have a more complete grammatical construction than the rest. They are three, viz., the Sanskrit, Greek, and Latin, which perhaps resemble each other nearly in an equal degree. The second group in this first class consists of languages very nearly allied to the Sanskrit, viz., the ancient languages of Persia and Media. They are, 1. The idiom in which the Persepolitan and other Persian cuneiform inscriptions are written, so nearly approaching the Sanskrit, that the meaning has been made out through this resemblance. 2. The Zend, in which the Zendavesta, or the Scriptures of the Fire-worshippers or followers of Zoroaster were written, is another language of this group, to which we may add the modern Persian. 3. The next branch, reckoning by the degrees of affinity, to the Sanskrit, is the Old Prussian family, including the Lettish and Lithuanian.

The Lettish and Lithuanian are said to resemble the Sanskrit more nearly than any other European dialect; and Von Bohlen, who has written a work on this subject, assures us that he could compose whole sentences in Sanskrit, which would be intelligible to the peasants of Lithuania. 4. The Germanic family constitutes a fourth group. 5. The Slavic or Slavonic, or Sarmatian languages, are a fifth section. They comprehend the languages of the eastern parts of Europe, the Russian, Polish, Bohemian, and the dialects of a great part of the countries *in Europe* subject to the Turkish empire.

I shall now stop to inquire what inferences can be drawn from these philological facts.

We know from history, that the nations above mentioned have been spread, from a remote age, over the regions which they now inhabit. The Teutonic and Scandinavian tribes of the German race were known to Pytheas, on the shores of the Baltic, in the time of Aristotle, and the Brahmans who spoke Sanskrit, to Megasthenes at the court of Palibothia, supposed to be Patna, soon after the same period. All ancient Germany, Sarmatia, Italy, Greece, Persia, Media, India, were then inhabited by independent races of people, speaking different languages, but languages strikingly analogous and palpably allied to each other. The question which now occurs to be solved, is, whether these circumstances prove the nations themselves to have descended from a common origin, or admit of any other explanation? Foreign conquests have often introduced new languages among nations, but it is hard to conceive any such hypothesis applicable to the facts now under consideration. If we suppose an Asiatic tribe, speaking any one idiom belonging to this dynasty of languages, to have made conquests ever so extensive in Europe, without leaving any traces in history, which is next to impossible, we could not imagine that they would introduce the German language among the German race, and the Slavonic among the widely-spread natives of Sarmatia, the Greek among the Greeks, the old Italic among the ancient nations of Italy. Any person who considers the nature of that deeply-rooted affinity which exists between these languages, will find convincing proof that their analogies are not engrafted, but spring out of their very fundamental structure. If we take into account the immense extent of the countries over which these nations were spread from so early a period, we cannot refer their affinity of speech to any circumstances accidental and necessarily of restricted and merely local influence. It must have been the result of a gradual deviation of one common language into a multitude of diverging dialects; and the conclusion that is forced upon us, when we take all the conditions of the problem into consideration, is, that the nations themselves descended from one original people, and, consequently, that the varieties of complexion, and other physical characters discovered among them, are the effects of variation from an originally common type.

Besides the languages which I have enumerated as the principal members of the Indo-European family, other groups have been more lately admitted, and some of them appear to be more remotely allied to that stock. One of these is the Celtic language, which was at one time asserted to be entirely distinct, and of separate origin from the Indo-European stock. Their affinity to that stock is now generally admitted, though some persons think that their descent is not genuine, and that they spring from an intermixture of an Indo-European with a more ancient aboriginal or perhaps a Finnish speech. In the east of Europe, the Skippetarians, or Arnauts, or Albanians, the descendants of the ancient Illyrians, and Epirots and Macedonians, speak a distinct idiom, which, by Ritter von Xylander, has been proved to be a particular branch of the great Indo-European stem. To the same stem belong the dialects of the Ossetes in Mount Caucasus, supposed to be descended from the ancient Avars, and those of the Lesgians, in the same mountainous region, the Armenians, all the Tájíks or real Persians, and, lastly, the Affghans or Patans, who speak the Pushtú language, and constitute an intermediate branch between the Persians and the Indians, more nearly allied, however, to the latter, but still distinct from both. Thus we find the Indo-European family to comprise nations which are spread –

Omnibus in terris quæ sunt a Gadibus usque
Auroram et Gangen.

2. The dialects which belong to the second great dynasty of languages in both parts of the great continent of the world – for thus we may term Asia and Europe – are not so obviously allied as are those of the former stock. Yet the proofs of their affinity are on the whole sufficiently marked. They are spread abroad

more widely even than the former languages, and occupy tracts lying to the northward, eastward, and westward, of the Indo-European countries. It is the opinion of many who have investigated these subjects, that the nations who speak dialects of the Ugrian or Tartarian family, were spread over vast regions of the world before the approach of the Indo-European nations, who drove them out towards the north, and east, and west. When the European nations, at a later period, approached them, they retired into the distant parts of Scandinavia, and in the Russian empire, beyond the Valdai Mountains, or the great Uwalli, a chain which divides the waters falling northward into the Baltic and Frozen Oceans, from those which, by a longer course, find their way to the Euxine and Caspian. The Valdai Mountains were for many ages the boundary which separated the Slavonic Russians from the people of this second race, who occupied the northern border of Europe and of Asia. The tribes who now belong to this class of nations in Europe, are the Finns, the Lappes, the Magyars in Hungary, and a variety of nations spread through all the northern regions of Russia, from the White Sea to far beyond the Uralian Mountains.

On the high table-land of Asia, other great divisions of people constitute the main part of the Tartarian stock. They are the Turkish, the Mongolian, and the Mantchu-Tartars. It was from this family that all those nations were descended who poured themselves down, during all the middle ages, upon Christendom and the East, who first overran the caliphat and the Asiatic parts of the Byzantine Empire, and afterwards under Tchingis Khan, conquered all the countries intervening between the Sea of Japan and the Danube. The discovery of a real and deeply rooted affinity between the languages of these nations, was a more difficult enterprise than the tracing of relations between the Indo-European languages. The nations of High Asia who belong to this stock, have passed under the general name of Tartars, given to the followers of Tchingis. The tribes of analogous speech in the northern parts of the Russian empire are termed, by the Russians, Tchudes and Ugres or Ogors. Hence the name of Ugro-Tartar, which comprehends the whole family. The writers who have explored the history of these idioms are Dobrowsky, Gyarmathi, a Hungarian, Rask, Vater, Abel Rémusat, and lastly Dr Schott of Berlin. The evidence of affinity between these nations themselves is principally that afforded by their languages. It may, however, be deemed historical, since history affords proofs that no other explanation can be found of the phenomena ascertained to exist, except that of primitive affinity. We must observe, that the connection of these languages is not merely or principally a resemblance of particular words, such as might have been borrowed by one people from another. It is a deeply-rooted affinity in the original elements of speech, or in the primitive vocables, and a striking analogy in grammatical construction. But beyond all this, there is a singular resemblance in the structure of words themselves. For example, in all these languages that euphonic principle prevails which was first pointed out by Viguier in the Turkish language, and was termed the "quadruple harmony of vowels." According to this principle, only vowels of certain sets can occur in the same word. There are four such sets in the Turkish language, and this law pervades all the dialects of the Turkish race spread from the confines of China to Constantinople. It also prevails in the idioms of the Mongoles and Kalmucks, and in those of the Tungusian and Mantchu Tartars, who are masters of China. It has likewise been noticed in the idioms of the Finnish and Lapponic nations; and Mr Norris, the learned secretary of the Asiatic Society, who is one of the greatest linguists in the world, assures me that it is equally prevalent in the language of the Japanese, which is likewise spoken in the Lieu-kieu islands.

How far towards the west the offsetts of this race extended themselves is as yet unknown. Professor Rask and others have thought the Euskaldunes or Euskarians, or the ancient inhabitants of Spain and the South of France, who are supposed to have occupied those countries before the Celts, might be referred to this stock of nations, but no sufficient proof has been afforded in support of this hypothesis, nor does it appear at all established that the aborigines of Britain were a Finnish race, though this has been conjectured, and is, I believe, the opinion of Dr Meyer, who has studied the Celtic languages and literature more successfully than any of his contemporaries. On this subject I shall say nothing at present, since I hope that we shall soon hear it most ably treated by that learned writer, with some of whose works on the Celtic history I have had occasion to become acquainted. It is no small confirmation of his views to observe that, in many parts of

Western Europe, the sepulchral remains of the oldest and most barbarous class of inhabitants display a type resembling that of the round-headed Tartar race. If these facts should be fully determined, we may find hereafter that the old British legend of Gog and Magog is at least true in a mythical sense. But this subject, though it involves the earliest history of our ancestors, is still involved in doubts which nobody has yet made any serious attempt to dispel, though it is within the reach of historical research.

On the present occasion, I have no opportunity of going fully into the ethnological results which present themselves on considering the history of the Ugro-Tartarian nations. I may just observe, that this survey brings together, and represents as branches of one stock, great tribes of people who differ physically from each other, as the Mongolians with broad lozenge-faced heads, flat noses, and projecting cheekbones, the various Turkish races, some of whom, as the Kirghises and other eastern tribes, resemble the Mongoles, while the Turks of Stamboul and Roum have a very different physiognomy; the little black-haired reindeer-feeding Lappes, and the phlegmatic fair-haired Finns; and lastly, the proud and lordly Magyars, who have almost a Grecian physiognomy.

3. The third family of nations reckoned among the principal races of the great Continent, are the Chinese and Indo-Chinese nations. They are brought into one department by the resemblance of their languages, all of which consist of monosyllabic words, incapable of grammatical inflection, and likewise by their great physical resemblance and geographical proximity.

4. The fourth great family of nations before alluded to are the Syro-Arabian, or, as German writers term them, the Semitic nations, to which stock the ancient Hebrews and Assyrians, and Syrians and Arabs belonged. The Arabian branch has spread its language over all the countries formerly occupied by these nations. Late researches into the languages of Northern Africa indicate, that the Syro-Arabian stock extended originally much farther into that part of the world than was formerly supposed.

I shall not now attempt to enumerate all the great families of languages or of nations in the world, and perhaps I have already trespassed too long on the time and patience of the Society. I shall sum up what remains to be said in a few general observations on the principal divisions of the human family.

The languages of Africa are not sufficiently known to be accurately classified or referred to particular groups, which we may consider with any degree of certainty as comprising the whole number. We may, however, reckon several great families. These are, 1. The North-African languages, more or less connected with the Syro-Arabian idioms. To this department are referrible with different degrees of evidence, 1. The Abyssinian languages, the Ghiz, Tigre, and Amhárá languages, and perhaps also the Galla dialects spoken by nomadic nations through an immense space to the southward of Abyssinia, including the idiom of the Somáli on the eastern coast. 2. The Berber, Kabylian, and Shillah languages, which are dialects of the ancient Lybian. Professor Newman, who has studied these languages with greater success than any other person, considers them as a branch of the Syro-Arabian family, correlative with the ancient Hebrew, Phœnician, and Syrian.

A third division in this North-African family is the idiom of the Hausa Negroes in the inland parts of Africa or Súdan. This language, as Professor Newman has proved, has grammatical affinities to the Syro-Arabian languages.

A second African family of languages, of perhaps equal extent, are the Kafir languages. More or less of affinity, both in words and in grammatical structure, pervades all the known languages of the black woolly-haired nations to the southward of the equator, including all the Kafir nations, the Suaheli on the eastern coast, and the nations of the so-termed Empire of Congo. It must be observed that some of the tribes belonging to this division have Negro features, while others have the Kafir figure and a physiognomy of a very different type.

3. The language of the Hottentots and Bushmen constitute a third group.

4. The languages of the Negro nations of Western Africa. The most correct enumeration of these languages as yet made, classified according to these vocabularies, is that which was laid before the Ethnological Section of the British Association by Dr Latham, two years ago, at York.

The languages of America, as yet generally known, belong to one type as far as grammatical structure is concerned, and that a very peculiar one, and strongly marked. It is possible that exceptions may hereafter occur to this remark, and Dr

Buschmann, the learned editor of Baron William von Humboldt's posthumous works, who has for several years been employed in preparing for the press a work on the American languages, written partly by William Humboldt, and partly, as I believe, by himself, informs me that he has found exceptions to the general character of these languages, though he does not consider as such the Othomi language which Naxera, a Mexican writer, supposed to be a monosyllabic idiom, and therefore very unlike the polysyllabic and polysynthetic languages, as they have been termed, of America. Several of the learned cultivators of philology, who have done credit to the rapidly increasing literature of the United States, have succeeded in classifying the native languages of North America, and referring them to a comparatively small number of families of great extent. These families are regarded by M. Gallatin as distinct from each other in relation to their vocabulary. Dr Latham, who has attentively studied their vocabularies, is of opinion that there is a greater connection between the different mother-tongues of the American nations, if we may use the expression, than M. Gallatin supposed. On this question I am unable to offer an opinion; but certainly the probability is on Dr Latham's side, since it is very unlikely, though perhaps the fact is not without example, that languages which have so great a similarity in structure as the American idioms, should yet display no proofs of affinity in their vocabulary.

I need not observe that the conclusion to be drawn in regard to the community or diversity of origin between the different American languages, is one very interesting in an ethnological point of view, especially if we take into account the very considerable physical differences which separate some of the American nations, as the Esquimaux, from the rest.

It is a matter of still greater interest to determine whether the American idioms bear any analogy to those of the Old Continent sufficient to furnish an argument of common origin. It has been observed that the Euskarian idiom, the old Iberian, probably the oldest known language of the west of Europe, has a resemblance in structure to the dialects of the American nations; and an American writer, Dr M'Culloh, has argued from this fact, that the nations of the New World had an European origin. But there are great diversities as well as resemblances between the Euskarian and the American languages, and nothing certain can be concluded from this argument, which, however, must not be entirely overlooked. It is observable that the races of people in the extreme north-east of Asia, beyond the river Kolyma, are described as differing considerably in physical conformation from the nations of Great Tartary. Very little is known of their languages; and it might possibly lead to some important discoveries if we could compare these unknown idioms with those of the hunting tribes on the opposite parts of America, particularly the Athabascas, and the nations bordering upon them. It has been long ago ascertained, that one language is common to the two continents. I mean that of the Esquimaux and the Fishing Tchuktchi in Asia, whose idioms certainly belong to the same stock.

In the South Sea there are, as I have observed, several distinct races. The most important of these are the Polynesians, descended from the Malays, from whom they differ physically. The history of the Papua races is very interesting. They resemble, in some particulars, the Africans of the Gold Coast, but differ widely in the shape of their heads from all the Negro races. Some Papua nations, whose idioms have been examined, have been found to speak dialects of the Polynesian language. Among them are the Figians. We may conclude that they are descended from Polynesians, though probably not without intermixture with people of the black or Papua race.

The Australians constitute a third race in these regions. Their dialects appear, from the researches of Captain Gray, to form a particular family of languages, displaying great varieties, but bearing traces of affinity among themselves, and derived from a common stock. One of the most interesting observations as yet made respecting them is the remark of Mr Norris, who has discovered indications of connection between the Australian dialects and the Tamilian spoken by the aboriginal inhabitants of the Dekhan.

I have endeavoured to explain what I believe to be the principles on which ethnological research must be conducted, if we would maintain for that study and its results the character of a really scientific and philosophical pursuit. The only certainty that can be obtained in the formation of groups and families of nations, must be founded mainly on historical proofs. We must begin by establishing the historical fact of relationship or consanguinity between tribes of people, before we venture to refer them to one race, or to assert their diversity of origin. The deviations which are known to have taken place within the limits of particular families, are too great to allow us to assume diversity of origin on the mere ground of physical difference; and it is equally obvious, that we cannot assume a near relationship on the simple evidence of physical resemblance.

It would carry me far beyond the limits of the subject of this paper if I were to attempt to sum up any general results, or trace the bearing of facts on the great question of the unity or diversity of human families; but I may be allowed to conclude with this remark, that the farther we explore the various paths of inquiry which lie open to our researches, the greater reason do we find for believing that no insurmountable line of separation exists between the now diversified races of men; and the greater the possibility, judging alone from such data as we possess, that all mankind are descended from one family.

THE RACES OF MEN
A Philosophical Enquiry into the Influence of Race over the Destinies of Nations

Robert Knox

Robert Knox (1791–1862) was of Scottish origin. Most of his ancestors were farmers. His father had managed to become a teacher of mathematics. Knox studied medicine at the University of Edinburgh and then at the extramural anatomical school run by John Barclay. In 1814 he took his MD. He enrolled as a doctor to the army. In 1817 his regiment was sent to the Cape where Knox undertook ethnological, zoological, meteorological, and medical researches. In 1821–2 he spent a year in Paris where he studied under Cuvier, Geoffroy Saint-Hilaire and others. In 1826 he took over the anatomical school of John Barclay in Edinburgh. But from the early 1830s, his popularity declined. After a period of unsettlement, in 1846 Knox started lecturing on race. He toured Newcastle-on-Tyne, Manchester and other towns. In 1850 he published the first edition of his *Races of Men*.

Physiological Question

Do races ever amalgamate? What are the obstacles to a race changing its original locality?

I have heard persons assert, a few years ago, men of education too, and of observation, that the amalgamation of races into a third or new product, partaking of the qualities of the two primitive ones from which they sprung, was not only possible, but that it was the best mode of improving the breed. The whole of this theory has turned out to be false: – 1st. As regards the lower animals; 2nd. As regards man. Of the first I shall say but little: man is the great object of human research; the philosophy of Zoology is not indeed wrapt up in him; he is not the end, neither was he the beginning: still, as he is, a knowledge of man is to him all-important.

The theories put forth from time to time, of the production of a new variety, permanent and self-supporting, independent of any draughts or supplies from the pure breeds, have been distinctly disproved. It holds neither in sheep nor cattle: and an author, whose name I cannot recollect, has refuted the whole theory as to the pheasant and to the domestic fowl. He has shown that the artificial breeds so produced are never self-supporting. Man can create nothing: no new species have appeared, apparently, for some thousand years; but this is another question I mean not to discuss here, although it is obvious that if a hybrid could be produced, self-supporting, the elaborate works of Cuvier would fall to the ground. The theory of Aristotle, who explained the variety and strangeness of the animal forms in Africa, on the grounds that a scarcity of water brought to the wells and springs animals of various kinds from whose intercourse sprung the singularly varied African Zoology, has been long known to be a mere fable.

Nature produces no mules; no hybrids, neither in man nor animals. When they accidentally appear they soon cease to be, for they are either non-productive, or one or other of the pure breeds speedily predominates, and the weaker disappears. This weakness may either be numerical or innate.

That this law applies strictly to man himself, all history proves: I once said to a gentleman born in Mexico, – Who are the Mexicans? I put the same question to a gentleman from Peru, as I had done before, to persons calling themselves Germans – neither could give a distinct reply to the question. The fact turns out to be, that there really are no such persons; no such *race*.

When the best blood of Spain migrated to America, they killed as many of the natives, that is, the copper-coloured Indians, indigenous to the soil, as they could. But this could not go on, labourers to till the soil being required. The old Spaniard was found unequal to this; *he could not colonize the conquered country*; he required other aid, native or imported. Then came the admixture with the Indian blood and the Celt-Iberian blood; the produce being the mulatto. But now that the supplies of Spanish blood have ceased, the mulatto must cease, too, for as a hybrid he becomes non-productive after a time, if he intermarries only with the mulatto: he can no longer go back to the Spanish blood: that stock has ceased; of necessity then he is forced upon the Indian breed. Thus, year by year, the

Spanish blood disappears, and with it the mulatto, and the population retrograding towards the indigenous inhabitants, returns to that Indian population, the hereditary descendants of those whom Cortes found there; whom nature seemingly placed there; not aliens, nor foreigners, but aboriginal. As it is with Mexico, so it is with Peru.

When Mr. Canning made his celebrated boast in Parliament, that he had created the republics of Mexico and Peru, Columbia, Bolivia, and Argentine, I made, to some friends, the remark, that to create races of men was beyond his power, and that the result of his measure would merely be to precipitate that return, sure to come at last, the return of the aboriginal Indian population, from whom no good could come, from whom nothing could be expected; a race whose vital energies were wound up; expiring: hastening onwards also to ultimate extinction.

If we look to the period of Rome's conquests, we shall find that no amalgamation of races ever happened; in Greece it was the same. It would seem, indeed, that happen what will, no race, however victorious they may be, has ever succeeded in utterly destroying a native population and occupying their place. Two laws seem to me the cause of this. Should the conquering party be numerous there is still the climate against them; and if few, the native race, antagonistic of the conquerors, again predominates; so that after most conquests the country remains in the hands of the original race.

Let us turn now to the ancient world, to Europe, and Asia, and Africa, and inquire into the history of the pretended amalgamation of races; the extinction of one race and the substitution of another; for these two questions may be considered together.

There has been no amalgamation of the Celtic and Saxon races in Ireland. They abhor each other cordially. When I publicly asserted this some years ago, I was as publicly contradicted. I call on those persons now to say whose opinion was the correct one; the Irish Celt is as distinct from the Saxon as he was seven hundred years ago. There is no mistaking the question now. Mr. Macaulay, in his Chronicles of the English People, will have it that the pitiable state of the Irish is owing to their religion; but the Caledonian Celt is an Evangelical Protestant, and so also is the Cymbrii, or Welsh: now I ask this plain question: Is the Caledonian Celt better off than the

The racialist Robert Knox did not like the Celts and their alledged descendants. The original caption to this picture reads: 'A Celtic Groupe [sic]; such may be seen at any time in Marylebone, London' (From Knox's *Races of Men*, 2nd ed., 1862).

Hibernian? is he more industrious? more orderly, cleanly, temperate? has he accumulated wealth? does he look forward to to-morrow? Though a seeming Protestant, can you compare his religious formula with the Saxon? It is the race, then, and not the religion; that elastic robe, modern Christianity, adapts itself with wonderful facility to all races and nations. It has little or no influence that I can perceive over human affairs, further than a great state engine serving political purposes; a tub for the whale. The great broad principles of the morality of man have nothing to do with any religion. The races of men still remain distinct – the gipsies mingle not, neither do the Jews. In Swedish and Russian Lapland, the Lappes remain apart; the Fins are Slavonians, they mingle not with the adjoining Saxon race; the Saxons remain distinct from the Slavonians in the Grand Duchy of Posen, and in all eastern Prussia. An attempt was made by the Germans to destroy the Slavonian race in Bohemia; it was a thirty years war, conducted by the savage and imbecile House of Hapsburgh against the Bohemians. It utterly failed, and the inhabitants are still Slavonian. The Muscovite has grasped all northern Asia, yet he has not succeeded in destroying any race, neither do they amalgamate with the Russ. The French Celt has never yet been able to live and thrive in Corsica; Algeria, he can, I fear, hold only as a military possession: a colonist, in the proper sense of the term, he never can become. On the banks of the Nile still wander in considerable numbers the descendants of the men who built the pyramids, and carved the Memnon and the Sphynx. Yet Egypt is in other hands, as if the destinies of the Coptic race had been decided. No one has yet clearly explained to the world the precise nature of the dominant race in Egypt; I mean here, the character of the great bulk of the population. They do not seem to increase in numbers; if this, then, be the case, their ultimate possession of Egypt may be doubted: the Coptic blood still lingers in the land, waiting the return of an Amenoph, a Sesostris, a Leader.

Let us attend now to the greatest of all experiments ever made in respect of the transfer of a population indigenous to one continent, and attempting by emigration to take possession of another; to cultivate it with their own hands; to colonize it; to persuade the world, in time, that they are *the natives* of the newly occupied land. Northern America and Australia furnished the fields for this, the greatest of experiments; already has the horse, the sheep, the ox, become as it were indigenous to these lands. Nature did not place them there at first, yet they seem to thrive, and flourish, and multiply exceedingly. Yet, even as regards these domestic animals, we cannot be quite certain; will they eventually be self-supporting?

will they supplant the llama, the kangaroo, the buffalo, the deer? or, in order to effect this, will they require to be constantly renovated from Europe? If this be the contingency, then the acclimatation is not perfect. How is it with man himself? The man planted there by nature, the Red Indian, differs from all others on the face of the earth; he gives way before the European races, the Saxon and the Celtic: the Celt-Iberian and Lusitanian in the south; the Celt and Saxon in the north. Of the tropical regions of the new world I need not speak; every one knows that none but those whom Nature placed there can live there: that no European can colonize a tropical country. But may there not be some doubts of their self-support in milder regions? take the Northern States themselves. There the Saxon and the Celt seem to thrive beyond all that is recorded in history. But are we quite sure that this success is fated to be permanent? Annually from Europe is poured a hundred thousand men and women of the best blood of the Scandinavian, and twice that number of the pure Celt; and so long as this continues he is sure to thrive. But check it;

The Saxons, by contrast, Knox regarded as a superior race; they were as intelligent as they were individualistic. In Knox's *Races of Man* this picture is presented as 'Anglo-Saxon house; it always, if possible, stands detached'.

arrest it suddenly, as in the case of Mexico and Peru; throw the *onus* of reproduction upon the population, no longer European, but native, or born on the spot; then will come the struggle between the European alien and his adopted fatherland. The climate; the forests; the remains of the aborigines not yet extinct; last, not least, that unknown and mysterious degradation of life and energy which in ancient times seems to have decided the fate of all the Phœnician, Grecian, and Coptic colonies. Cut off from their original stock they gradually withered and faded, and finally died away. The Phœnician never became acclimatized in Africa, nor in Cornwall, nor in Wales; vestiges of his race, it is true, still remain, but they are mere vestiges. Peru and Mexico are fast retrograding to their primitive condition; may not the Northern States, under similar circumstances, do the same? Already the United States man differs in appearance from the European: the ladies early lose their teeth; in both sexes the adipose cellular cushion interposed between the skin and the aponeuroses and muscles disappears, or, at least, loses its adipose portion; the muscles become stringy, and show themselves; the tendons appear on the surface; symptoms of premature decay manifest themselves. Now what do these signs, added to the uncertainty of infant life in the Southern States, and the smallness of their families in the Northern, indicate? Not the conversion of the Anglo-Saxon into the Red Indian, but warnings, that the climate has not been made for him, nor he for the climate. See what even a small amount of insulation has done for the French Celt in Lower Canada. Look at the race there! small men; small horses; small cattle; still smaller carts; ideas smallest of all; he is not even the Celt of modern France! He is the French Celt of the Regency; the thing of Louis XIII. Stationary, absolutely stationary, his numbers, I believe, depend on the occasional admixture of fresh blood from Europe. He has increased to about a million since his first settlement in Canada; but much of this has come from Britain, and not from France. Give us the statistics of the aboriginal families who keep themselves apart from the fresh blood imported into the province; let us have the real and solid increase of the original habitants, as they are pleased to call themselves, and then we may calculate on the result. Had the colony been left to itself, cut off from Europe for a century or two, it is my belief that the forest, the buffalo, the *wilde*, and the Red Indian, would have pushed him into the

St. Lawrence, from the banks of which he never had the courage to wander far; amalgamating readily with the Red Indian by intermarriage, (for the Celt has not that antipathy to the dark races which so peculiarly characterize the Saxon); – amalgamating with the Red Indian, the population would speedily have assumed the appearance it has in Mexico and Peru; to follow the same fate, perish or return to the original Indian; and finally, to terminate in the all but utter destruction of the original race itself.

Lecture II

Physiological Laws Regulating Human Life

In the rapid sketch of the dominant races of men I am about to submit to you (of the Saxon I have already spoken), I have endeavoured to comprise an outline of their history, viewed, as I have long been in the habit of viewing them, not as *nations*, but as *races*. I am well aware that when these lectures were first delivered, about five years ago, the opinions they contained were opposed to all the received opinions of the day. The world was so *national*, and *race* had been so utterly forgotten, that for at least two years after delivering my first course of lectures at Newcastle I had the whole question to myself. But *now* the press, even in insular England, has been, most reluctantly I believe, forced to take it up; to make admissions which I never supposed could have been wrung from them; to confess it to be possible that man, after all, may be subject to some physiological laws hitherto not well understood; that *race*, as well as "democracy,"[1] or socialism,[2] or bands of peripatetic demagogues,[3] or evil spirits,[4] may have had something to do with the history of nations, and more especially with the last revolutions in Europe. It is true that Englishmen will not admit its application to Ireland or to our *colonies*. "Persons," they say, "situated as the Irish, so favoured by Divine Providence as to be permitted to live under our glorious institutions in church and state, should dismiss from their minds all questions of race;

[1] Guizot.
[2] English aristocracy.
[3] Russell.
[4] Metternich.

such questions may and do apply to the continental people, but we happy islanders have nothing to do with them." Of the various ways in which, with a view to suit the English palate, the great question of the day, the question of race, has been touched on by ponderous quarterlies and sprightly weeklies, some admitting most of my views already proven, others qualifying them in a variety of ways, they are yet unanimous, I think, on this one point, that the physiological laws proposed by me are not applicable to the Irish nor to the Jews – tabooed races, which must not be touched. But the question with me is simply, What is truth? Man, Celtic or Judean, is either subject to physiological laws or he is not. By happy conceit, the Jew has been withdrawn from the influence of these laws; and English statesmen and English men cherish the fond belief that the Celtic natives of Ireland, Scotland, and Wales, may yet be converted into good Saxons, by means of the "Estates Encumbered Bill," aided by Divine Providence. The latter, no doubt, is an all-powerful auxiliary, could they but calculate on it; the former is also a powerful measure, and may do much. The extent of soil in Celtic Ireland to be converted from Romanism (Paganism?) is limited, measured. It is not a continent; it is an island. Sell the island to Saxon men. It is a powerful measure. It has succeeded seemingly against some of the dark races of men, whom it has brought to the verge of destruction. Caffre and Hottentot, Tasmanian and American: why not against a fair race – the Celtic natives of Ireland, Wales, and Caledonia, for they must be classed together? They are one; the same fate, whatever it be, awaits all. Placed front to front, antagonistic in fact with a stronger race, our reason, aided, as it would at first appear, by past history, might hastily decide in foretelling their extermination and ruin. On the other hand, the more I inquire into the history of race, the more I doubt all theorists who neglect or despise this grand element; who speak of "European civilization and a Caucasian race;" of all nature's works being unalterable, excepting man, who is ever changing.[5] But man is also a part of nature; he must obey certain laws. The object of the present inquiry is to discover these laws. They have never been honestly sought for, but conjecture offered instead; from the climatic theory of Hippocrates to the Caucasian dream of Blumenbach – wild

[5] Quarterly, Nov. 1849.

hypotheses have been assumed as truths. Instinctive, animal man, a part and parcel of nature's great scheme, has been lost sight of; because he has built ships and cities, it has been surmised that his nature changes with circumstances! – that under a wise and liberal government his mind and frame expand! Look at France; look at Ireland; look at Canada; at Southern Africa. Ask Pretorius and his bold Saxon boors how they like the mild and free government of our "best light-cavalry officer!" Ask the United States men, who forces them already to introduce an oppressive and cruel tariff into their laws? A few years ago they were clamorous against England's restrictive laws; they blamed the English government. "See," said they, "the British, the selfish British, refuse to modify their navigation laws!" Knowing well *the race*, I ventured, even then, to declare the whole to be a false pretence, a delusion, and a mockery. They were Saxons; that was enough – they wanted no free tariff. A commercial war against the world is what they aim and aimed at; but it served their purpose to declaim against England; hypocrisy and unscrupulous selfish-ness are blemishes, no doubt, in the Saxon element of mind; they lead to sharp practices in manufactures, which have, somehow or other, a strange connexion with dishonesty; they give to Saxon commerce a peculiar character, and to Saxon war a vulgar, low, and mercenary spirit, cold and calculating; profitable wars, keenly taken up, unscrupulously followed out. The plains of Hindostan have been the grand field for Saxon plunder: the doings there are said to be without a parallel in history.

Scarcely five years have elapsed since I announced the general principle, that he who would not or could not see, in the dominant races of Europe, distinct elements of mind, could never read aright the history of the past, understand the present, nor rightly guess the future. And now the truth of this principle, so stoutly denied by the chronicler of the *Times*, is already fully admitted. There is still an unwillingness to admit some other laws announced at the same time: the physiological laws which regulate the destinies of mankind and of race. Let me here consider some of these laws.

Physiological Laws
It was Hippocrates who wrote that pleasing fiction, which, embodying the scattered notions of his day (for he was a

compiler, and a most extensive one, too), gave to theories, based on no proofs, a *quasi* philosophical character. He assumed that external circumstances modified human structure and human character. His actual observations were few, and made on a narrow field – Greece, I presume, and a portion of Asia Minor. Like most medical men, he was a great theorist, and has the credit of having first separated medicine from philosophy. And so I think he did, much to its disadvantage. What it was before this unlucky event can scarcely now be known; since then it has almost rivalled theology in the wildness of its conjectures, its contradictory views, its conflicting theories. Let us return to Hippocrates.

That the minds and bodies of men are influenced, *to a certain extent*, by external circumstances, I see no reason to deny. But this is not the real question: the question is, *to what extent?* Let us first consider the effects of climate. Hippocrates was enough of a philosopher to see that it was not merely to the atmosphere that was to be assigned the supposed influence exercised by external circumstances over man's form and mind. Accordingly, he entitles his work, Περι υδατων, αερον, και τοπον – which may be thus translated, On the Influence of the Atmosphere, the Waters and the *Locality*, over Man. These heads were meant to include all possible physical elements affecting man. Man's mind he traces to his bodily frame; if he believed in a heaven and a future state, he had no faith in Olympus, nor in a thundering, material Jove, nor Styx, nor Pluto. He was a sort of anatomist, and had probably seen the brain – a sight of which tends no doubt to remove many prejudices.

That the hypotheses sanctioned by his great name existed long before his period we need not doubt; it is sufficient for our present purpose to trace them to him. In his writings we find hypotheses – 1st, That climate or external circumstances make men brave or cowardly, freemen or slaves; in other words, that man's *mind* was the result of *climate*. 2ndly, That to climate and to other external circumstances, summed up in the expression, "Air, Water, and Place," (Hippocrates!) might be traced all differences in the form, complexion, and mental qualifications of men; the varieties, in short, observable everywhere in their physical structure and mental dispositions; that race, in short, depends on climate. And 3rdly, That such alterations in form and mind, the result of external influences, thus constituting a race, become in time permanent, transmissible by hereditary descent, and so independent of their original producing causes; and lastly, that the head itself, the very brain, by means of which we lay claim to the character and title of intellectual beings, might be so altered by mechanical means, by external pressure, as scarcely to be recognizable for a human head; and that this most extraordinary of all forms, once produced, becomes transmissible by hereditary descent, requiring no longer the influence of the mechanical cause producing it.

To Hippocrates was ascribed the honour of having first separated medicine from philosophy; these are some of the results of this disunion – hypothesis heaped on hypothesis, unsupported by observation, based on no truths. To him, or at least to those from whose works he compiled, we owe some, at least, of these conjectures. He is supposed (for in ancient history all is supposition) to have flourished some 470, say 500 years before the present æra, that is, at the least, 2300 years ago: he has been usually called a physician – to me he seems to have been a surgeon, and his success was probably equal to any of the present day. The opinions he has collected are much older than the period he lived in; medical theories and theorists had been already tested and appreciated by the philosophers of his times – Thucydides, the historian, knew them well. But Hippocrates, at all events, embodied some of these theories into a sort of system, handing them down to posterity in classic language, bestowing on error immortality. That his mind was philosophic on the whole, cannot be questioned; but so was that of Descartes, of Pythagoras, of Voltaire; all philosophic minds, all impatient of the calm investigation of physical truths. Like many great and good men, some modern fanatics have accused him of atheism; those, in fact, and they belong to all denominations, who accuse of atheism all who refuse joining their outrageously ridiculous anthropomorphical notions of a First Cause. He denied the discrepancy of divine and physical causes, merging them in one; he treated all phenomena as at once divine and scientifically determinable. This doctrine he applied to disease: my object is to apply it to all living nature – to man, the most important of all – to man, the antagonistic animal of nature's works; to that animal who wages perpetual war with nature's fairest productions. It is in vain that theologians endeavour to divert the attention of men's minds from this great question, How are the races of men produced? whence come they? wither tend they? Already a learned divine[6] has stretched the link between the 2nd and 3rd verses of the Mosaic record to a coil so extended, so elastic, as to leave on the part of the scientific nothing to desire; and whilst I write this passage, a friend has pointed out to me that a learned theologian, if not an orthodox divine,[7] who writes on a subject of which I fear he does not know much, – "the Unity of Man" – cautions his readers not to mistake the chronology of Bishop Usher for the true chronology of man, which he candidly admits has never yet been discovered: he prepares his readers for a lengthening of the *period* to account for the different races! I knew it must come to this – another version of the Mosaic record to the hundreds already existing. For the present, I leave the chronological part in their hands, proceeding with the inquiry into the physiological laws regulating human life.

That by mere climate, giving to the expression its utmost range of meaning, a new race of men can be established in perpetuity, is an assertion which for the present is contradicted by every well-ascertained physiological law, and by all authentic history. On the limited habitable territory of the Cape of Good Hope, shut in by deserts and by the sea, lived, when the Saxon Hollander first landed there, two races of men, as distinct from each other as can be well imagined, the Hottentot, or Bosjeman, and the Amakoso Caffre. To these was added a third, the Saxon Hollander. What time the Bosjeman child of the desert had hunted these desert and arid regions, for what period the Hottentot had listlessly tended his flocks of fat-tailed sheep, how long the bold Caffre had herded his droves of cattle, cannot now be ascertained: the Saxon Hollander found them there 300 years ago, as they are now in respect of physical structure and mental qualifications, inferior races, whom he drove before him, exterminating and enslaving the coloured man; destroying mercilessly the *wilde* which nature had placed there; and with the *wilde*, ultimately the coloured *man*, in harmony with all around him – antagonistic, it is true, but still in harmony to a certain extent; non-progressive; races which mysteriously had run their course, reaching the time appointed for their destruction.

---

6   Buckland.

7   British Quarterly, for Nov. – Editor, Rev. Dr. Vaughan.

To assert that a race like the Bosjeman, marked by so many peculiarities, is convertible, by any process, into an Amakoso Caffre or Saxon Hollander, is at once to set all physical science at defiance. If by time, I ask what time? The influence of this element I mean to refute presently: the Dutch families who settled in Southern Africa three hundred years ago, are now as fair, and as pure in Saxon blood, as the native Hollander; the slightest change in structure or colour can at once be traced to intermarriage. By intermarriage an individual is produced, intermediate generally, and partaking of each parent; but this mulatto man or woman is a montrosity of nature – there is no place for such a family: no such race exists on the earth, however closely affiliated the parents may be. To maintain it would require a systematic course of intermarriage, with constant draughts from the pure races whence the mixed race derives its origin. Now, such an arrangement is impossible. Since the earliest recorded times, such mixtures have been attempted and always failed; with Celt and Saxon it is the same as with Hottentot and Saxon, Caffre and Hottentot. The Slavonian race or races have been deeply intercalated for more than twice ten centuries with the South German, the pure Scandinavian, the Sarmatian, and even somewhat with the Celt, and with the Italian as conquerors: have they intermingled? Do you know of any mixed race the result of such admixture? Is it in Bohemia? or Saxony? or Prussia? or Finland?

This seems to be the law. By intermarriage a new product arises, which cannot stand its ground; 1st, By reason of the innate dislike of race to race, preventing a renewal of such intermarriages; 2nd, Because the descendants will of necessity fall back upon the stronger race, and all traces, or nearly so, of the weaker race must in time be obliterated. In what time, we shall afterwards consider. If a pure race has appeared to undergo a permanent change when transferred to a climate materially differing from their own, such changes will be found, on a closer inquiry, to be delusive. It has been asserted of the West-Indian Creole; of the Mexican, Peruvian, and Chilian Creole; and of the North-American or Saxon Creole, now called a United States man; but the pretended changes we shall find are either trifling, or not permanent, or do not exist. When speaking of the races so located, that is, dislocated from the climate and land of their origin, and from the pure race which sent them forth, swarms of living beings, in search of new lands, I shall endeavour to apply those laws practically which are here merely announced, discussing also, in separate sections, some of the leading doctrines applicable to all men. Of other animals I speak not here, for this obvious reason – the species of animals as they now exist, have their specific laws regulating their existence. What is true of one may or may not be true of another. Sheep have their specific laws; so have cattle and horses, pigs and elephants. Some of the laws regulating their existence are applicable to man in a general way – others, and the greater part, are not. When I am told that there is a short-legged race of sheep somewhere in America, the product of accident, my reply is simple – I do not believe it, even although, to make the story look better, it has been also added, that from among the few short-legged sheep *accidentally* produced in the flock, the owner was careful to extrude the long-legged ones, and so at last his whole flock became short-legged, and he *had no more trouble with it*. It is the old fable of Hippocrates and the Macrocephali reduced to something like a scientific formula; transferred from sheep, it has been made the basis of a theory of race, of mankind – reducing all to *accident*. By accident, a child darker than the rest of the family is born; when this happens in the present day, it is also, by courtesy, called an accident, but its nature is well understood; not so in former times. This dark child, a little darker than the others, separates, with a few more, from the rest of the family, and sojourns in a land where a hot sun enbrowns them with a still deeper hue. In time they become blacker and blacker, or browner and browner. Should they travel north instead of south, it is all the same, for extreme cold produces the same effect as extreme heat! This is ancient and modern physiology! it is the old fable of Hippocrates revived. Men's minds seem to move in circles, ever reverting to ancient errors; it is as the struggle of a small body of men against the gloomy forest, the bog, the spreading desert; lovers of truth vainly endeavouring to clear away the accumulated ignorance of fifty centuries.

For my own part, I do not think such theories worthy a serious refutation. Man is not a ruminant; he has his own physiological laws, which ought long since to have been traced. But the statement in question is not even true of sheep, for by no effort, saving that of a *constant* never-ceasing intermixture, or draught on the pure breeds, can a mixed breed be maintained. Leave it to itself, and it ceases to be. It is the same with man; with fowls; with cattle; with horses. Distinct breeds, when not interfered with, mark them all. Man can create nothing permanent; modify, he may for a time, but he can create no new living element. It is said that the cattle fed on the pampas of South America have assumed three distinct forms; be it so – the fact proves nothing, for they are constantly interfered with by man. I have been assured that our domestic cattle, imported into New Zealand and New Holland, return after a generation or two to the primitive breeds – nothing more likely, this, in fact, being the physiological law. In Britain we have a white breed of cattle, confined within the domains of two wealthy families; they remain *white*, merely because all calves which show other colours are destroyed. See how difficult the simplest physiological question becomes. We talk freely of men's destiny and races, and their laws, as if we knew them, whilst as yet no one has solved so simple a question as the origin of the white cattle of Britain and of Wales. But to return to man.

Add to the hypothesis of *accidental* origin of a variety in family, its separation from its tribe, yet even this explanation will fail; for the family so separated, by the very law which produced the variety, will be fertile in other varieties; they therefore must also appear in numbers at least equal to the others. In the history of the Jewish and Gipsy races I shall consider this question at greater length, and endeavour to show that the application of the doctrines of transcendental anatomy made in this direction is also false.

"Time and development change all things;" this is my own belief: but what is the time required? when was man different from what we find him now? Development is positive: time has no existence. The existing order of things we see, though imperfectly; of the past, but little has been preserved in human records – that little is not understood. One thing, however, is certain – the Pyramids exist, and the ancient tombs of Egypt; the ruins of Karnâc; the paintings on the walls of these tombs; some Etruscan remains; the Egyptian mummies; the Cyclopean walls – these are nearly all the sure data which man has to depend on whilst tracing back his history, and the history of the existing order of life, towards that unknown past from which he sprung. Now what do these amount to? What do they prove? They are but as yesterday, compared with the period through which the globe has rolled in space; through which life has undergone its ever succeeding developments; yet they announce one fact at least, that man, up to the earliest recorded time, did not differ *materially* from what he is now; that there were races then as now; that they seemed to be identical (but of this we are not quite certain) with those now existing, and that neither over them, nor over the living world around, has climate or external circumstances effected any serious changes, produced any new species, any new groups of animal or vegetable life, any new varieties of mankind. To the important fact, if it really be one, thus made out, the illustrious and cautious Cuvier first drew men's attention; but his reserve, his position, his habitual caution, induced him to omit all mention of man. So long as he excluded him from his line of observation, the Sorbonne, he was aware, cared not what he did with the rest. It was his practice to leave untouched whatever he thought speculative, unsafe, transcendental – whatever he fancied shocked too much the present feelings. Satisfied with the refutation of St. Fond and the geologists of his day, he desired to proceed no further. "He had formed an æra – he constituted an æra:" to his positive opinions and well-ascertained facts were tacked theories by the theologico-geological school of England, which he never acknowledged, which he never admitted, which he never sanctioned by word or writing. We shall consider these matters in a future section; in the meantime one thing remains certain, which he either did not notice or avoided mentioning – man has changed no more than other animals: as they were in Egypt when the pyramids were built, so are they now, men and animals: man seems different, it is true: at first it would appear as if a race had become extinct; we shall find it is not so. The Coptic race is no more extinct that is the ancient Mexican, and even now it is questionable whether the mixed barbarian and savage race of slaves, now called Egyptians, will ultimately stand their ground, fed though they be by imports from Nubia and the White Nile – from Greece and Asia Minor. They are not Arabs: a motley crew, as I understand, destined to cease when the imports are withdrawn, and to assume a form traceable to the dominant blood now circulating, be it Copt or Arab, Nubian or Negro.

But in claiming for the races of men an antiquity coeval with the historic period, and with man's earliest appearance on the earth, I venture to caution you from accepting of this deduction or that of M. Cuvier in respect of animals, as being rigorously accurate. Neither men nor animals seem to have changed; as regards the latter, Cuvier asserted that they had not in the slightest degree. Admitting the expression to be sufficiently accurate for his and our purpose, yet I think it strong, perhaps too strong. Data sufficiently accurate and extensive are wanting to enable us to institute a very rigorous comparison. I do not mean to cavil at the expression: the changes undergone in five or six thousand years are so small as to escape notice; but it does not absolutely follow that no changes whatever have taken place. On the tombs of Egypt, the most valuable of all existing records, there stands the Negro, the Jew, the Copt, the Persian, the Sarmatian, nearly as we find them now; this is enough for our purpose. Herodotus says that the Egyptians of his days were black men: very possibly; but neither before nor since his period has this remark been found to be true. The paintings on the tombs and the mummies entombed alike refute his assertion, if extended beyond his period. He gossiped, I am afraid, like some other travellers, and talked a good deal about what he did not understand. Was he ever in Egypt? I feel disposed to doubt it. His story about the Persian skull reminds me of the next assertion of ancient and modern physiologists, of the supposed influence of external, even mechanical, means over the human form.

It is to Hippocrates we owe the story of the Macrocephali, inhabiting at that time the shores of the Euxine. They were a race with narrow, elongated, elevated heads and depressed foreheads, like the American Indians, or copper-coloured race, and more especially like the Carib and the Chenook. This variety in form the illustrious Greek explains in this way – for of the unity of mankind he never doubted any more than any other strictly scientific man: he fancied, for it was mere fancy, that this extraordinary form of head was at first produced by pressure, but that in time this pressure became unnecessary, the malformation becoming permanent by hereditary descent. Two hypotheses in a breath, both opposed to well-ascertained physiological laws. That the Carib and Chenook, and the ancient Macrocephali, fancied that by pressure they could give to the human head what form they chose, is certain enough; but does it follow that they could do so? The form of the head I speak of is peculiar to the race; it may be exaggerated somewhat by such means, but cannot be so produced: neither will such deformation become hereditary. For four thousand years have the Chinese been endeavouring to disfigure the feet of their women: have they succeeded in making the deformation permanent? Corsets have been worn time out of mind: Galen complains of them; he ascribes to them all sorts of bad results, deformities of spine and chest. Have such become hereditary? All matrons still produce virgin daughters. For how long have the Jews, with most African and Eastern nations, practised circumcision? Has the deformation become hereditary? Is there any instance of such accidental or mechanical deformities becoming transmissible by hereditary descent?

The varieties of form classed under the law of deformation, and dependent on the operation of the great law of unity of organization, belong to a different category, as will be explained in a distinct chapter on that head; but even they are kept in constant check by the laws of specialization, restoring man and animals to their specific shapes, else what would life terminate in? Varieties in form proceed only to a certain length – they are constantly checked by two laws, the laws maintaining *species as they exist* – 1, the tendency to reproduce the specific form instead of the variety; 2, non-viability or non-reproduction, that is, extinction. This it is which checks deformations of all kinds, and I even think I have observed varieties in form to be more common in those who died young than in those reaching adult years, as if the very circumstance of these internal deformations or varieties, however unimportant they may seem, coincided at least, if they were not the efficient cause of early decay of the vital powers and of premature death. Had the heads of the Macrocephali of ancient times, and of the Carib and Chenook and Peruvian of modern, owed their forms to mechanical means, that form would and must have ceased with their immediate descendants, or the race would have perished. How much more singular is the *fact*, that there should exist naturally men with heads and brains so singularly shaped; that it should be in their nature; that the form should still persist – unalterable, dependent on no climate, Asiatic – American; ancient and modern. This curious question we shall discuss when speaking of the American race; let us in the meantime bring this lecture to a close: the great laws announced in it will fall to be examined again in their application to race and to human history.

It was Herodotus who said, that on a field of battle it was easy to distinguish the Egyptian from the Persian skull, the former being hard, the latter soft. Herodotus must, I think, have studied medicine; he gives a reason in such a pleasant, off-hand way for all natural phenomena. The reason he assigns for this difference is, that the Persians covered the head – the Egyptians used no head-dress. Admitting both facts to be true, and I doubt them both, the reason given explains nothing; if there was a difference, it depended on race. The Copt was African; the Persian, Asiatic: they were different races of men – that is all. The *black* Egyptians of Herodotus have not been seen since his time.

The theories and errors of Hippocrates and Herodotus linger in the physiological schools to this day. M. Foville, for example, ascribes to mechanical pressure on the head of the infant, the wide hollow groove occasionally traversing it over the region of the vertex, and so frequently persisting to the adult state – a deformation wholly independent of such a cause, and occurring in all countries. The late Mr. Key persisted in blaming tight and short shoes for the most common deformity of the feet; and Dr. Combe,[8] still lingering on the gossip of Herodotus, finds a Bœotia in Holland, with all its presumed results – a marshy, foggy, wet, and heavy land, giving rise to phlegm and dulness – the grave and witless, plodding Dutchman. I put these three observations, but not the writers, under the same category; the last is refuted by every observation, and is below notice. But to return.

To Hippocrates, then, as representing the entire class of physiologists, we owe most of the medical, philosophical, and theo-philosophical notions of the present day; the theories which teach that cities looking to the west differ very materially from cities looking to the east, as also their inhabitants; the reason why Asiatics differ from Europeans – not one word of which is true; how in a country where the seasons and climates differ much, the inhabitants also must differ much, the reverse of which is nearer the truth: to him we owe the theory, that people living under a monarchy are servile and cowardly, whilst republicans are bold and brave – a doctrine which certainly has some little show of truth, and which we may afterwards discuss. His theories he transmitted to the scholars

---

6 Combe on Digestion.

of Greece; they affected even Aristotle, a master mind, who ought to have known better; but it is difficult to shake off the prejudices of centuries and of education. Aristotle assigns as a cause for the variety of strange and fantastic forms of animal life with which Africa abounds, and abounded also in his time, the scarcity of water, which, bringing to the same wells and springs all sorts of animals, gave rise to an endless variety of offspring! And this reminds me of a mysterious law in nature, not yet fully investigated, to which I next beg to call your attention. I know that I have little or no occasion now to tell you, that the climate in no way influences man's form or colour permanently; some of the exceptions to this statement, which will no doubt occur to you, fall to be explained in the next section.